Lewis Hamilton

World Champion

For my father.
Thanks for getting me into cars.

First edition published in October 2007
Second edition published in November 2008

A catalogue record for this book is available from the British Library

ISBN 978 1 84425 699 0

Library of Congress control no. 2008941046

Design and layout by Richard Parsons

Published by Haynes Publishing,
Sparkford, Yeovil, Somerset BA22 7JJ, UK.
Tel: 01963 442030 Fax: 01963 440001
Int. tel: +44 1963 442030
Int. fax: +44 1963 440001
E-mail: sales@haynes.co.uk
Website: www.haynes.co.uk

Haynes North America Inc., 861 Lawrence Drive,
Newbury Park, California 91320, USA

Printed and bound in Britain by J. H. Haynes & Co. Ltd,
Sparkford, Yeovil, Somerset BA22 7JJ

PHOTOGRAPH CREDITS

Action Images: 21, 26 inset, 130 top, 146–147, 148 top
Chris Walker Karting Images: 20 top, 26 main
DPPI: 24 top, 25, 89 inset, 96
Getty Images: Front jacket, 17, 114–115, 124 bottom, 125, 128–129, 139 top, 148 bottom, 150–151, 152 top, 153, 160, 173 inset, 187, 190 top, 192–193, 203, 233
GP2 Series Media Service: 56–57, 58 bottom, 59, 60, 61 top left, 62–65, 66 main, 67
LAT: Rear jacket, 3, 4–5, 6, 16 bottom, 20 bottom, 22 bottom, 23, 36 bottom, 37 top, 38–39, 42 bottom, 43, 44 inset, 45 bottom, 46–47 top, 47 bottom, 48 top and middle, 50, 52, 53 bottom, 54–55, 70, 71 main, 76–77, 78 bottom, 80 top and middle, 81, 84 top, 85, 86–87, 89 main, 90–91, 92 top and middle, 97, 98–99, 100–103, 106, 107 middle and bottom, 108, 110–111, 112 main and top, 116, 117,120 top, 121, 122–123, 124 top, 126, 127, 130 middle and bottom, 131, 132–133, 135 main, 136–137, 140–141, 142 left pair, 145, 156–159, 16–167,168 lower pair, 169–172, 173 main, 174–186, 188–189, 190 bottom, 191, 194–194 main, 195 right upper and lower, 196 top, 198–199, 200–201, 202, 204–207, 210–213, 214 top left, 214–215 main, 216–231, 232, 234–240
Rex Features: 8–9, 10, 12, 13, 14, 15, 16 top
Schlegelmilch: 107 top, 118 top
sutton-images.com: 11, 18–19, 22 top, 24 bottom, 27, 28–29, 30–35, 36 top and middle, 37 bottom, 40–41, 42 top, 44 main, 45 top, 46 bottom, 48 bottom, 49, 51, 53 top and middle, 58 top and middle, 61 top right and bottom, 66 inset, 68–69, 71 inset, 72, 73, 74–75, 78 top, 79, 80 bottom, 82–83, 84 bottom, 88, 92 bottom, 93, 94–95, 104–105, 109, 113 inset, 118–119, 120 middle and bottom, 134, 135 inset, 138, 139 main, 142–143 main, 144, 149, 152 lower pair, 168 top, 195 right middle, 196 bottom, 197, 208–209, 214 lower

ACKNOWLEDGEMENTS

Thanks to: Chris Walker, Dino Chiesa, Robert Ladbrook, Kevin Wood, Jim Holder, Matt James, Andy Bothwell, John McIlroy, David Malsher, Johnny Restrick, Charles Bradley, Tim Bowdler, Martin Hines, Mark Hughes, Steve Cooper, Jonathan Noble.

Lewis Hamilton
World Champion

Andrew van de Burgt

Santander
vodafone
HAMILTON
BOSS
JOHNNIE WALKER
Mobil 1
algo

Contents

vodafone

Introduction

"I think he's the best ever. He'll go on to beat all the records of Schumacher or Senna." These are the words of Marc Hynes, renowned driver coach, ex-British Formula 3 champion, and one of the men who helped Lewis Hamilton make the leap from being a highly ambitious kid from Stevenage into the youngest World Champion in Formula 1's 58-year history.

Hynes was on hand to offer advice to 16-year-old Hamilton as he stepped up from a glittering career racing karts into the super-competitive world of single-seater racing. It was the first stage in a sensational journey – one that took Lewis to the brink of the F1 World Championship in his sensational first season at the pinnacle of motor racing, and then to the main prize a year later in the most dramatic finale there's ever been.

Along the way he has become a sporting hero, one of Britain's few genuine world-class performers. His winning smile and positive attitude transformed people's perceptions of Formula 1 as an aloof playground for rich kids, while being F1's first-ever mixed-race driver opened up motor racing to a whole new audience.

It is a stunning achievement for a 23-year-old and fully justifies the faith and investment the McLaren team placed in him.

The story of Lewis's rise to become Britain's first World Champion since Damon Hill in 1996 is unique. Never before has a Formula 1 team taken such a keen interest in a junior karter, and McLaren's decision to back a toothy 13-year-old has been justified a million times over. Their faith and finances removed the biggest hurdle standing in his way – with little worry about how the bills would be paid, Lewis's talents were able to shine through.

Along with his sheer speed, he's probably the best overtaker there's ever been. From Formula Renault through F3, GP2 and into F1, his passing ability – the way he is instinctively able to size up a situation and act on it – has made him stand out from the crowd even more than his bright yellow helmet.

This book charts Lewis's career from his first brush with fame racing radio-controlled cars on *Blue Peter* to a race-by-race account of his amazing drive to the 2008 World Championship.

As a journalist working for *Autosport*, I have been following Lewis's progress since he started in Formula Renault back in 2002. That year I was reporting on the British Touring Car Championship, but I had the chance to watch many Formula Renault outings and couldn't help but notice the performances of the grey car with the driver in the yellow lid. In 2004 I covered his switch to the F3 Euroseries, and was there at Zandvoort a year later when he wrapped up the title in style.

I'd already been the GP2 correspondent for a season when Lewis arrived in 2006, and by then I'd become the magazine's Editor. It was an incredible season, and twice I made the call to put this virtual unknown on the cover. It's rare that anyone outside F1 gets that sort of exposure, but it was clear to me that here was a once-in-a-generation talent I could not ignore.

The 2008 title was a fantastic achievement but, like Marc, I have the feeling there's a lot more to come.

Andrew van de Burgt
November, 2008

Lewis
PLAYSCAPE
Pi Research
STP
PI RESEARCH

Growing up

FIRM FOUNDATIONS

Ron Dennis was still celebrating his first Formula 1 title win as boss of McLaren when Lewis Carl Hamilton was born on 7 January 1985. After many years of trying, Anthony Hamilton, the son of a Grenadian immigrant, and wife Carmen had the son they had been hoping for, and, against a backdrop of a booming economy in Mrs Thatcher's Britain, they optimistically named their first-born after an athlete who had become an international superstar.

Carl Lewis was the star of the show at the Olympic Games in Los Angeles in 1984, claiming a record four track and field gold medals (100m, 200m, 100m relay and long jump). By the time Lewis Hamilton was at school, Carl Lewis had added a second Olympic 100m title at the infamous Seoul Games in South Korea (1988), where winner Ben Johnson was excluded for steroid use. Meanwhile, McLaren had won three of the past four F1 drivers' titles under Ron Dennis's stewardship.

By then Lewis Hamilton was already carving out a career for himself as a sportsman, albeit in a discipline not yet recognised by the International Olympic Committee: radio-controlled car racing. Such was Hamilton's ability with a controller in hand that he was invited to appear on the BBC's long-running children's programme *Blue Peter*. A cherubic-faced six-year-old Hamilton was pitted against a group of adult racers and duly trounced them all!

Lewis was by now living with his mother in Stevenage, Hertfordshire. His parents had separated when he was two, but they nevertheless remained

LEFT Lewis poses for a photoshoot with his kart at the Kimbolton circuit in December 1995, after becoming the youngest-ever winner of the British Cadet Championship at the age of just ten.

close, and that Christmas Anthony spent the best part of his month's wages from the London Underground buying Lewis his first go-kart.

Lewis's passion for racing was obvious, and as he became increasingly serious about making it his life's ambition, so it became apparent that he would be better served by going to live with his dad, who was by now a 'weekend warrior', playing engineer and mechanic on Lewis's kart. So, at the age of ten, Lewis moved back in with Anthony, who had started a new family with his second wife, Linda, with whom he'd had another son, Nicholas.

"It didn't damage Lewis," Carmen told the *Daily Telegraph* regarding her separation from Anthony. "He is probably better for it than if we had stuck together in an unhappy marriage. I couldn't see myself in that busy, hectic motor racing lifestyle, but I didn't stop Anthony making sure Lewis got what he wanted."

Despite the break-up Lewis and his mother remain close, and he was delighted by his extended family. "I always wanted a brother and I remember when my parents [Anthony and Linda] first told me they were going to have a boy, I was well excited," he told *The Observer*.

Nicholas was born with cerebral palsy, and his striving to overcome his handicap and live a normal life has been a great inspiration to Lewis as he has fought to make his way up the motorsport ladder. "It's quite a cool feeling to watch someone grow up, to see the difficulties and troubles he's had, the experiences he's had. To go through them with him and see how he pulls out of them. I think he's just an amazing lad and I really love to do things for him."

LEFT, FROM TOP A beaming Lewis, aged eight, looks delighted after winning his first ever kart race in 1993; posing for the camera again, whilst driving for the Zip works kart team, aged 12; Lewis leads a race driving his McLaren-Mercedes-liveried kart at the Trent Valley circuit in 1998.

RIGHT Lewis poses with Ron Dennis at the 1998 Belgian Grand Prix, which he attended as a guest of McLaren-Mercedes. During the weekend at Spa, Dennis would sign Lewis to a long-term future with the McLaren-Mercedes team.

"Unlike so many people, he looked me square in the face and informed me where he was going in his life."

Ron Dennis

JBJ

As Lewis started to enjoy more success in karting, so he attracted the attention of bullies at the school he attended in Stevenage. Rather than hide away, Lewis decided to take up karate. With his excellent natural balance coming to the fore, just as it did in karting, he soon made his way through the grades, gaining his first black belt at the age of 12. His racing career had also really taken off now, but in order to cover the costs Anthony was having to work up to three jobs at a time. Thus a bargain was struck: Anthony would do what it took to pay the bills so long as Lewis got his head down and worked hard at school.

It was a deal that worked well, and Lewis passed his GCSEs, although there was one unsavoury incident when he was one of a group of children expelled from school after a fellow pupil was attacked. However, it was later proven that it was a case of mistaken identity: Lewis was cleared of any involvement and his family was issued with an official apology.

Lewis next attended Cambridge College of Arts and Science, where he studied for his A-levels. Somehow, despite racing full-time and studying, Lewis still found time to do part-time jobs. One was serving at a pub near the new family home in Tewin, Hertfordshire; another was in car valeting, for which he soon earned a reputation as the best in the area.

It seemed that whatever he turned his hand too, he had to be the best: "I think at a young age I did everything competitively," Lewis told *The Observer*. "I wanted to win and I hated not being the best at any sport I did. When I competed against anyone

LEFT **Lewis takes a leap at Earls Court in September 1997, during a photoshoot to promote the Joe Bloggs clothing brand, one of his main sponsors at the time. He had just won the McLaren-Mercedes Champion of the Future award for the second time.**

ABOVE RIGHT **Dreaming of a bright future – even at the age of 12 Lewis was acquiring PR skills which would stand him in good stead in the high-pressure world of Formula 1.**

RIGHT **The former Hamilton family home, in Peartree Way, Stevenage.**

LEFT Lewis has always been competitive, no matter what the sport. Here he provides another winning smile whilst posing in his rugby kit.

OPPOSITE, TOP LEFT Twelve-year-old Lewis poses in the garden at home with the Formula Junior Yamaha Winner 1997 trophy.

OPPOSITE, BOTTOM LEFT Surrounded by an impressive collection of karting trophies at the age of 13, after being signed to the McLaren-Mercedes Young Driver Support Programme.

OPPOSITE, FAR RIGHT Schoolboy Lewis, in 1998, shortly after being signed by Ron Dennis to the McLaren-Mercedes Young Driver Support Programme. Although his future career in motorsport already seemed assured, Lewis worked hard at school, passing all his GCSEs before going to college to study A-levels.

West McLaren Mercedes

RIGHT Lewis poses with his father, Anthony, after winning the ICA Italian Industrials series in 1999.

BELOW Lewis's younger brother, Nick, congratulates him on clinching the Formula 3 Euroseries title at Zandvoort in 2005.

OPPOSITE A winning team – Anthony, Nick and Lewis Hamilton at the *Autosport* Awards in December 2006.

I thought "I've got to win". But I've got to a point now that if I play golf and lose, I can deal with it."

Lewis also had to deal with being one of the very few black faces in the motor racing world. While he's proud of potentially opening up the sport to a sector of British society that may have been alienated from it before, he'd also rather be recognised for just being a great sportsman *per se*, not a great black sportsman. "Because I've come from nothing, I have a big drive," he told *Autosport*. "Because of my colour I can probably have an influence on another culture. That's a big bonus. I'd love to be able to do something for other people and have them say 'Oh yeah, that was him that opened the gateway'. That would be great.

"But I don't get treated as if I'm different – maybe occasionally by some people, but by most people I get treated normally, so it never really occurs to me unless someone mentions it. I'm just here doing what I love."

team mbm
AMG
mbm
15
20
15
HAMILTON
BRIDGESTONE
AMG

AMG

ABOVE The shape of things to come – Lewis leads the pack during a Cadet Class Super One race in 1995.

LEFT Ten-year-old Lewis with Jacques Villeneuve at the *Autosport* Awards in 1995 – the event at which Lewis famously told Ron Dennis that he would one day drive a McLaren F1 car.

OPPOSITE Lewis celebrates winning the McLaren-Mercedes Champions of the Future title with a delighted Ron Dennis at Buckmore Park kart circuit in 1996.

"If you're a novice racer you have to wear a black number plate for your first six races," recalls Hines. "Normally that means you're at the back, because they don't have enough experience to get through the field. But one day I saw Lewis Hamilton, with his black plate, and he was battling it out at the front. I knew straight away that he was a bit special."

Hines has a history of backing young British talent and by the end of the year he had reached an agreement to supply Lewis with one of his Zip chassis. With growing support and a burgeoning reputation, Hamilton started to make an impact on the domestic karting scene. In 1995, at the age of just 10, he became the youngest-ever British Cadet Champion. He backed that up with victory in the STP series too, and earned himself an invite to the end-of-season *Autosport* Awards dinner, where young karters collect their trophies and the great and the good of world motorsport meet to eat, drink and celebrate the year on track. It was here that Lewis famously approached McLaren boss Ron Dennis and told him "I'm going to race one of your cars one day".

Hamilton would be back at the Awards a year later, this time as the Champions of the Future series champion. His growing CV also boasted victory in the Sky TV Masters series and the Five Nations title.

By the age of 12 the time had come for Lewis to leave the Cadet scene and take the next step in his career. Junior Yamaha was his chosen path as part of the Zip works team, and victory in the Super 1 series was the reward. But, more importantly, he also took the honours again in the McLaren-Mercedes-backed Champions of the Future series.

The young pretender who had the guts to approach Ron Dennis that evening at London's Grosvenor Hotel was constantly being talked about. Dennis couldn't ignore the signs and invited Lewis to the 1998 Belgian Grand Prix. There, at just 13 years of age, Lewis signed a long-term deal with McLaren that would eventually catapult him into the big time. It was an unprecedented move by Dennis and his team. Formula 1 outfits had backed young drivers in the past, but normally they were at the Formula 3 stage of their careers – supporting a 13-year-old schoolboy was unheard of.

Lewis switched to Junior Intercontinental A (JICA) for 1998 and veteran kart mechanic Johnny Restrick was brought in to bolster the engineering

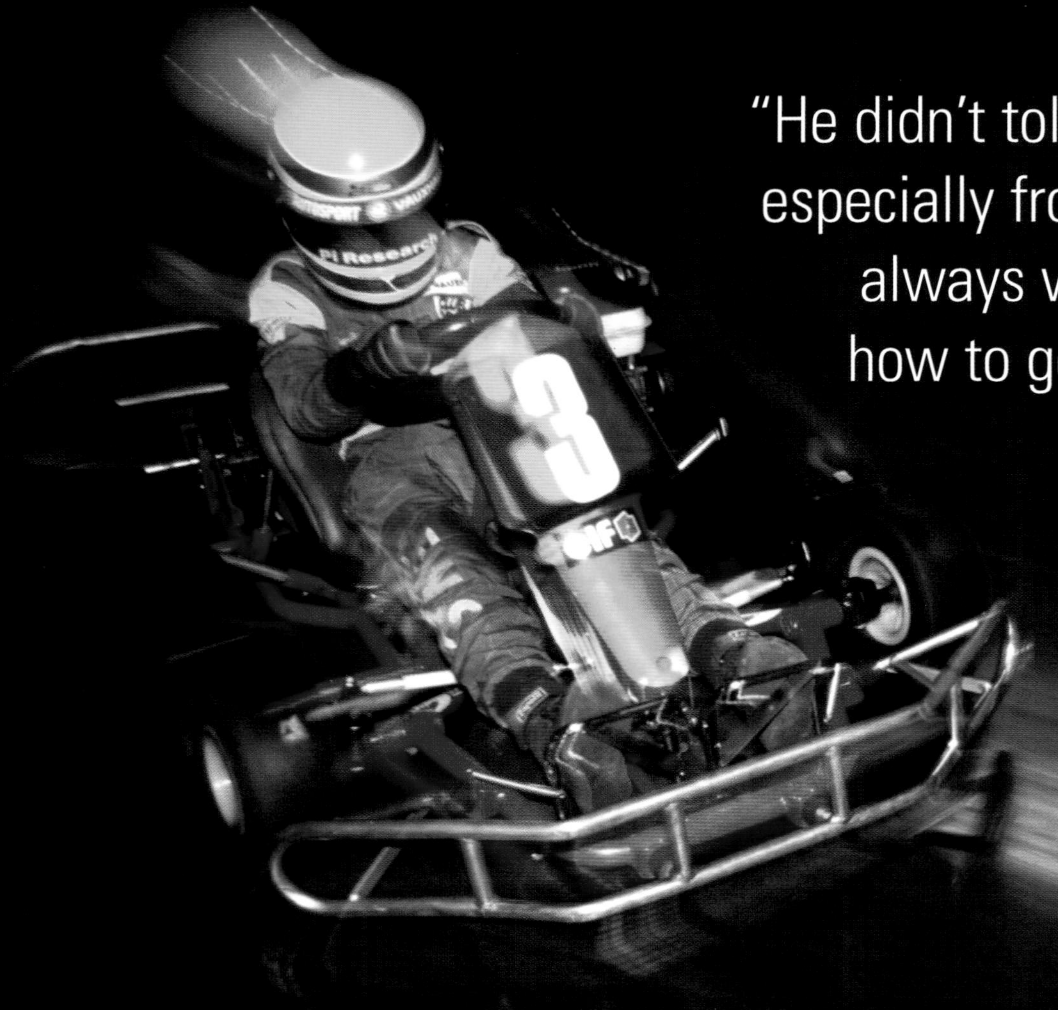

"He didn't tolerate mistakes, especially from himself, and always wanted to know how to get the very best from the kart."

Johnny Restrick

team. It didn't take long for Restrick to see that young Hamilton was the outstanding driver of his generation. "Working in karting you can often switch from one driver to another," he says, "and when I first started working with Lewis I thought 'this is just another driver', but by the end of the day it was clear that wasn't the case – he was a special one.

"He didn't tolerate mistakes, especially from himself, and always wanted to know how to get the very best from the kart. If he heard us talking about a way of possibly finding some extra performance, he didn't want to wait a session for us to put it on, he wanted it now. But it's very inspiring to work with someone like that and it's very unusual to find that in someone who's 12 or 13 years old.

"He was always very mature for his age and I think being part of that McLaren programme forced him to grow up quick too. I remember there was never a time when he was thinking of 'if I get to F1' it was always '*when* I get to F1'. It seemed to be part of his destiny to get to Formula 1 and become World Champion."

Despite victory in the final race, Lewis was just pipped for the Champions of the Future title in what would be his final season of full-time racing in the UK karting scene. Now international racing, and the European karting scene, beckoned. "In Britain, you can race against the same drivers for five years, and for me it was getting really boring," Lewis admitted at the time. "I've always wanted to go abroad, and you get to meet and race against a lot of different people and learn a different language. You're not just against the best in Britain, you're against the best in the world, so it motivates you a bit more."

Mercedes-Benz and McLaren established a squad for Lewis's European adventure, in the form of Teammbm.com, which would be run by 1982 Formula 1 World Champion Keke Rosberg with help from renowned Italian karting expert Dino Chiesa. With Nico Rosberg – Keke's son – as his team-mate, Teammbm.com became the one to beat.

"The McLaren-Mercedes link is the most important in my career," Lewis told *Motoring News*. "Ron Dennis wants me to finish my education before I concentrate full-time on my racing. All my friends say 'you've got your life sorted already, what are you doing at school?' but it isn't like that. I still have to work for it. There's more than just getting in the kart and driving."

Lewis was now a serious player in European karting and in 1999 he took his first international title, coming out on top in the ICA Italian Industrials series. He backed this up by taking second in the JICA European Championship and with victory in the prestigious Trophy de Pomposa. His hectic schedule also included the Italian Open series, in which he took fourth.

By now Chiesa had been won over by Lewis's talents: "Lewis is one of the best I've ever had. Karting is different to other racing. Giorgio Pantano was one of the best ever but he made political mistakes, whereas you see Lewis and he had a different attitude. He had the talent too. If you look at the two seasons with Nico, Nico probably was quicker 75 per cent of the time in qualifying but in the races it was always Lewis in front of him. Karting isn't like cars where if you make pole you win, it's all about fighting, and Lewis in the fight would win every time. And you see that now in F1 – he's the only driver who can really overtake. For sure he takes a risk, but he never crashes and that's what makes him so good.

OPPOSITE, TOP Racing indoors at the *Autosport* International Show at the NEC, Birmingham in January 1997.

OPPOSITE, BOTTOM At the 1996 *Autosport* International Show with, L to R, Oliver Gavin, Niki Cleland, Jos Verstappen, Dario Franchitti, Jason Watt, Andy Hallbery, Jan Magnussen, Jonny Kane, Lewis, Ian Flux, Will Hoy, Ralph Firman Jnr. and Allan McNish.

ABOVE Receiving another trophy for the cabinet at the 1997 *Autosport* Awards.

"For sure it was two of my best years in my karting career with Lewis and Nico. Both of them are still good friends and if you don't have a good time with people you don't remain friends for six or seven years. In the race they were very competitive, but out of the race they were always together. It was like a family and we are still in contact. He tells me one day he would like to have another go in the kart. I think that's because you never forget karting, because it's the first thing you do when you are young in motorsport."

Formula A has long been the top level of karting and in 2000 Lewis Hamilton entered its ranks with stunning effect. In a sensational season, the 15-year-old claimed the CIK-FIA European Championship. Added to this was victory in the one-off World Cup meeting at Motegi in Japan, where he produced an amazing drive after problems in qualifying left him

"All my friends say 'you've got your life sorted already, what are you doing at school?' but it isn't like that. I still have to work for it."

well down the grid. He was in line for a magnificent victory in the World Championship, when, in a thrilling battle with Colin Brown and Clivio Piccione, he was in the thick of the dice for the lead when a con rod broke in his kart with just four laps to go. These results meant he was the number-one ranked driver in the world, which he backed up in style with a great win in the end-of-season invitational race at Bercy in Paris.

Now aged 16, 2001 would be his final year in karts. The Formula Super A World Championship was the destination, with Teammbm.com again running the show. A pre-season decision was taken to switch chassis, but the Parloin kart and Lewis never really gelled, and while the season was punctuated by good results and strong performances, his previous consistency was missing and he just made the top 15. Still, there remained one last opportunity to showcase his karting skills: the season finale in Kerpen, Germany.

The Kerpen track is partly owned by Michael Schumacher, who at the time had just taken his fourth Formula 1 world title. An excellent karter himself in his junior days, Schumacher decided to enter the event with the works Tonykart team. This meant that for the only time in their racing careers Hamilton and Schumacher would go head-to-head. "It will be an opportunity of a lifetime to race against Michael," said Lewis before the event. "We've had a bad year so far, but we should have a new chassis for the race and I'm hoping I'm competitive so I can have a good race with him."

With the new chassis performing as expected, Lewis was able to give a true account of his potential. In a field that included a host of professional karters, and eventual series champion

OPPOSITE, TOP Lewis and Nico Rosberg swap four wheels for one to try their hands at unicycling at the World Kart Championship meeting at Braga in 2000.

OPPOSITE, BOTTOM Ready for action at the annual Elf Karting Masters event at Bercy in 2000.

ABOVE Racing at Val d'Argenton in 2000 in the CIK-FIA European Championship.

Vitantonio Liuzzi, Lewis bagged a pair of seventh-place finishes. It may not sound like a stellar performance, but it caught the eye of Schumacher: "He's a quality driver, very strong and only 16," he told *Motoring News*. "If he keeps this up I am sure he will reach F1. It's something special to see a kid of his age out on circuit. He's clearly got the right racing mentality."

Hamilton was stunned: "I wasn't aware he was paying such close attention to me. But hearing those comments gives me a great deal of hope for the future and proves I must be doing something right."

It would be the last competitive kart race for Lewis for the foreseeable future, but, like Schumacher, he didn't rule out a comeback: "It is very sad to leave karting behind, but I hope I can come back in the future and have another go. Coming back like Schumacher as World Champion would be pretty nice..."

ABOVE **14-year-old Lewis talks to Prince Charles at the McLaren Formula 1 factory in March 1999.**

BELOW **Using a rain visor – note the hastily applied duct tape holding it in place – at a wet race in 2001.**

KARTING
1995–2001 RESULTS

1995

British Super One Cadet Karting Championship	1st place
STP Cadet Karting Championship	1st place

1996

McLaren Mercedes Champions of the Future series	1st place
Sky TV Kart Masters Champion	
Five Nations Champion	

1997

Junior Yamaha Super One British Championship	1st place
McLaren Mercedes Champions of the Future series	1st place

1998

Italian Open Junior ICA Championship	4th place
McLaren Mercedes Champions of the Future series	2nd place
Signed by McLaren and Mercedes-Benz to Young Driver Support Programme	

1999

European ICA Junior Championship	2nd place
Italian Open ICA Junior Championship	4th place
Italian 'Industrial' ICA Championship	1st place
Trophy de Pomposa winner	

2000

World Formula A Championship	20th place
European Formula A Championship	1st place
World Cup Formula A Championship	1st place
Karting Masters at Paris Bercy	1st place
Karting World No 1	
Awarded BRDC 'Rising Star' Membership	

2001

World Formula Super A Championship	15th place

Flag
sistance
TAGHeuer
TAGHeuer
TAGHeuer
3
elf

Formula Renault

A FAST LEARNER

"The motor racing history books are littered with stories of drivers that were excellent in karts, but only average when they moved to cars. I didn't want to join that list."

It's hard to believe now, but before Lewis Hamilton made his single-seater debut driving a Manor Motorsport Tatuus in the opening round of the 2001 Formula Renault UK Winter Series, he had doubts about his ability to make the grade.

After conquering all before him in karting, his backers at McLaren felt that at 16 Lewis was ready to start racing cars. Even though he was still a few months away from being able to drive legally on the road, McLaren approached Manor boss John Booth and arranged for Lewis to have his first car test. Manor was an obvious for McLaren: over the previous decade it had enjoyed considerable success in FRenault, winning multiple titles with drivers like Kimi Räikkönen and Antonio Pizzonia.

Lewis's first test took place at Mallory Park near Leicester with no real fanfare – which was just as well, as he crashed after only three laps! But the Manor mechanics soon rebuilt the car, and he went out again and started setting times that showed what he was capable of. On the back of this, the

LEFT Race winner Lewis in action during the British Formula Renault Championship round at Snetterton in August 2003, a race which he dominated from pole position, also setting fastest lap.

"The motor racing history books are littered with stories of drivers that were excellent in karts, but only average when they moved to cars. I didn't want to join that list."

LEFT Looking forward to his first-ever race in a single-seater racing car at the British Formula Renault Winter Series meeting at Rockingham on 11 November 2001.

decision was made for Lewis to compete in the four-race Winter Series. There would be time for a handful of further tests prior to his debut, and also time for another shunt, this time a 100mph crash at Turn 1 of the challenging Oulton Park track in Cheshire.

Lewis qualified 14th for his first-ever car race, at Rockingham, near Corby, on 11 November 2001 – steady but unspectacular. In the race itself, despite an overly cautious approach he was caught up in a first-lap incident which dropped him to 15th, where he finished in the crash-shortened event. However, it was double-header meeting and in the second race he showed a glimpse of what the future held in store. Already tenth by lap two, he steadily worked his way up the order and passed series returnee Alex Kapadia on the final lap to bag fourth place. It was an impressive charge, of which Lewis was rightly proud. "This was the best race of my life," he told *Motorsport News*. "It was one of the first times I have driven the car and felt totally relaxed. Everything felt very natural and I enjoyed it greatly. This was the first car race of my career and it has taken me to another level. It wasn't an easy race, but it's all about channelling any negativity into positive energy and putting that to use."

The second round of the Winter Series took Lewis to Donington Park. Lewis qualified on the front row for the first race and was dicing for the lead when he clattered over a kerb and spectacularly damaged his undertray with terminal effect. In race two he was involved in an entertaining battle for third with Andrew Thompson, but lost out when they banged wheels in the final laps, dropping him back to fifth.

With the Winter Series experiment clearly a success, McLaren agreed a deal with Manor to compete in the full UK Championship in 2002, with an occasional outing in the highly competitive Euro Cup added in to maximise his experience. Lewis got his UK challenge off to a fine start at Brands Hatch, with an aggressive pass on Jamie Green earning him third place and his first-ever car racing podium. "We wanted points in the bag," he said after the race. "Third place is what I was hoping for; it's a good start."

Lewis tangled with Luciano Garcia at the next

ABOVE A portent of things to come. Lewis in action in the Manor Motorsport Renault FR2000, on his way to a hard-fought fourth place, during the second race of the double-header British Formula Renault Winter Series meeting at Rockingham.

ABOVE **After securing pole position for the first time, Lewis charges towards his maiden car race victory in Round 5 of the British Formula Renault Championship at Thruxton in June 2002.**

round at Donington Park and finished back in 15th. He was back in the points with fourth at Thruxton, and was in inspired form a month later at Silverstone. Engine problems left him 28th on the grid, but he fought back in style, setting fastest lap on his way to ninth place.

Things got even better when the series returned to Thruxton for round six. Lewis was fastest throughout practice and in qualifying scored his first single-seater pole. After a great start, he led every lap around the super-fast Hampshire track to record his maiden car racing win. "Every time I've been getting in the car I've learnt something new," he told *Motorsport News*. "I've changed my approach slightly and the team have also made some changes to the set-up and it shows."

Lewis crashed out of the next round at Brands, but was back at the sharp end with sixth at Croft. Then there was controversy at Snetterton when he clashed with championship leader Danny Watts as they disputed the lead. Watts was sent flying into the air, while Lewis was forced to pit with damage and dropped out of the points. Both drivers blamed the other for the clash, but ultimately the race stewards deemed it to be a 'racing accident' and no further action was taken. The incident nevertheless took the shine off the day's earlier race, in which Lewis returned to the podium with a battling second place.

He more than made amends at the Brands Hatch Indy circuit next time out with a crushing victory from pole position. He followed up that success with another win, this time in the Euro Cup round at Donington Park. "This feels fantastic," he beamed. "I had a great start and just kept pushing, I wanted to get the biggest gap I could and that's what I did."

Lewis made it three straight wins with victory in the penultimate race of the UK series, again at Donington Park. He backed this up with fourth in the final race, but fell just short of taking the runner-up spot in the championship. Still, his late-season form made him the hot tip for the title in 2003 after McLaren overruled an early switch to Formula 3 in favour of a championship attack.

RIGHT **Lewis looks delighted as he displays the trophy for his first Formula Renault win, after a dominant weekend at Thruxton.**

RENAULT
MICHELIN
MICHELIN

LEFT A lock-up on his way to a win in the British Formula Renault Championship meeting at Brands Hatch in August 2002.

ABOVE & RIGHT On his way to a lights-to-flag victory in Round 12 of the European Formula Renault Championship at Donington Park in October 2002.

"Every time I've been getting in the car I've learnt something new. I've changed my approach slightly and the team have also made some changes to the set-up and it shows."

Lewis started out the right way with pole for the 2003 season-opener at Snetterton, but lost the lead to Mike Conway when he was delayed by a backmarker. However, he took third in race two to hold third place in the standings. Lewis crashed out of round three at Brands before it finally all came together at a wet Silverstone, where he was the class of the field in difficult conditions.

Starting fourth on the grid, he worked his way up to third with a clever move on Alex Lloyd. On slick tyres on a wet track, Lewis was the fastest car out there, and he used that pace to overtake James Rossiter around the outside through the fast Maggotts sweepers. Lewis was running a second a lap quicker than early leader Tom Sisley and it wasn't long before he shot into the lead. With conditions deteriorating, and crashed cars littering the circuit, the race was stopped and Lewis was declared the winner.

With the 2003 victory jinx broken, Lewis swept to an emphatic win at Rockingham, coming home over seven seconds ahead of championship leader Rossiter. The result took Lewis to within three points of the series lead – it would be the last time he would be behind...

Pole position at Donington Park was squandered when a computer glitch meant he didn't know what gear he was in at the start, but he atoned for that disappointment in style with his third win of the year in the meeting's second event. The wins flowed now for Lewis, and his rivals barely got a look in as he routinely led from start to finish after having begun the race from pole. A double victory at Brands all but assured him of the title, and it was confirmed at the next round at Donington, where he scored two more wins – his ninth and tenth of the season. At just 18 years old he was the youngest champion in the series' history. "I'm really happy," he admitted afterwards. "It's a fantastic feeling to have sealed the title at last. Formula Renault has been such a great stepping stone in my career, and I've learnt a lot in this series – more than I could have imagined at the start of the year."

With the championship already secure, Lewis skipped the season finale, which denied him the opportunity of breaking Pizzonia's UK series record of 11 wins in a season, set with Manor in 1999. But it gave his rivals a chance to sip the victory champagne for once, while Lewis set about his next goal: conquering Formula 3.

OPPOSITE, FROM TOP Another win, another interview, at Croft in July 2003; James Rossiter (2nd) sprays winner Lewis with champagne as Susie Stoddart (3rd) looks on at Snetterton in August 2003; lining up on pole at Donington in September 2003.

ABOVE Leading the chasing pack away at Croft in July 2003.

RIGHT Proudly displaying the Formula Renault UK Champion 2003 trophy.

FORMULA RENAULT
2001–2003 RESULTS

2001

British Formula Renault Winter Series

Lewis Hamilton Race No 21
Manor Motorsport
Renault FR2000

Round 1 Rockingham

Race 1 – Qualifying

1	Robert Bell	-

Race 1

1	Robert Bell	8m29.93s
2	Julien Piguet	+1.110s
3	Alex Kapadia	+4.914s
15	Lewis Hamilton	
F/L	Robert Bell	1m23.000s

Race 2 – Qualifying

1	Robert Bell	-

Race 2

1	Robert Bell	19m30.23s
2	Julien Piguet	+6.810s
3	Martin Steyn	+9.632s
4	Lewis Hamilton	+14.067s
F/L	Robert Bell	1m22.451s

Round 2 Donington

Race 1 – Qualifying

1	Robert Bell	-

Race 1

1	Robert Bell	15m08.920s
2	Julien Piguet	+2.933s
3	Colin Brown	+4.184s
R	Lewis Hamilton	
F/L	Robert Bell	1m07.075s

Race 2 – Qualifying

1	Robert Bell	-

Race 2

1	Robert Bell	17m14.351s
2	Jamie Green	+2.090s
3	Andrew Thompson	+13.718s
5	Lewis Hamilton	+14.067s
F/L	Robert Bell	1m07.850s

Final Championship Positions

1	Robert Bell	136 points
2	Julien Piguet	106 points
3	Alex Lloyd	70 points
8	Lewis Hamilton	46 points

2002

British Formula Renault 2000 Championship

Lewis Hamilton Race No 25
Manor Motorsport
Renault FR2000

Round 1 Brands Hatch

Qualifying

1	Danny Watts	1m23.783s
2	Mark McLoughlin	1m24.141s
3	Jamie Green	1m24.423s
4	Lewis Hamilton	1m24.462s

Race

1	Danny Watts	24m19.774s
2	Mark McLoughlin	+1.473s
3	Lewis Hamilton	+7.784s
F/L	Mark McLoughlin	1m24.682s

Round 2 Oulton Park

Qualifying

1	Katherine Legge	1m19.292s
2	Danny Watts	1m19.355s
3	Robert Bell	1m19.522s
9	Lewis Hamilton	1m19.796s

Race

1	Danny Watts	26m21.952s
2	Ryan Sharp	+9.300s
3	Mark McLoughlin	+10.174s
15	Lewis Hamilton	+47.474s
F/L	Danny Watts	1m20.264s

Round 3 Thruxton

Qualifying

1	Robert Bell	1m11.155s
2	Will Davison	1m11.326s
3	Danny Watts	1m11.351s
9	Lewis Hamilton	1m11.574s

Race

1	Mark McLoughlin	33m27.216s
2	Lewis Hamilton	+0.440s
3	Will Davison	+2.218s
F/L	Lewis Hamilton	1m11.739s

Round 4 Silverstone

Qualifying

1	Jamie Green	1m20.318s
2	Danny Watts	1m20.569s
3	Ryan Sharp	1m20.677s
28	Lewis Hamilton	1m22.742s

Race

1	Danny Watts	26m02.735s
2	Jamie Green	+5.392s
3	Mark McLoughlin	+7.254s
9	Lewis Hamilton	+16.455s
F/L	Lewis Hamilton	1m21.363s

Round 5 Thruxton

Qualifying

1	Lewis Hamilton	1m11.576s
2	Matt Griffin	1m11.950s
3	Jamie Green	1m11.971s

Race

1	Lewis Hamilton	30m36.084s
2	Jamie Green	+3.310s
3	Danny Watts	+3.856s
F/L	Lewis Hamilton	1m12.058s

Round 6 Brands Hatch

Qualifying

1	Danny Watts	44.961s
2	Jamie Green	45.026s
3	Patrick Long	45.167s
9	Lewis Hamilton	45.347s

Race

1	Danny Watts	24m42.331s
2	Jamie Green	+5.340s
3	Alex Lloyd	+8.021s
20	Lewis Hamilton	+39.648s
F/L	Danny Watts	45.328s

Round 7 Croft

Qualifying

1	Danny Watts	1m18.397s
2	Will Davison	1m18.402s
3	Lewis Hamilton	1m18.405s

Race

1	Danny Watts	24m00.563s
2	Jamie Green	+2.748s
3	Will Davison	+10.862s
6	Lewis Hamilton	+14.325s
F/L	Jamie Green	1m19.295s

Round 8 Snetterton

Qualifying

1	Patrick Long	1m06.423s
2	Gary Turkington	1m06.445s
3	Lewis Hamilton	1m06.528s

Race

1	Patrick Long	22m29.707s
2	Lewis Hamilton	+1.106s
3	Danny Watts	+1.743s
F/L	Danny Watts	1m06.536s

Round 9 Snetterton

Qualifying

1	Danny Watts	1m06.596s
2	Lewis Hamilton	1m06.641s
3	Patrick Long	1m06.660s

Race

1	Jamie Green	31m31.889s
2	Patrick Long	+1.179s
3	Will Davison	+7.521s
R	Lewis Hamilton	
F/L	Jamie Green	1m06.703s

Round 10 Knockhill

Qualifying

1	Jamie Green	50.089s
2	Lewis Hamilton	50.109s
3	Danny Watts	50.166s

Race

1	Jamie Green	17m56.807s
2	Lewis Hamilton	+2.910s
3	Danny Watts	+4.061s
F/L	Danny Watts	1m01.149s

Round 11 Brands Hatch

Qualifying

1	Lewis Hamilton	44.422s
2	Danny Watts	44.527s
3	Jamie Green	44.702s

Race

1	Lewis Hamilton	25m00.180s
2	Danny Watts	+7.637s
3	Jamie Green	+14.505s
F/L	Lewis Hamilton	45.020s

Round 12 Donington

Qualifying

1	Lewis Hamilton	1m32.324s
2	Danny Watts	1m32.507s
3	Robert Bell	1m32.605s

Race

1	Lewis Hamilton	17m14.119s
2	Danny Watts	+3.239s
3	Robert Bell	+4.338s
F/L	Lewis Hamilton	1m33.255s

Round 13 Donington

Qualifying

1	Robert Bell	1m32.698s
2	Danny Watts	1m32.706s
3	Lewis Hamilton	1m32.794s

Race

1	Danny Watts	23m34.468s
2	Ryan Sharp	+3.868s
3	Pat Long	+7.024s
4	Lewis Hamilton	+9.582s
F/L	Danny Watts	1m32.828s

Final Championship Positions

1	Danny Watts	333 points
2	Jamie Green	279 points
3	Lewis Hamilton	274 points

2002

Formula Renault Eurocup

Lewis Hamilton Race No 69
Manor Motorsport
Renault FR2000

Round 6 Spa-Francorchamps

Qualifying

1	Neel Jani	-

Race

1	Neel Jani	22m49.917s
2	José Maria López	+8.610s
3	Mike den Tandt	-
7	Lewis Hamilton	-
F/L	Hannes Lachinger	2m29.272s

Round 7 Imola

Qualifying

1	José Maria López	-

Race

1	Eric Salignon	20m20.526s
2	Lewis Hamilton	+3.582
3	Nicolas Lapierre	
F/L	Lewis Hamilton	2m10.729s

Round 8 Donington Park

Qualifying

1	Lewis Hamilton	-

Race

1	Lewis Hamilton	27m55.397s
2	Christian Klien	+12.001
3	Roberto Streit	-
F/L	Lewis Hamilton	1m32.440s

Round 9 Estoril

Qualifying

	Neel Jani	-

Race

	Neel Jani	28m45.048s
	Lewis Hamilton	**+6.130s**
	José Maria López	-
F/L	Neel Jani	1m40.692s

Final Championship Positions

1	Eric Salignon	182 points
2	Neel Jani	178 points
3	Nicolas Lapierre	120 points
5	**Lewis Hamilton**	**92 points**

NB: Lewis Hamilton competed in 4 rounds in the 9-round series.

2003

British Formula Renault 2000 Championship

Lewis Hamilton Race No 3
Manor Motorsport
Renault FR2000

Round 1 Brands Hatch

Qualifying

	Lewis Hamilton	**1m05.909s**
	Mike Conway	1m05.917s
	Alex Lloyd	1m05.945s

Race

	Mike Conway	20m03.459s
	Lewis Hamilton	**+8.959s**
	James Rossiter	+9.903s
F/L	Mike Conway	1m05.931s

Round 2 Snetterton

Qualifying

	Mike Conway	1m05.989s
	Tom Sisley	1m06.039s
	Mike Spencer	1m06.133s
	Lewis Hamilton	**1m06.149s**

Race

	Alex Lloyd	20m23.632s
	Mike Conway	+0.355s
	Lewis Hamilton	**+1.392s**
F/L	Mike Conway	1m06.919s

Round 3 Brands Hatch

Qualifying

	Tom Sisley	45.265s
	Lewis Hamilton	**45.415s**
	Alex Lloyd	45.477s

Race

	Tom Sisley	32m28.289s
	Alex Lloyd	+1.592s
	Mike Conway	+2.059s
R	**Lewis Hamilton**	
F/L	Mike Conway	45.149s

Round 4 Thruxton

Qualifying

1	James Rossiter	1m11.973s
2	Alex Lloyd	1m12.124s
3	**Lewis Hamilton**	**1m12.183s**

Race

1	James Rossiter	20m40.504s
2	**Lewis Hamilton**	**+0.687s**
3	Stefan Söderberg	+2.922s
F/L	**Lewis Hamilton**	**1m12.282s**

Round 5 Silverstone

Qualifying

1	Tom Sisley	1m20.452s
2	James Rossiter	1m20.818s
3	Mike Conway	1m20.958s
4	**Lewis Hamilton**	**1m20.966s**

Race

1	**Lewis Hamilton**	**23m35.434s**
2	Tom Sisley	+0.500s
3	James Rossiter	+1.497s
F/L	Tom Sisley	1m22.257s

Round 6 Rockingham

Qualifying

1	**Lewis Hamilton**	**1m33.933s**
2	James Rossiter	1m34.126s
3	Tom Sisley	1m34.182s

Race

1	**Lewis Hamilton**	**32m51.362s**
2	James Rossiter	+7.547s
3	Alex Lloyd	+10.476s
F/L	**Lewis Hamilton**	**1m24.345s**

Round 7 Croft

Qualifying

1	**Lewis Hamilton**	**1m19.028s**
2	James Rossiter	1m19.308s
3	Mike Spencer	1m19.487s

Race

1	**Lewis Hamilton**	**18m54.090s**
2	Mike Spencer	+1.400s
3	Alex Lloyd	+2.798s
F/L	Mike Spencer	1m20.115s

Round 8 Croft

Qualifying

1	**Lewis Hamilton**	**1m19.091s**
2	James Rossiter	1m19.314s
3	Mike Spencer	1m19.652s

Race

1	**Lewis Hamilton**	**21m34.248s**
2	James Rossiter	+4.467s
3	Mike Spencer	+9.837s
F/L	**Lewis Hamilton**	**1m20.281s**

Round 9 Donington

Qualifying

1	**Lewis Hamilton**	**1m33.202s**
2	Tom Sisley	1m33.359s
3	James Rossiter	1m33.412s

Race

1	Tom Sisley	23m43.688s
2	Alex Lloyd	+3.580s
3	James Rossiter	+5.859s
R	**Lewis Hamilton**	
F/L	Mike Spencer	1m34.231s

Round 10 Donington

Qualifying

1	**Lewis Hamilton**	**1m33.205s**
2	Tom Sisley	1m33.529s
3	James Rossiter	1m33.547s

Race

1	**Lewis Hamilton**	**26m07.078s**
2	Tom Sisley	+6.844s
3	James Rossiter	+10.056s
F/L	**Lewis Hamilton**	**1m33.874s**

Round 11 Snetterton

Qualifying

1	**Lewis Hamilton**	**1m05.654s**
2	James Rossiter	1m05.756s
3	Tom Sisley	1m05.758s

Race

1	**Lewis Hamilton**	**27m11.357s**
2	James Rossiter	+3.296s
3	Susie Stoddart	+7.883s
F/L	**Lewis Hamilton**	**1m06.435s**

Round 12 Brands Hatch

Qualifying

1	**Lewis Hamilton**	**44.772s**
2	Alex Lloyd	44.942s
3	Tom Sisley	44.950s

Race

1	**Lewis Hamilton**	**22m59.593s**
2	Alex Lloyd	+1.761s
3	James Rossiter	+2.648s
F/L	**Lewis Hamilton**	**45.447s**

Round 13 Brands Hatch

Qualifying

1	**Lewis Hamilton**	**44.854s**
2	Tom Sisley	44.980s
3	Alex Lloyd	44.983s

Race

1	**Lewis Hamilton**	**24m14.902s**
2	Tom Sisley	+3.360s
3	Alex Lloyd	+7.360s
F/L	**Lewis Hamilton**	**45.165s**

Round 14 Donington

Qualifying

1	**Lewis Hamilton**	**1m08.507s**
2	James Rossiter	1m08.661s
3	Mike Spencer	1m08.739s

Race

1	**Lewis Hamilton**	**13m50.961s**
2	James Rossiter	+2.272s
3	Mike Spencer	+9.612s
F/L	**Lewis Hamilton**	**1m08.458s**

Round 15 Donington

Qualifying

1	**Lewis Hamilton**	**1m08.515s**
2	Alex Storckenfeldt	1m08.793s
3	Mike Spencer	1m08.825s

Race

1	**Lewis Hamilton**	**18m35.217s**
2	Alex Storckenfeldt	+3.205s
3	Stefan Söderberg	+6.754s
F/L	**Lewis Hamilton**	**1m08.888s**

Final Championship Positions

1	**Lewis Hamilton**	**419 points**
2	Alex Lloyd	371 points
3	James Rossiter	347 points

NB: Lewis Hamilton did not enter Rounds 16 and 17 at Oulton Park – title already won.

2003

Formula Renault Masters

Lewis Hamilton
Manor Motorsport
Renault FR2000

Round 1 Assen

Race 1

Lewis Hamilton competed in 2 races, both at Assen. The first race was stopped after four laps and declared void due to time restrictions at the circuit.

Race 2

1	Simon Pagenaud	26m45.096s
2	**Lewis Hamilton**	**+1.254s**
3	Toni Vilander	-
F/L	Simon Pagenaud	1m19.968s

Final Championship Positions

1	Esteban Guerrieri	124 points
2	Robert Schlünssen	88 points
3	Simon Pagenaud	86 points
12	**Lewis Hamilton**	**24 points**

2003

German Formula Renault Championship

Lewis Hamilton
Manor Motorsport
Renault FR2000

Round 2 Hockenheim

Race 1 – Qualifying

1	Ryan Sharp	-

Race 1

1	Ryan Sharp	25m48.845s
2	Marc Walz	-
3	Reinhard Kofler	-
9	**Lewis Hamilton**	-
F/L	Franck Perera	-

Race 2 – Qualifying

1	Ryan Sharp	-

Race 2

1	Ryan Sharp	25m47.554s
2	Hendrik Vieth	-
3	Robert Schlünssen	-
8	**Lewis Hamilton**	-
F/L	Ryan Sharp	-

Final Championship Positions

1	Ryan Sharp	300 points
2	Hendrik Vieth	257 points
3	Robert Schlünssen	242 points
27	**Lewis Hamilton**	**25 points**

F/L = Fastest lap R = Retired D = Disqualified

YOKOHAMA
27
MACAU
TAG

Formula 3

THE GRADUATE

With graduates such as double World Champions Emerson Fittipaldi and Mika Häkkinen, triple world title holders Nelson Piquet and Ayrton Senna, and the record-smashing Michael Schumacher, Formula 3 has long been established as an integral step on the ladder to motor racing superstardom.

Given that Lewis Hamilton had just clinched the Formula Renault UK Championship it was logical that he, too, would follow in the wheel tracks of those illustrious names. And it made perfect sense that his F3 debut should be behind the wheel of a car from two-time British F3 title winners Manor Motorsport, with whom he'd had so much success in FRenault.

Initial testing went encouragingly, with Lewis 12th fastest in the Dallara-Mugen at Donington Park, just 0.7 seconds behind future champion Alan van der Merwe. With the team and McLaren confident of Lewis's ability to run competitively in F3, a deal was done for him to make a one-off appearance at the 2003 British F3 season finale at Brands Hatch.

Qualifying went well, and Lewis lined up a promising seventh on the grid. He made a strong start and had worked his way up to third when a puncture forced him out. Things got considerably worse in the second race when team-mate Tor Graves was caught out by the car ahead of him slowing. As Graves swerved to avoid an accident he lost control and spun across the track just as Lewis was approaching. With nowhere to go there was a huge collision and Hamilton thumped into the barriers. It was a big impact – big enough to send a

LEFT Lewis in action in the Manor Motorsport Dallara F302 Mugen-Honda on possibly the most challenging and unforgiving street circuit in the world during the Macau Grand Prix in November 2003.

concussed Hamilton off to hospital for X-rays, where he was held overnight for observation.

His next turn in an F3 car was in a wet test session at Croft, where he lapped "a second a lap" quicker than the rest according to Manor boss John Booth. With his performances blossoming, the decision was taken to enter Lewis in the season-ending races at the classic Macau street circuit and the Korean Superprix.

Macau is arguably the greatest street track in the world. It's certainly one of the fastest and least forgiving, as Lewis found to his cost in two separate accidents in free practice. With his track time compromised he could do no better than 18th.

No matter, in the first of the two heats that made up the race itself he showed his true colours. A charging run, which included intelligent avoidance of a collision up ahead, took him into fifth place.

Things looked even better in heat two, when he used his typical brilliance under braking to pass two cars in one go and moved into third. Alas, he ran

slightly wide, which gave Robert Kubica a shot at a podium position and the Pole grabbed it, but was going way too fast and slammed into the tyre barrier. Lewis somehow avoided hitting him, but was not so fortunate when Richard Antinucci spun as he tried to take advantage of the situation and clipped Hamilton's right rear wheel, damaging his suspension.

So Lewis left Macau empty-handed, but with the chance to make amends in Korea two weeks later. It was chilly, to say the least, in Changwon as the F3 cars went out for qualifying. With the drivers struggling to get heat into their tyres the track was "like driving on ice". In such situations car control comes to the fore, and that was the cue for Lewis to produce a stunning performance to grab pole position. Lewis's race didn't last past lap three, however, a collision with Nelson Piquet Jr taking him out. "It was really disappointing because we could have come away with a win," he commented ruefully.

During the trip to the Far East, McLaren, Mercedes and Manor made the decision to take Lewis into the F3 Euroseries in 2004. It was a bold move, as it would take Manor and Lewis away from the tracks they knew and into unfamiliar territory. But at least they would have Mercedes's HWA-built engine, which was starting to come to the fore in the Euroseries. When Euroseries testing began in March 2004 the decision seemed justified. On his first run in the Dallara-Mercedes, Lewis set the fastest time at Valencia in Spain.

The season kicked off in front of thousands of Mercedes guests at Hockenheim in Germany. While pre-season expectations were high, reality bit hard in qualifying. Lewis never really got to grips with the track and the Kumho tyres and qualified only 14th for the first of the two races. Things got worse when he was forced onto the grass on the opening lap and dropped to 19th. But his fighting spirit shone through, and in a charging drive he forced his way up to 11th at the flag. No points, but a pointer of things to come.

OPPOSITE, TOP Lewis's distinctive yellow helmet design has always marked him out.

OPPOSITE, BOTTOM With the car of Tor Graves in the foreground, marshals work to extract a concussed Lewis from his damaged car at Brands Hatch in September 2003.

ABOVE Nelson Piquet Jr knocks Lewis into the air during the 2003 Korean Superprix at Changwon.

RIGHT **Lewis displays characteristic professionalism as he participates in a world record attempt at filling tarts during the Food Festival at the 2003 Macau Grand Prix.**

BELOW **Lewis and Danny Watts on top of the world at the Macau Tower during the Macau Grand Prix weekend in November 2003.**

He started ninth for race two, but again lost out at the start. This triggered another fightback, which this time yielded seventh place and his first F3 points. "It's been a very positive experience," he said. "I think I can take most of the blame for qualifying."

There would be no points at the next round in Estoril, although sixth on the grid for race two showed that he was starting to get to grips with the one-lap qualifying pace. Lewis also lined up sixth for the first race at the next round, at Adria, but in truth it should have been third, but for a harsh penalty for cutting over a kerb. The unusual and tight Adria track isn't great for passing, and even Lewis struggled to make up places from ninth on the grid for race two. Still, he didn't look a gift-horse in the mouth when Giedo van der Garde was told by his team that he was on the last lap when there was in fact a lap to

go, and when the Dutchman backed off after what he thought was the finish Lewis went up to fifth for his best result of the season to date.

He went one better at the next round, held at the historic Pau street circuit. Torrential rain meant the race was started under the safety car, and a misunderstanding with the team over the restart procedure meant a gap of almost 20 seconds had opened up ahead of him before he got going. But his form on the tricky wet track was stunning and he soon closed that gap down and then started passing the people ahead of him. By the flag he'd worked his way up to fifth, which became fourth when race winner Alex Prémat was excluded for a yellow flag infringement.

Lewis started from 13th in race two, but once again found passing places that others struggled to find. This took him to seventh, completing his first double points finish. However, a cloud initially hung over the result and Lewis was temporarily excluded, only to be later reinstated after Manor successfully argued that the aluminium 'Gurney flap' used on his front wing was, in fact, legal.

Ahead of the next Euroseries round at Norisring in Germany, Manor went testing at the French Grand Prix venue of Magny-Cours. The aim of the test was to get a set-up that Lewis was happy with not just for the race but for qualifying – the team suspected that he was using his talent to compensate for shortcomings in the car, and F3 is so competitive that sometimes talent just isn't enough. The test was a breakthrough, and enabled Lewis to claim his first pole position at the unique Norisring street track, though the session was marred by a controversial collision with champion-elect Jamie Green.

Nicolas Lapierre jumped the start and led initially, but he was soon punished, leaving Lewis to fend off the attentions of Prémat. The Frenchman passed Lewis but couldn't pull away, try as hard as he might. Eventually something broke in the suspension of

RIGHT, TOP **Chewing the fat with long-time rival Nelson Piquet Jr during the Marlboro Masters meeting at Zandvoort in 2004.**

RIGHT **Winner Lewis congratulates second-placed Loic Duval at the end of the Formula 3 Euroseries race at Norisring in June 2004.**

his car, and Lewis was left with a clear lead that he held to the flag. From fifth on the grid for race two he worked his way up to third by the flag, for a double podium finish and a tally of 16 points for the weekend.

It was back to Magny-Cours with a bump for the next round. Lewis lost out in the wet/dry qualifying lottery and started back in 20th. Back in the pack is a bad place to be in a quick car, and so it proved here, as Lewis was punted into a spin and retirement. In the second race he was again in trouble, losing a lap in a multi-car tangle at the first corner. Many drivers would just park the car in this situation, but not Lewis, who kept on pushing to the flag, setting the fastest lap of the race on his way to a frustrating 17th place. However, he returned to the podium with a typically gritty drive next time out at the Nürburgring, where he backed up third in race one with a solid drive to fourth in race two.

The F3 Masters race at Zandvoort brings together the best drivers from Britain and the Euroseries for a one-off winner-takes-all affair in the summer sun at

the classic Dutch track. ASM took the honours for the Euroseries, while Manor and Hamilton were never a factor and seventh was the best Lewis could do.

Then it was back to Zandvoort for the next round of the Euroseries itself, and in race one he claimed another podium finish with a spirited drive to third. Brno in the Czech Republic played host to the penultimate round of the series. Pre-race testing at the long, undulating track hadn't gone well for Lewis, and was reflected in him lining up ninth for race one. A brave move around the outside took him into seventh at the flag. However, things improved in the second race, in which a stunning opening lap charge took Lewis from seventh to fourth and another tidy points haul.

Hockenheim was the venue for the season finale, and back on familiar asphalt Lewis excelled once again. A storming drive in the first race was rewarded with third, which became second when Hannes Neuhauser was disqualified. Despite starting tenth for the second race Lewis was in inspired form and had a brilliant dice with Kubica on his way to sixth, which

FAR LEFT Lewis, looking pensive, with his father, Anthony before the qualifying session for the Formula 3 Euroseries round at Magny-Cours in July 2004.

ABOVE Three abreast, jostling for position with Alex Prémat (middle) and Nico Rosberg (background) during the second race of the Formula 3 Euroseries meeting at Nürburgring in August 2004.

LEFT Preparing for battle in the Marlboro Masters of Formula 3 event at Zandvoort in 2004.

ABOVE Lewis leads the field away, followed by team-mate Robert Kubica, and went on to win the qualifying race for the 2004 Macau Grand Prix.

RIGHT Lewis's British Bulldog mascot provides support at the 2004 Macau Grand Prix.

RIGHT Lewis displays his 'never-say-die' spirit as he pushes his car up the pitlane during the wet qualifying session for the 2004 Bahrain F3 Superprix, a race which would provide him with a memorable win.

was enough to take fifth in the final standings. "We were disappointed in the season," he admitted. "We expected a lot more from ourselves."

All that remained for 2004 was the end-of-season races. After a year that had promised much more than it delivered, Lewis wanted to sign off in style, and winning at Macau, he thought, would be the perfect tonic ahead of graduation to the new GP2 series in 2005. McLaren and Mercedes thought otherwise. They didn't see the benefit in Macau and Bahrain, and thought another season in F3 would be better than stepping up without the championship on his CV. So Lewis and his family set about finding their own backing to compete in the year's final two F3 races, and had exploratory discussions with a number of GP2 teams before reaching a provisional agreement with Super Nova. It was a close-run thing, but ultimately a deal was done and Lewis and Manor were off to Macau.

From the moment Lewis and new team-mate Kubica hit the track the Manor cars were the quickest things out there. In the end it was Kubica who took pole, just 0.2 seconds faster than Lewis – the rest of the field was more than half a second behind them.

Lewis won the qualifying race, comfortably ahead of Nico Rosberg. In the race proper, he and Rosberg shot off the line and through the first series of corners, but at the first heavy braking point Lewis left it a little late and ran wide and into the tyres – where he was promptly joined by Rosberg. It was a disaster. Still, he'd have a chance to make it right two weeks later in Bahrain...

His odds of winning didn't look too enticing when he qualified 21st. A typically forceful performance in the qualifying race took him to 11th – respectable, but hardly what he was hoping for – but an amazing start in the final took him to fourth by the first corner, and the impossible beckoned. When leaders Jamie Green and Nico Rosberg made a hash of the restart following a late safety-car period, Lewis went through for the biggest win of his career to date.

In the weeks that followed he relinquished his hopes of an early graduation to GP2 and another deal was done with McLaren. This took him to ASM – the dominant team of the 2004 season – and instantly meant he would be pre-season title favourite.

BELOW Qualifying at the 2004 Bahrain F3 Superprix, with Bahrain University in the background.

ABOVE Number One again, after a spectacular drive from 11th on the grid to win in Bahrain.

ABOVE **Into the light – emerging from the tunnel at Monaco on the way to a brace of wins in the Formula 3 Euroseries races supporting the 2005 Monaco Grand Prix.**

OPPOSITE **The champagne flies as Lewis celebrates victory at Monaco under the watchful eyes of the Formula 1 team bosses.**

Lewis instantly justified his billing by taking pole by almost a second for the opening race of the season, at Hockenheim, and then converting it into a comfortable win. He was caught out by excessive tyre wear in the wet second race, but still claimed third to take a title lead he would never lose. "It has been the perfect start to the season," he said. "I've scored many valuable championship points."

His rivals didn't get a look in at the second round of the series at Pau. Starting from pole again he led into the first corner and was never headed. He was made to work for victory in the second race, however, as team-mate Adrian Sutil got the jump on him at the start. But the pressure from Lewis was relentless and eventually Sutil cracked and had a half-spin, and Lewis was home and dry for his third win in four races.

The classic Spa-Francorchamps circuit in Belgium played host to round three, and, as is often the case in the Ardennes regaion, it was raining come race day. Rain or shine, Lewis was still on top, although this time Sutil was a constant thorn in his side, finishing just a second behind at the flag. In fact the German was later declared the winner, as Lewis was one of seven drivers disqualified for a technical infringement.

The loss of his win stung Lewis, and after Sutil led away at the start of race two he was determined to show everybody who was boss. Picking up a great slipstream on the downhill run into the challenging Eau Rouge corner, Lewis demonstrated why he is probably the best overtaker in motor racing today, with an audacious pass around the outside! Once ahead, he duly rattled off another win.

The glamour of Monaco can be a distraction for any young driver, but with the F1 fraternity looking on Lewis showed them all that he was a future star by bagging another pair of wins. Sutil pushed him hard throughout, but Lewis was ultimately too strong.

Given his Euroseries form, Lewis went to the Marlboro Masters in Zandvoort as the clear favourite, and once again he brushed the competition aside. Pole position was again converted into the lead, and he led every lap to put his name on a roll of honour alongside David Coulthard, Jos Verstappen and Takuma Sato.

"There has been a lot of pressure this year. But once you get experience, you learn to cope with it and block it out."

The return to the Euroseries brought Lewis the unusual experience of defeat, when, at Oschersleben in eastern Germany, Lewis's replacement at Manor Motorsport, Lucas di Grassi, scored his maiden win after leading all the way from pole, while Lewis ran home in third. Normal service was resumed in race two, where, back on his familiar pole, Lewis raced away to victory. "The car felt fantastic today and I just kept pushing to the end," he said.

One year on from his breakthrough victory, Lewis Hamilton returned to the Norisring at the head of the championship. Fittingly he was on top all weekend, posting a pair of commanding wins, and with closest title rival Sutil retiring from race one Lewis's points total now stretched past 40 – it seemed to be all over bar the shouting.

But fortunes can change quickly in motorsport, and at the next round, at the Nürburgring, Lewis made his first real error of the year, clipping Paul di Resta's car on the opening lap and sending both of them into a spin. Lewis recovered to 12th, but Sutil won and breathed life back into the title fight – well, until race two, that is. In what remains the most comprehensive victory in Euroseries history, Lewis decimated the field. In just 21 laps he built up a winning margin of over 19 seconds,

including the fastest lap of the race on the very last lap. "I knew after yesterday people were saying 'He's going to crack', so I wanted to make a point," he said.

The point was rammed home at the next round, at Zandvoort, where Lewis claimed the title – with four races still to go. But the weekend was not without its dramas, especially in race one, where Lewis and Sutil collided on the run out of the first corner, taking each other out. "There's no point in creating a bad atmosphere, so we just need to draw a line under it and move on," was Lewis's mature response.

Race two was copybook, with pole turned into the lead and a comfortable win that sealed the championship – to his surprise. "I hadn't even realised I won it until the team hung out a 2005 Champion banner," he said. "I think it's been well-deserved."

With the title pressure off, Lewis reeled off two more dominant wins at the EuroSpeedway in Lausitz, Germany, and repeated the feat at the season finale back at Hockenheim. It was a stunning season, and with the Euroseries having changed its race format in 2006 with the introduction of reverse grids for race two it's likely that Hamilton's record of 15 wins in 20 races will never be beaten.

"There has been a lot of pressure this year," he told *Autosport*. "But once you get experience, you learn to cope with it and block it out. But I needed to win, and I needed to do it in dominant style."

And that's exactly what he did.

OPPOSITE, TOP Another road leading to victory – conquering the street circuit during qualifying at Norisring in July 2005.

OPPOSITE, BOTTOM Battling with ASM team-mate Adrian Sutil at the start of Round 10 of the 2005 Formula 3 Euroseries at Norisring.

TOP LEFT Lewis demonstrates his impressive ability to avoid distractions during an interview.

MIDDLE LEFT The flag flies for Lewis after securing victory in the 2005 Formula 3 Euroseries at Zandvoort in August.

BELOW Reflecting on a job well done at the end of a stunning 2005 season.

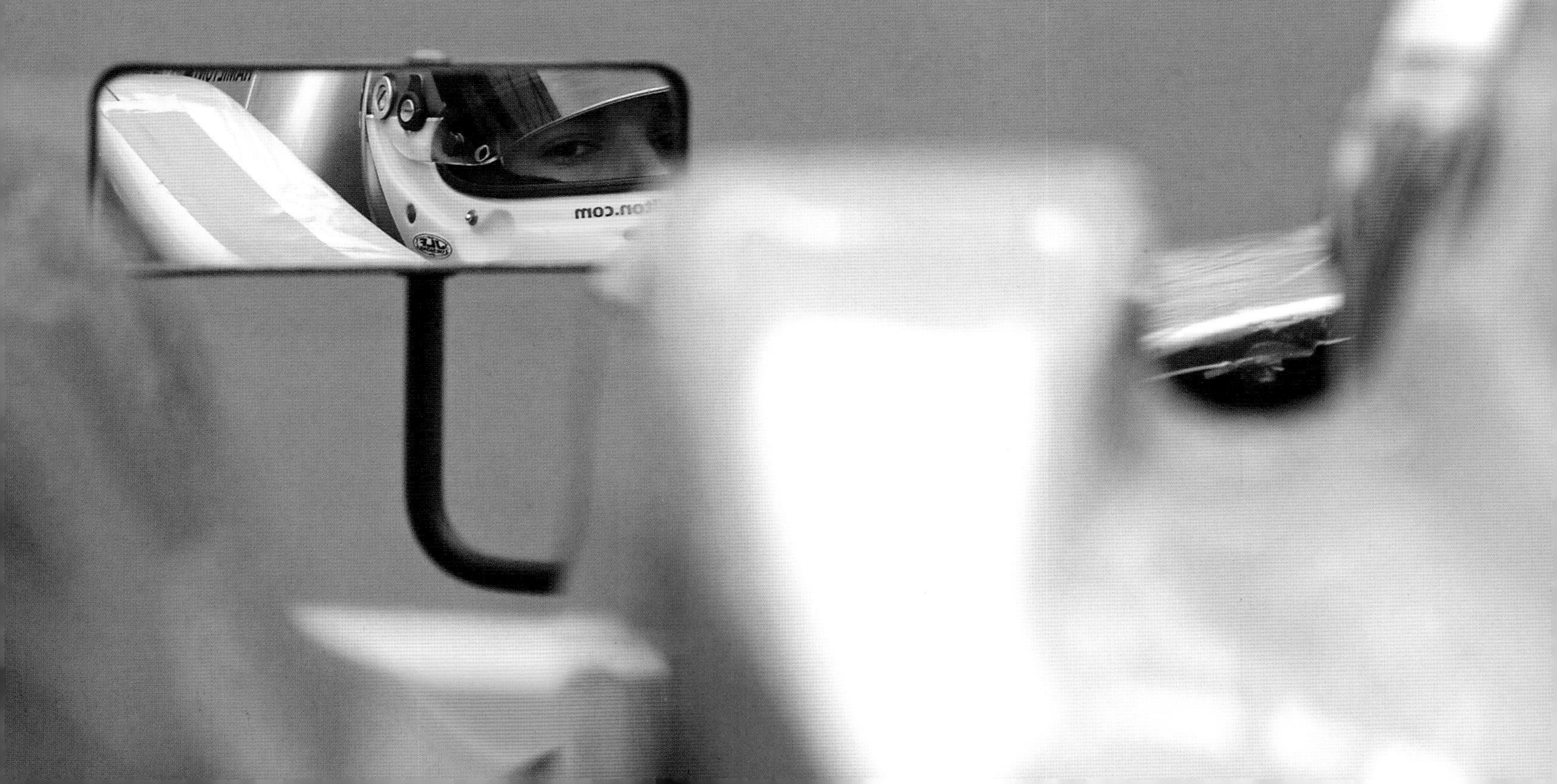

FORMULA 3 2003–2005 RESULTS

2003

British F3 Championship

Lewis Hamilton Race No 23
Manor Motorsport
Dallara F302 Mugen-Honda

Round 12 Brands Hatch

Race 1 – Qualifying

1	Nelson Piquet Jr	1m19.073s
2	Will Davison	1m19.139s
3	Eric Salignon	1m19.159s
7	**Lewis Hamilton**	**1m19.461s**

Race 1

1	Nelson Piquet Jr	20m4.063s
2	Will Davison	+5.579s
3	Danny Watts	+9.688s
R	**Lewis Hamilton**	
F/L	Robert Doornbos	1m19.127s

Race 2 – Qualifying

1	Nelson Piquet Jr	1m18.823s
2	Robert Doornbos	1m18.993s
3	Billy Asaro	1m19.063s
25	**Lewis Hamilton**	**No time**

Race 2

1	Nelson Piquet Jr	16m5.169s
2	Robert Doornbos	+11.798s
3	Jamie Green	+16.206s
R	**Lewis Hamilton**	
F/L	Nelson Piquet Jr	1m18.865s

2003

Macau Grand Prix

Lewis Hamilton Race No 27
Manor Motorsport
Dallara F302 Mugen-Honda

Combined Qualifying

1	Fabio Carbone	2m13.016s
2	Ryan Briscoe	2m13.223s
3	James Courtney	2m13.232s
18	**Lewis Hamilton**	**2m15.160s**

Qualifying Race

1	James Courtney	25m43.212s
2	Nicolas Lapierre	+4.607s
3	Richard Antinucci	+9.056s
5	**Lewis Hamilton**	**+13.312s**
F/L	James Courtney	2m13.381s

Feature Race

1	Nicolas Lapierre	1hr2m48.597s
2	Fabio Carbone	+5.416s
3	Katsuyuki Hiranake	+15.382s
R	**Lewis Hamilton**	
F/L	James Courtney	2m12.937s

2003

Korean F3 Superprix

Lewis Hamilton Race No 27
Manor Motorsport
Dallara F302 Mugen-Honda

Combined Qualifying

1	**Lewis Hamilton**	**1m9.989s**
2	Nelson Piquet Jr	1m10.536s
3	Richard Antinucci	1m10.196s

Race 1

1	Richard Antinucci	28m37.027s
2	Nelson Piquet Jr	+1.651s
3	Robert Doornbos	+2.929s
R	**Lewis Hamilton**	
F/L	Nelson Piquet Jr	1m10.350s

Race 2

1	Richard Antinucci	27m25.208s
2	Robert Doornbos	+1.982s
3	Nelson Piquet Jr	+2.473s
14	**Lewis Hamilton**	**+40.947s**
F/L	James Courtney	1m10.647s

Combined Race Classification

1	Richard Antinucci	56m2.235s
2	Robert Doornbos	+1.962s
3	Nelson Piquet Jr	+2.473s
N/C	**Lewis Hamilton**	

2004

F3 Euro Series

Lewis Hamilton Race No 35
Manor Motorsport
Dallara F302 Mercedes

Round 1 Hockenheim

Qualifying

1	Alexandre Prémat	1m33.880s
2	Nico Rosberg	1m34.039s
3	Jamie Green	1m34.169s
14	**Lewis Hamilton**	**1m35.038s**

Race

1	Nico Rosberg	28m50.559s
2	Alexandre Prémat	+1.114s
3	Franck Perera	+5.566s
11	**Lewis Hamilton**	**+25.680s**
F/L	Alexandre Prémat	1m34.979s

Round 2 Hockenheim

Qualifying

1	Jamie Green	1m34.332s
2	Alexandre Prémat	1m34.432s
3	Nico Rosberg	1m34.518s
9	**Lewis Hamilton**	**1m35.091s**

Race

1	Nico Rosberg	28m31.991s
2	Jamie Green	+0.883s
3	Alexandre Prémat	+8.331s
6	**Lewis Hamilton**	**+12.989s**
F/L	Jamie Green	1m33.892s

Round 3 Estoril

Qualifying

1	Alexandre Prémat	2m14.431s
2	Nico Rosberg	2m14.614s
3	Franck Perera	2m14.640s
25	**Lewis Hamilton**	**2m16.342s**

Race

1	Alexandre Prémat	30m12.123s
2	Jamie Green	+3.436s
3	Nicolas Lapierre	+15.122s
R	**Lewis Hamilton**	
F/L	Jamie Green	1m34.556s

Round 4 Estoril

Qualifying

1	Nicolas Lapierre	2m13.186s
2	Eric Salignon	2m13.232s
3	Jamie Green	2m13.394s
6	**Lewis Hamilton**	**2m13.667s**

Race

1	Eric Salignon	30m3.472s
2	Jamie Green	+6.587s
3	Nicolas Lapierrre	+7.217s
9	**Lewis Hamilton**	**+21.181s**
F/L	Eric Salignon	1m34.067s

Round 5 Adria

Qualifying

1	Adrian Sutil	1m20.843s
2	Jamie Green	1m20.898s
3	Roberto Streit	1m20.971s
6	**Lewis Hamilton**	**1m21.186s**

Race

1	Jamie Green	31m4.084s
2	Katsuyuki Hiranaka	+6.940s
3	Giedo van der Garde	+10.551s
R	**Lewis Hamilton**	
F/L	Nico Rosberg	1m11.039s

Round 6 Adria

Qualifying

1	Jamie Green	1m10.338s
2	Eric Salignon	1m10.350s
3	Nico Rosberg	1m10.422s
8	**Lewis Hamilton**	**1m10.785s**

Race

1	Eric Salignon	31m10.846s
2	Franck Perera	+1.630s
3	Daniel La Rosa	+3.945s
5	**Lewis Hamilton**	**+6.445s**
F/L	Bruno Spengler	1m11.029s

Round 7 Pau

Qualifying

1	Eric Salignon	1m10.990s
2	Jamie Green	1m11.104s
3	Robert Kubica	1m11.274s
11	**Lewis Hamilton**	**1m11.751s**

Race

1	Jamie Green	30m2.398s
2	Nicolas Lapierre	+24.586s
3	Robert Kubica	+27.313s
4	**Lewis Hamilton**	**+33.697s**
F/L	Jamie Green	1m28.433s

Round 8 Pau

Qualifying

1	Nicolas Lapierre	1m11.673s
2	Nico Rosberg	1m11.668s
3	Eric Salignon	1m11.721s
12	**Lewis Hamilton**	**1m11.976s**

Race

1	Nicolas Lapierre	30m47.121s
2	Robert Kubica	+4.172s
3	Jamie Green	+4.654s
7	**Lewis Hamilton**	**+14.537s**
F/L	Nicolas Lapierre	1m12.412s

Round 9 Norisring

Qualifying

1	**Lewis Hamilton**	**48.977s**
2	Nicolas Lapierre	48.994s
3	Alexandre Prémat	49.057s

Race

1	**Lewis Hamilton**	**29m8.759s**
2	Löic Duval	+2.046s
3	Franck Perera	+3.872s
F/L	Alexandre Prémat	49.316s

Round 10 Norisring

Qualifying

1	Jamie Green	49.206s
2	Alexandre Prémat	49.228s
3	Robert Kubica	49.305s
5	**Lewis Hamilton**	**49.372s**

Race

1	Alexandre Prémat	29m9.469s
2	Jamie Green	+0.487s
3	**Lewis Hamilton**	**+0.751s**
F/L	**Lewis Hamilton**	**49.324s**

Round 11 Magny-Cours

Qualifying

1	Jamie Green	1m34.411s
2	Alexandre Prémat	1m34.672s
3	Eric Salignon	1m34.842s
20	**Lewis Hamilton**	**1m35.841s**

Race

1	Jamie Green	30m59.788s
2	Eric Salignon	+2.707s
3	Löic Duval	+7.771s
R	**Lewis Hamilton**	
F/L	Jamie Green	1m36.996s

Round 12 Magny-Cours

Qualifying

1	Nico Rosberg	1m34.116s
2	Alexandre Prémat	1m34.271s
3	Nicolas Lapierre	1m34.282s
9	**Lewis Hamilton**	**1m34.755s**

Race

1	Alexandre Prémat	29m57.534s
2	Nico Rosberg	+0.794s
3	Bruno Spengler	+5.152s
21	**Lewis Hamilton**	**1 Lap**
F/L	**Lewis Hamilton**	**1m35.917s**

Round 13 Nürburgring

Qualifying

1	Jamie Green	1m22.621s
2	Nico Rosberg	1m22.634s
3	Eric Salignon	1m22.701s
4	**Lewis Hamilton**	**1m22.741s**

Race

1	Nico Rosberg	30m54.367s
2	Jamie Green	+5.075s
3	**Lewis Hamilton**	**+13.021s**
F/L	Nico Rosberg	1m23.356s

Round 14 Nürburgring

Qualifying

1	Nico Rosberg	1m22.863s
2	Robert Kubica	1m22.868s
3	Jamie Green	1m22.986s
4	**Lewis Hamilton**	**1m22.999s**

Race

1	Jamie Green	30m50.736s
2	Robert Kubica	+0.846s
3	Nico Rosberg	+3.072s
4	**Lewis Hamilton**	**+4.511s**
F/L	Jamie Green	1m23.415s

Round 15 Zandvoort

Qualifying

1	Eric Salignon	1m32.267s
2	Nicolas Lapierre	1m32.483s
3	Giedo van der Garde	1m32.554s
4	**Lewis Hamilton**	**1m32.850s**

Race

1	Eric Salignon	28m58.299s
2	Nicolas Lapierre	+0.486s
3	**Lewis Hamilton**	**+0.803s**
F/L	Eric Salignon	1m33.203s

Round 16 Zandvoort

Qualifying

1	Eric Salignon	1m32.171s
2	Jamie Green	1m32.186s
3	Alexandre Prémat	1m32.478s
5	**Lewis Hamilton**	**1m32.871s**

Race

1	Jamie Green	29m59.938s
2	Eric Salignon	+0.207s
3	Alexandre Prémat	+7.855s
6	**Lewis Hamilton**	**+17.374s**
F/L	Eric Salignon	1m33.723s

Round 17 Brno

Qualifying

1	Alexandre Prémat	1m50.619s
2	Jamie Green	1m50.701s
3	Franck Perera	1m51.516s
9	**Lewis Hamilton**	**1m51.825s**

Race

1	Jamie Green	28m31.884s
2	Alexandre Prémat	+5.486s
3	Franck Perera	+19.084s
7	**Lewis Hamilton**	**+23.894s**
F/L	Jamie Green	1m53.176s

Round 18 Brno

Qualifying

1	Alexandre Prémat	1m50.976s
2	Jamie Green	1m51.402s
3	Bruno Spengler	1m51.455s
7	**Lewis Hamilton**	**1m51.835s**

Race

1	Jamie Green	28m20.149s
2	Alexandre Prémat	+7.817s
3	Giedo van der Garde	+19.194s
4	**Lewis Hamilton**	**+25.046s**
F/L	Jamie Green	1m52.595s

Round 19 Hockenheim

Qualifying

1	Nicolas Lapierre	1m47.097s
2	Hannes Neuhauser	1m47.142s
3	Maximillian Götz	1m47.228s
4	**Lewis Hamilton**	**1m47.343s**

Race

1	Nicolas Lapierre	28m59.962s
2	**Lewis Hamilton**	**+4.200s**
3	Charles Zwolsman	+9.870s
F/L	Alexandre Prémat	1m35.629s

Round 20 Hockenheim

Qualifying

	Adrian Sutil	1m34.533s
	Nicolas Lapierre	1m34.630s
	Roberto Streit	1m34.664s
0	Lewis Hamilton	1m35.036s

Race

	Nicolas Lapierre	28m40.437s
	Jamie Green	+0.735s
	Roberto Streit	+5.958s
	Lewis Hamilton	+13.094s
/L	Nicolas Lapierre	1m34.683s

Final Championship Positions

	Jamie Green	139 points
	Alexandre Prémat	88 points
	Nicolas Lapierre	85 points
	Lewis Hamilton	68 points

2004

Marlboro Masters F3 – Zandvoort

Lewis Hamilton Race No 7
Manor Motorsport
Dallara F302 Mercedes

Qualifying

	Alexandre Prémat	1m32.767s
	Eric Salignon	1m32.974s
	James Rossiter	1m32.816s
4	Lewis Hamilton	1m33.353s

Race

	Alexandre Prémat	43m20.752s
	Eric Salignon	+2.130s
	Adam Carroll	+4.105s
	Lewis Hamilton	+15.103s
/L	Eric Salignon	1m34.220s

2004

Macau Grand Prix

Lewis Hamilton Race No 21
Manor Motorsport
Dallara F302 Mercedes

Combined Qualifying

	Robert Kubica	2m12.155s
	Lewis Hamilton	2m12.344s
	Richard Antinucci	2m12.512s

Qualifying Race

	Lewis Hamilton	33m18.341s
	Nico Rosberg	+2.284s
	Alexandre Prémat	+3.982s
/L	Lewis Hamilton	

Feature Race

	Alexandre Prémat	37m13.731s
	Robert Kubica	+0.675s
	Lucas Di Grassi	+1.178s
4	Lewis Hamilton	+7.267s
/L	Robert Kubica	2m13.215s

2004

Bahrain F3 Superprix

Lewis Hamilton Race No 21
Manor Motorsport
Dallara F302 Mercedes

Combined Qualifying

	Franck Perera	1m53.938s
	Jamie Green	1m53.972s
	Fabio Carbone	1m54.078s
2	Lewis Hamilton	1m55.227s

Qualifying Race

	Jamie Green	15m17.488s
	Fabio Carbone	+3.357s
	Nico Rosberg	+5.552s
1	Lewis Hamilton	+15.575s
/L	Jamie Green	

Feature Race

	Lewis Hamilton	47m11.528s
	Nico Rosberg	+0.794s
	Jamie Green	+4.701s
/L	Jamie Green	1m54.048s

2005

F3 Euro Series

Lewis Hamilton Race No 1
ASM Formule 3
Dallara F305 Mercedes

Round 1 Hockenheim

Qualifying

1	Lewis Hamilton	1m37.725s
2	Adrian Sutil	1m38.657s
3	Giedo van der Garde	1m38.660s

Race

1	Lewis Hamilton	28m43.886s
2	Adrian Sutil	+6.132s
3	Marco Bonanomi	+18.106s
F/L	Lewis Hamilton	1m35.135s

Round 2 Hockenheim

Qualifying

1	Paul Di Resta	2m1.194s
2	Loïc Duval	2m1.498s
3	James Rossiter	2m1.582s
5	Lewis Hamilton	2m2.090s

Race

1	James Rossiter	31m18.125s
2	Loïc Duval	+14.192s
3	Lewis Hamilton	+18.291s
F/L	Richard Antinucci	1m45.101s

Round 3 Pau

Qualifying

1	Lewis Hamilton	1m10.490s
2	Adrian Sutil	1m11.069s
3	Franck Perera	1m11.078s

Race

1	Lewis Hamilton	30m26.815s
2	Loïc Duval	+9.390s
3	James Rossiter	+10.952s
F/L	Lewis Hamilton	1m11.353s

Round 4 Pau

Qualifying

1	Lewis Hamilton	1m11.021s
2	Adrian Sutil	1m11.806s
3	Loïc Duval	1m11.152s

Race

1	Lewis Hamilton	30m15.999s
2	Adrian Sutil	+4.087s
3	Loïc Duval	+7.263s
F/L	Lewis Hamilton	1m11.668s

Round 5 Spa-Francorchamps

Qualifying

1	Lewis Hamilton	2m33.705s
2	James Rossiter	2m34.164s
3	Adrian Sutil	2m35.248s

Race

1	Adrian Sutil	31m21.675s
2	James Rossiter	+11.291s
3	Guillaume Moreau	+17.916s
D	Lewis Hamilton	
F/L	Adrian Sutil	2m34.526s

Round 6 Spa-Francorchamps

Qualifying

1	Adrian Sutil	2m14.641s
2	Lewis Hamilton	2m14.932s
3	Esteban Guerrieri	2m15.548s

Race

1	Lewis Hamilton	26m56.524s
2	Adrian Sutil	+2.160s
3	Lucas Di Grassi	+17.562s
F/L	Lewis Hamilton	1m13.844s

Round 7 Monaco

Qualifying

1	Lewis Hamilton	1m28.593s
2	Adrian Sutil	1m29.202s
3	Loïc Duval	1m29.316s

Race

1	Lewis Hamilton	28m42.069s
2	Adrian Sutil	+1.777s
3	Loïc Duval	+12.525s
F/L	Adrian Sutil	1m28.017s

Round 8 Monaco

Qualifying

1	Lewis Hamilton	1m28.593s
2	Adrian Sutil	1m29.202s
3	Loïc Duval	1m29.316s

Race

1	Lewis Hamilton	39m4.191s
2	Loïc Duval	+7.644s
3	Franck Perera	+10.513s
F/L	Lewis Hamilton	1m28.797s

Round 9 Oschersleben

Qualifying

1	Lucas Di Grassi	1m17.781s
2	Paul Di Resta	1m17.953s
3	Adrian Sutil	1m18.133s
4	Lewis Hamilton	1m18.207s

Race

1	Lucas Di Grassi	31m3.925s
2	Adrian Sutil	+1.473s
3	Lewis Hamilton	+2.262s
F/L	Giedo van der Garde	1m19.384s

Round 10 Oschersleben

Qualifying

1	Lewis Hamilton	1m17.747s
2	Lucas Di Grassi	1m17.918s
3	Adrian Sutil	1m18.312s

Race

1	Lewis Hamilton	29m18.523s
2	Lucas Di Grassi	+7.205s
3	Adrian Sutil	+8.218s
F/L	Lewis Hamilton	1m19.183s

Round 11 Norisring

Qualifying

1	Lewis Hamilton	48.874s
2	Adrian Sutil	49.110s
3	Sebastian Vettel	49.123s

Race

1	Lewis Hamilton	30m35.173s
2	Sebastian Vettel	+3.040s
3	Paul Di Resta	+4.607s
F/L	Lewis Hamilton	49.262s

Round 12 Norisring

Qualifying

1	Lewis Hamilton	49.038s
2	Adrian Sutil	49.273s
3	Sebastian Vettel	49.345s

Race

1	Lewis Hamilton	28m51.233s
2	Adrian Sutil	+2.709s
3	Franck Perera	+11.643s
F/L	Adrian Sutil	49.035s

Round 13 Nürburgring

Qualifying

1	Paul Di Resta	1m22.463s
2	Lucas Di Grassi	1m22.575s
3	Lewis Hamilton	1m22.638s

Race

1	Adrian Sutil	30m49.380s
2	Lucas Di Grassi	+0.594s
3	Kohei Hirate	+16.216s
12	Lewis Hamilton	+30.512s
F/L	Paul Di Resta	1m23.147s

Round 14 Nürburgring

Qualifying

1	Lucas Di Grassi	1m23.009s
2	Lewis Hamilton	1m23.115s
3	Paul Di Resta	1m23.134s

Race

1	Lewis Hamilton	30m18.782s
2	Sebastian Vettel	+19.615s
3	Adrian Sutil	+22.411s
F/L	Lewis Hamilton	1m22.744s

Round 15 Zandvoort

Qualifying

1	Lewis Hamilton	1m31.259s
2	Adrian Sutil	1m31.512s
3	Lucas Di Grassi	1m31.774s

Race

1	Guillaume Moreau	30m5.230s
2	Sebastian Vettel	+3.393s
3	Franck Perera	+6.319s
R	Lewis Hamilton	
F/L	Paul Di Resta	1m33.497s

Round 16 Zandvoort

Qualifying

1	Lewis Hamilton	1m31.592s
2	Lucas Di Grassi	1m32.189s
3	Adrian Sutil	1m32.198s

Race

1	Lewis Hamilton	30m8.794s
2	Sebastian Vettel	+1.077s
3	Giedo van de Garde	+12.687s
F/L	Luca Di Grassi	1m34.134s

Round 17 Lausitzring

Qualifying

1	Giedo van der Garde	1m20.813s
2	Sebastian Vettel	1m20.944s
3	Lewis Hamilton	1m21.230s

Race

1	Lewis Hamilton	31m10.310s
2	Giedo van de Garde	+8.410s
3	Sebastian Vettel	+16.442s
F/L	Esteban Guerrieri	1m23.024s

Round 18 Lausitzring

Qualifying

1	Paul Di Resta	1m33.496s
2	Lewis Hamilton	1m34.039s
3	Franck Perera	1m34.196s

Race

1	Lewis Hamilton	30m54.350s
2	Adrian Sutil	+11.177s
3	Lucas Di Grassi	+15.575s
F/L	Lewis Hamilton	1m16.546s

Round 19 Hockenheim

Qualifying

1	Lewis Hamilton	1m49.698s
2	Lucas Di Grassi	1m50.154s
3	Maximillian Götz	1m50.179s

Race

1	Lewis Hamilton	31m16.906s
2	Lucas Di Grassi	+14.230s
3	Maximillian Götz	+16.553s
F/L	Sebastian Vettel	1m47.439s

Round 20 Hockenheim

Qualifying

1	Lewis Hamilton	1m34.132s
2	Lucas Di Grassi	1m34.360s
3	Guillaume Moreau	1m34.588s

Race

1	Lewis Hamilton	28m37.411s
2	Guillaume Moreau	+3.990s
3	Sebastian Vettel	+5.772s
F/L	Lewis Hamilton	1m34.528s

Final Championship Positions

1	Lewis Hamilton	172 points
2	Adrian Sutil	94 points
3	Lucas Di Grassi	68 points

2005

Marlboro Masters F3 – Zandvoort

Lewis Hamilton Race No 1
ASM Formule 3
Dallara F305 Mercedes

Qualifying

1	Lewis Hamilton	1m31.175s
2	Adrian Sutil	1m31.441s
3	Paul Di Resta	1m31.811s

Race

1	Lewis Hamilton	39m2.045s
2	Adrian Sutil	+6.477s
3	Lucas Di Grassi	+7.254s
F/L	Lewis Hamilton	1m32.866s

F/L = Fastest lap R = Retired D = Disqualified N/C = Not Classified

RICHARD
2
RICHARD

GP2 Series

A STAR ASCENDS

"That was the best race of my life!" – Lewis Hamilton's verdict on his stunning fightback from 18th to second in the GP2 sprint race at Istanbul.

His drive was of such verve and brilliance that as he walked back from the podium, seven-times World Champion Michael Schumacher made his way over to the 21-year-old to offer his congratulations. It was the only time the two were to meet in the F1 paddock while the German legend was still an active Grand Prix driver. Two weeks later, at Monza, just a few hours after Lewis claimed the GP2 title with a pair of podium positions, an emotional Schumacher announced his retirement in front of Ferrari's passionate *tifosi* fans.

It was a symbolic changing of the guard. The old master stepping aside as the man who would be King moved out of his shadows. It would also leave open an intriguing question: how would Hamilton have fared against Schumacher? Or should that be how would Schumacher have coped with Hamilton?

Lewis's stunning debut in F1, just six months after clinching the GP2 title, was proof positive of the effectiveness of the latter series as a feeder formula. When its predecessor, Formula 3000, began losing its way in the early 2000s, F1 boss Bernie Ecclestone and Renault F1's talismanic leader Flavio Briatore decided that a new junior category was needed to prepare drivers for the final step into the big time. GP2 was the result, and when series one champ Nico Rosberg set fastest lap on his F1 debut for Williams, GP2 became the place to be for all young drivers aspiring to Formula 1.

LEFT Lewis locks up as he pushes hard during the penultimate round of the 2006 GP2 Series in Istanbul – a weekend that would provide two of the finest drives of his pre-Formula 1 career.

It's hard to comprehend now, given how well GP2 prepared Hamilton for F1, but there was a time when his participation in the series was in doubt, as McLaren evaluated the benefit of slotting him in as an F1 test and reserve driver rather than funding him to race in the Renault-backed series. But Hamilton was always clear that he wanted to race and GP2 was the obvious place to be. "Of course I would love to drive an F1 car, but F1 is not crucial at the moment," he said as he headed to Jerez in southern Spain for his first GP2 test outing in November 2005. "I need to be focused on GP2 and not get distracted by anything else."

Having claimed the Formula 3 Euroseries title in dominant fashion with the crack French ASM Formule team, it was natural that his maiden GP2 test would be with its sister ART Grand Prix squad, which had taken Rosberg to the first GP2 Championship.

Hamilton sat out the first day of the test, but used the time to monitor the performance of the cars and in particular their F1-esque grooved tyres. Along with double the horsepower of his F3 car, getting to grips with this unusual type of tyre would be his biggest challenge. Yet within half a dozen laps of his first run in the car, he was at the top of the timesheets – and he stayed there until the end of the test. Team boss Frederic Vasseur was mightily impressed: "What Lewis did was excellent considering it was his first time in the car. Hopefully we will find out soon if he is doing the season, because for sure he is the best option for us."

Although there had been no official confirmation, Hamilton's appearance at the next GP2 test session, at Paul Ricard in France, was a sure-fire sign of his 2006 ambitions. Here he encountered wet conditions for the first time, but naturally it didn't faze him, and once again the red-and-white ART car with the driver in the yellow helmet was at the head of the times.

Lewis had clearly shown himself a force to be reckoned with, and with ART running probably the best car in the series he was instantly acknowledged

LEFT, FROM TOP Lewis heads out for his first GP2 test, on grooved tyres, at Jerez in November 2005; interpreting telemetry data is a vital part of the job; trying the GP2 simulator during testing at Paul Ricard.

RIGHT Profile of a champion – a face that would soon be recognised throughout the world.

"Of course I would love to drive an F1 car, but F1 is not crucial at the moment. I need to be focused on GP2 and not get distracted by anything else."

BELOW Lewis acknowledges his delighted crew as he crosses the line to win at the Nürburgring in May.

OPPOSITE, CLOCKWISE FROM TOP LEFT Qualifying against the breathtaking Monaco backdrop; Lewis gives the thumbs-up after claiming pole position at Monaco; tunnel vision – at 160mph – during a faultless drive to Monaco victory, a turning point in the GP2 Series title fight.

as pre-season favourite. But not everyone expected a title tilt. His record in Formula Renault and Formula 3 had shown him to be a second-year driver: in both series he'd been strong at times in his rookie year, but had upped his game considerably in his second. Why should GP2 be any different?

However, this argument failed to take into account his increasing maturity, not to mention his excellent relationship with ASM/ART, where he slotted perfectly into the team's rigorously prepared F1-style mentality. His chances were further boosted when GP2 decided to switch to more conventional slick tyres. While Lewis had no problem in getting up to speed on the grooves, he still lacked experience at managing them through a whole race. In terms of performance and wear characteristics the slicks would be much closer to the tyres he'd been used to throughout the rest of his racing career.

GP2 2006 kicked off with a stand-alone event in Valencia. F1 supremo Bernie Ecclestone was in attendance in a prelude to an eventual Valencia F1 street race, giving the meeting a sense of occasion, and an impressive launch party in the city's futuristic downtown added extra gravitas. But it's what happened on the track that really matters, and there it was Nelson Piquet Jr who laid down a marker by taking pole position and scorching to an emphatic win, 17 seconds up the road from Lewis, who fluffed his start from third on the grid and dropped to the tail end of the top ten. But a combination of a good early pit call and some robust overtaking moved him up to second and his first GP2 podium finish.

GP2 reverses the finishing order of the top eight in the feature race for the starting order of the second, shorter sprint race. Thus Lewis lined up seventh for his second GP2 race, although his start was pretty much the same, as he again bogged down and lost a couple of places.

With no pit stops, he had to do all his passing on the track. The tight, slow-speed Valencia circuit was built for motorcycle racing and does little to facilitate overtaking by cars, but Lewis forced his way back up the order to take sixth at the flag. With one round over he was third in the points, behind Piquet and French A1GP star Nicolas Lapierre.

San Marino was next up, and it would be a bittersweet weekend for Lewis. Again he qualified third and again there were problems at the start. After creeping on the line he was adjudged to have jumped the start, and was penalised with a stop-go penalty. He was called in to take this just as the safety car was deployed after chaos erupted further down the order. Unsure of where he was when he rejoined, Hamilton passed the safety car along with the two cars in front on him that were waved through. But unbeknown to him he was actually leading the race at the time and was subsequently disqualified for his infringement.

This meant he started from last in the sprint, but he was in inspired form and stormed back from 26th to tenth. It wasn't enough for a point, but he was far from downhearted: "We've shown we've got the pace and I feel that sooner or later it's all just going to come right and I'm going to take pole, fastest lap and the win..."

Two weeks later at the Nürburgring he did just that. Well, not exactly. Piquet took pole – as he would do at most races that season. But from third on the grid (again) Lewis got it just right at the start, snatched the lead from the superfast-starting Hiroki Yoshimoto at Turn 3 and disappeared into the distance. Even a drive-through penalty for speeding in the pit lane – "It was my mistake, I took my finger off the button too early" – couldn't remove him from the lead. His eventual

POTENZA
UNIQA
Insurance Group
MARTINI
MARTINI
MARTINI
Marlboro
Marlboro
RENAULT

Mobil
BRIDGESTONE
L.Hamilton

ABOVE Taking the chequered flag to win Saturday's feature race at the Silverstone British Grand Prix meeting. Sunday would provide an even more impressive performance, bringing the crowd to its feet.

winning margin was 19 seconds – it could have been double that.

His first win was soon followed by his second. And what a win it was! From eighth on the grid he made another good start and was fifth by the end of lap one. On lap five he passed José Maria López for fourth, getting a great run out of the final turn and outbraking the Argentine into the tight first corner. A few laps later he pulled the same move on Adam Carroll. Lapierre also succumbed soon after, leaving only Yoshimoto in the way of an astonishing double. For three laps the Japanese clung on before he fell in the same way, powerless to resist Hamilton's superiority on the brakes. After these two stunning wins Lewis was up to second in the championship, just a point behind Piquet.

One golden rule in motor racing is that you don't hit your team-mate, but that's exactly what happened to Hamilton at the next GP2 round in Barcelona. After another poor start, ART pitted Lewis early and the strategy worked brilliantly. Lapping way faster than the rest of the field, he moved into the lead when they came in for their mandatory stops. But stopping so early meant the tyre wear was marginal and in the

RIGHT The banner says it all, as Lewis's reputation spread throughout the motorsport world and beyond.

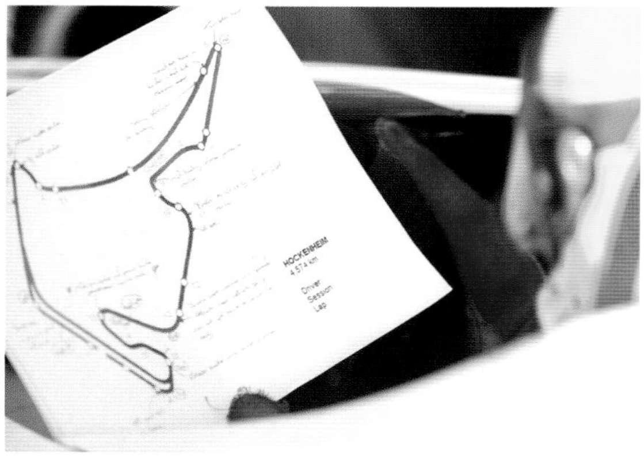

FAR RIGHT Lewis studies his circuit notes during qualifying at Hockenheim.

closing stages he became a sitting duck on his badly worn Bridgestones. But with team-mate Alexandre Prémat behind him, surely he was safe? Prémat had other ideas, and on the final lap he dived inside under braking for the hairpin. There was contact as the Frenchman clipped Hamilton's left rear wheel. It was minor, but enough to send Hamilton spinning. He recovered to take second, and managed fourth in the sprint, but the lost points allowed Piquet to retain the championship lead.

Monaco came next and it proved to be a turning point in the title fight. From the only GP2 pole of his career, Hamilton drove a faultless race. Franck Perera, one of his old karting rivals, kept the pressure on, but Lewis never faltered and achieved an impressive win. With Piquet off-colour and out of the points the title lead shifted to Lewis for the first time.

He was denied pole for his home race at Silverstone by just four thousandths of a second by another Brit, Adam Carroll. But he passed Carroll around the outside into the first corner and what followed was an exhibition of pure speed and control. Timo Glock put up a challenge after a mid-race safety-car restart, but Hamilton held on for an emotional win.

But if anyone thought that was good, they needed only to wait until the sprint race to see something even better. Hamilton's drive in front of the packed grandstands as people were ushered in for the Grand Prix will go down in Silverstone history. Indeed, his three-abreast pass of Clivio Piccione and Piquet into Maggotts must surely rate as one of the finest passes of all time.

Coming out of Copse, Lewis picked up a great tow from the pair duelling ahead. Then, as they approached the challenging sequence of high-speed turns at Maggotts and Becketts, he flicked to the right of Piccione as Piquet went to the left, and in one fell swoop he passed them both. From there he continued his charge, clearing the remaining cars ahead of him with devastating aplomb. When he crossed the line to take a landmark triumph the crowd erupted in spontaneous applause and a new British racing hero was born. His championship lead was 21 points and Hamilton's momentum seemed unstoppable. Stories about McLaren bringing Lewis into its F1 line-up began to gather pace...

His first real mistake of the season followed at Magny-Cours, when he misjudged a passing move

BELOW Lewis battles with Adam Carroll at Hockenheim, where he came second in the feature race and third in the sprint event to stretch his lead over Nelson Piquet Jr in the championship table.

ABOVE **Lewis ponders the uphill struggle ahead after crashing on his first flying lap during qualifying in Hungary, leaving him at the back of the grid.**

RIGHT **Leading title rival Nelson Piquet Jr during the sprint race in Istanbul. Lewis drove a stunning race to finish second after a spin on the opening lap dropped him to 18th place**

on Carroll and spun. He fought back to 19th and took the point for fastest lap, and stemmed the flow of points lost to Piquet by a strong run to fifth in the sprint.

His title lead stretched out with two strong podium finishes in Germany, while Piquet had a disaster with two non-scores. With the championship looking all but over, the series headed for Hungary.

In the crucial free practice session – drivers get just 30 minutes of running before qualifying in GP2 – Lewis made an uncharacteristic error and spun into the barriers, causing heavy damage to his car: "That's the first time I've crashed a GP2 car and it wasn't a good time to do it," he admitted. An even worse time to do it was on his first flying lap in qualifying, but that's exactly what he did – and in exactly the same place! This left him 26th and last on the grid, while Piquet was on his customary pole.

Piquet dominated the race, but a brave drive by Lewis took him from last to tenth on a track where overtaking is all but impossible. This earned him no points, but placed him in a position from which it was possible to salvage something in the sprint. An inspired Piquet won again in torrential conditions, but he was followed home by Hamilton. With his back against the wall Lewis had proved his mettle, and with potential disaster averted he headed for Turkey and his date with destiny...

The fantastic new Istanbul Park facility was the setting for Hamilton's finest moment of his pre-F1 career. In qualifying he was a surprisingly lowly fifth, while Piquet was on pole as usual and with the wind really in his sails. As he had in Hungary, Piquet made a textbook start and roared away into the lead.

It took Hamilton seven laps to work his way up to second, by which time Piquet was over seven seconds up the road. With the bit between his teeth, Lewis started to claw back Piquet's advantage – a little at a time, but enough to set up a tantalising battle between the championship contenders. With the race on the verge of a classic battle, ART called Lewis in for new tyres. It was a make or break move

but a sticking wheel nut cost him valuable time and he rejoined in the cut and thrust of the top six fight. In a taster of what was to come in the sprint, he scythed his way back up to second, but by now Piquet was out of reach – but almost in touch in the title race.

When Lewis spun on the opening lap of the sprint, dropping back to 18th place, his grip on the GP2 title appeared to be weakening. But the spin – caused by cold rear tyres and a set-up of minimum downforce, designed to make him super quick on the straights – only spurred him on to greater things.

Lap after lap, corner after corner, Hamilton dispatched one rival after another. Only Timo Glock in fourth offered staunch resistance, the pair running wheel-to-wheel through three corners before Lewis finally took him. That delay may have ultimately cost Lewis the win. He blasted by Carroll on the final lap to take second, but Andi Zuber was just a fraction too far away to be caught. "I think that's the best I've ever driven," an emotional Hamilton said afterwards. With just Monza to go, the championship lead was back to ten points and his to lose.

In the end the title was sealed in pretty straightforward fashion. Needing only to keep Piquet in check, Lewis did just that in the opening race, trailing the Brazilian home in third place to become the 2006 GP2 Champion. Second in the sprint – after an amazing start – was the icing on the cake.

"I can't explain just how good it feels to be champion," he exclaimed. "It's been such a good fight with Nelson and this has been such a competitive series."

RIGHT Celebrating after clinching the championship at Monza.

FAR RIGHT Nick Hamilton congratulates his big brother on his championship victory.

GP2 SERIES 2006 RESULTS

Lewis Hamilton Race No 2
ART Grand Prix
Dallara GP2 Renault

Round 1 Valencia

Qualifying

1	Nelson Piquet Jr	1m17.886s
2	Tristan Gommendy	1m18.360s
3	**Lewis Hamilton**	**1m18.400s**

Race 1

1	Nelson Piquet Jr	1hr3m15.360s
2	**Lewis Hamilton**	**+16.655s**
3	Adrián Vallés	+19.490s
F/L	Nicolas Lapierre	1m22.168s

Race 2

1	Michael Ammermuller	38m44.066s
2	Ernesto Viso	+9.756s
3	Nicolas Lapierre	+10.213s
6	**Lewis Hamilton**	**+18.510**
F/L	Andreas Zuber	1m21.244s

Round 2 Imola

Qualifying

1	Gianmaria Bruni	1m32.691s
2	José Maria López	1m32.940s
3	**Lewis Hamilton**	**1m32.990s**

Race 1

1	Gianmaria Bruni	1h1m13.889s
2	Michael Ammermuller	+10.907s
3	Nicolas Lapierre	+14.514s
D	**Lewis Hamilton**	
F/L	Adrián Vallés	1m35.261s

Race 2

1	Ernesto Viso	45m17.116s
2	Nelson Piquet Jr	+0.596s
3	Hiroki Yoshimoto	+25.001s
10	**Lewis Hamilton**	**+33.366s**
F/L	Ernesto Viso	1m34.431s

Round 3 Nürburgring

Qualifying

1	Nelson Piquet Jr	1m40.799s
2	Franck Perera	1m41.241s
3	**Lewis Hamilton**	**1m41.325s**

Race 1

1	**Lewis Hamilton**	**1h1m26.097s**
2	Alexandre Prémat	+19.642s
3	Adam Carroll	+28.756s
F/L	**Lewis Hamilton**	**1m42.782s**

Race 2

1	**Lewis Hamilton**	**41m18.772s**
2	Nicolas Lapierre	+1.034s
3	José Maria López	+3.821s
F/L	Alexandre Prémat	1m40.983s

Round 4 Barcelona

Qualifying

1	Nelson Piquet Jr	1m23.704s
2	**Lewis Hamilton**	**1m23.371s**
3	Alexandre Prémat	1m23.758s

Race 1

1	Alexandre Prémat	57m24.150s
2	**Lewis Hamilton**	**+2.187s**
3	Michael Ammermuller	+10.963s
F/L	Adrián Vallés	1m25.550s

Race 2

1	Ernesto Viso	37m37.277s
2	Nelson Piquet Jr	+0.730s
3	Alexandre Prémat	+1.581s
4	**Lewis Hamilton**	**+2.443s**
F/L	Gianmaria Bruni	1m25.970s

Round 5 Monaco

Qualifying

1	**Lewis Hamilton**	**1m20.430s**
2	Franck Perera	1m20.717s
3	Gianmaria Bruni	1m21.155s

Race

1	**Lewis Hamilton**	**1hr3m50.768s**
2	Franck Perera	+8.445s
3	Alexandre Prémat	+36.312s
F/L	Lucas Di Grassi	1m22.563s

Round 6 Silverstone

Qualifying

1	Adam Carroll	1m29.104s
2	**Lewis Hamilton**	**1m29.108s**
3	Alexandre Prémat	1m29.134s

Race 1

1	**Lewis Hamilton**	**37m27.225s**
2	Timo Glock	+5.014s
3	Adam Carroll	+6.145s
F/L	**Lewis Hamilton**	**1m32.505s**

Race 2

1	**Lewis Hamilton**	**1hr53.888s**
2	Adam Carroll	+10.040s
3	Clivio Piccione	+11.025s
F/L	**Lewis Hamilton**	**1m31.313s**

Round 7 Magny-Cours

Qualifying

1	José Maria López	1m23.910s
2	Timo Glock	1m24.031s
3	Giorgio Pantano	1m24.057s
4	**Lewis Hamilton**	**1m24.100s**

Race 1

1	Timo Glock	1hr1m14.285s
2	Alexadre Prémat	+5.988s
3	José Maria López	+17.100s
19	**Lewis Hamilton**	**1 Lap**
F/L	**Lewis Hamilton**	**1m27.418s**

Race 2

1	Giorgio Pantano	40m55.810s
2	Nelson Piquet Jr	+0.500s
3	Alexandre Prémat	+9.667s
5	**Lewis Hamilton**	**+12.199s**
F/L	José Maria López	1m26.513s

Round 8 Hockenheim

Qualifying

1	Gianmaria Bruni	1m22.588s
2	Timo Glock	1m22.910s
3	Nelson Piquet Jr	1m22.928s
8	**Lewis Hamilton**	**1m23.169s**

Race 1

1	Gianmaria Bruni	57m40.763s
2	**Lewis Hamilton**	**+1.238s**
3	Timo Glock	+16.319s
F/L	Alexandre Prémat	1m23.774s

Race 2

1	Timo Glock	38m36.598s
2	José Maria López	+1.322s
3	**Lewis Hamilton**	**+12.610s**
F/L	Lucas Di Grassi	1m24.477s

Round 9 Hungaroring

Qualifying

1	Nelson Piquet Jr	1m29.464s
2	José Maria López	1m30.081s
3	Michael Ammermuller	1m30.274s
26	**Lewis Hamilton**	**No time**

Race 1

1	Nelson Piquet Jr	1hr5m13.884s
2	Timo Glock	+32.795s
3	Giorgio Pantano	+34.019s
10	**Lewis Hamilton**	**1m13.818s**
F/L	Nelson Piquet Jr	1m30.711s

Race 2

1	Nelson Piquet Jr	45m59.804s
2	**Lewis Hamilton**	**+12.921s**
3	Alexandre Prémat	+26.202s
F/L	Nelson Piquet Jr	1m51.716s

Round 10 Istanbul

Qualifying

1	Nelson Piquet Jr	1m34.741s
2	José Maria López	1m34.744s
3	Giorgio Pantano	1m35.068s
5	**Lewis Hamilton**	**1m35.169s**

Race 1

1	Nelson Piquet Jr	55m59.398s
2	**Lewis Hamiliton**	**+17.879s**
3	Alexandre Prémat	+23.964s
F/L	Nelson Piquet Jr	1m36.334s

Race 2

1	Andreas Zuber	37m54.990s
2	**Lewis Hamilton**	**+2.938s**
3	Adam Carroll	+3.826s
F/L	**Lewis Hamilton**	**1m36.822s**

Round 11 Monza

Qualifying

1	Nelson Piquet Jr	1m30.161s
2	Giorgio Pantano	1m30.390s
3	**Lewis Hamilton**	**1m30.488s**

Race 1

1	Giorgio Pantano	51m31.171s
2	Nelson Piquet Jr	+5.054s
3	**Lewis Hamilton**	**+6.887s**
F/L	**Lewis Hamilton**	**1m31.038s**

Race 2

1	Giorgio Pantano	32m8.597s
2	**Lewis Hamilton**	**+0.411s**
3	Clivio Piccione	+14.075s
F/L	**Lewis Hamilton**	**1m30.528s**

Final Championship Positions

1	**Lewis Hamilton**	**113 points**
2	Nelson Piquet Jr	101 points
3	Alexandre Prémat	66 points
4	Timo Glock	57 points
5	Giorgio Pantano	43 points
6	Ernesto Viso	42 points

F/L = Fastest lap R = Retired D = Disqualified

Lewis
SAP
SIEMENS
at&t

F1 Testing

LIVING THE DREAM

Had fiery Colombian Juan Pablo Montoya not walked away from Formula 1 after crashing out of the US Grand Prix midway through the 2006 season, things could have turned out very differently for Lewis Hamilton.

Had Montoya stuck it out with McLaren for the rest of the year, he would have been in pole position to claim the seat next to Fernando Alonso in the 2007 line-up. With McLaren famously averse to offering one of its seats to a rookie – twice bitten by the crashing exploits of Andrea de Cesaris in 1981 and the crushing under-achievement of Michael Andretti in 1993 – Montoya's experience and undoubted speed would have been a near-unbeatable combination once it became clear that Ron Dennis's dream pairing of Alonso with Kimi Räikkönen could not happen, as the Finn was off to Ferrari. In that scenario Lewis would have been left with the prospect of a year on the testing sidelines or placed with a team further down the grid.

But Montoya decided his future lay in NASCAR stock-car racing in the US, and this opened up the possibility for Lewis of a race drive in one of the best teams in F1, his title-winning performance in GP2 marking him out as a major talent of the future. Lewis's only real rival for the drive was McLaren test driver Pedro de la Rosa, who'd done a commendable job standing in for Montoya in the second half of 2006. And while everyone in the team was at pains to stress it wasn't a shoot-out, with Alonso still contracted to Renault, end-of-season testing would

LEFT The sun sets at the end of another hard day's work testing at Barcelona in November 2006, Lewis's first test after the announcement that he would be racing in F1 for McLaren-Mercedes in 2007.

RIGHT Wearing McLaren-Mercedes F1 livery for the first time at Silverstone in September 2006.

BELOW Lewis's first taste of F1 power was at the *Autosport* Young Driver Test at Silverstone in December 2004.

give the team the perfect opportunity to assess the merits of the two candidates.

The first of these outings was at Silverstone a week after Hamilton clinched the GP2 title in the final round at Monza. The British press was out in force at the Northamptonshire track, but would be disappointed. A shortage of engines meant that Lewis was restricted to a handful of in-and-out 'shakedown' laps. It may not have been a full-blown test, but it was an experience he savoured. "I know it's only a shakedown, but being in my own gear, knowing that I can focus just on this, I really enjoyed it," he said. "When the car started I couldn't help but smile. I tried to stay serious, but got this big grin on my face."

The engine situation was rectified for the following two days. During the first, Lewis managed 64 laps of the British GP venue, recording a time just under a second slower than de la Rosa's best. The next day Lewis managed 47 laps, but his best time was a tenth faster than the experienced Spaniard, who had 71 grands prix under his belt for Arrows, Prost, Jaguar and McLaren. It was a taste of things to come and a signal to Ron Dennis and McLaren Chief Operating Officer Martin Whitmarsh that he was up to the task in hand. "I don't feel any pressure and the team have told me there is no need for me to feel pressure," said Lewis. "I'm just living my dream at the moment."

While the test was the first opportunity for Lewis to show his outright speed in an F1 car, it wasn't his first run. That came back in December 2004, not long after he claimed the Formula Renault UK title. McLaren sponsors the BRDC McLaren *Autosport* driver award, and part of the prize for the winner is a test in one of its cars. While Lewis was ineligible for the award thanks to his late-season F3 drives, he was given 21 laps in the car at Silverstone, alongside 2003 winner Jamie Green and 2004's recipient Alex Lloyd. But the outing is about the experience, not speed, and the drivers are under strict instructions not to crash the car, above all else.

Lewis had also conducted some straightline work for McLaren in the interim. These outings take place on airfields and are used to bed in brakes or evaluate launch and traction control software. And most importantly of all, he had spent many hours on McLaren's fabled F1 simulator, a high-tech piece of kit able to recreate tracks from all over the world, complete with g-forces.

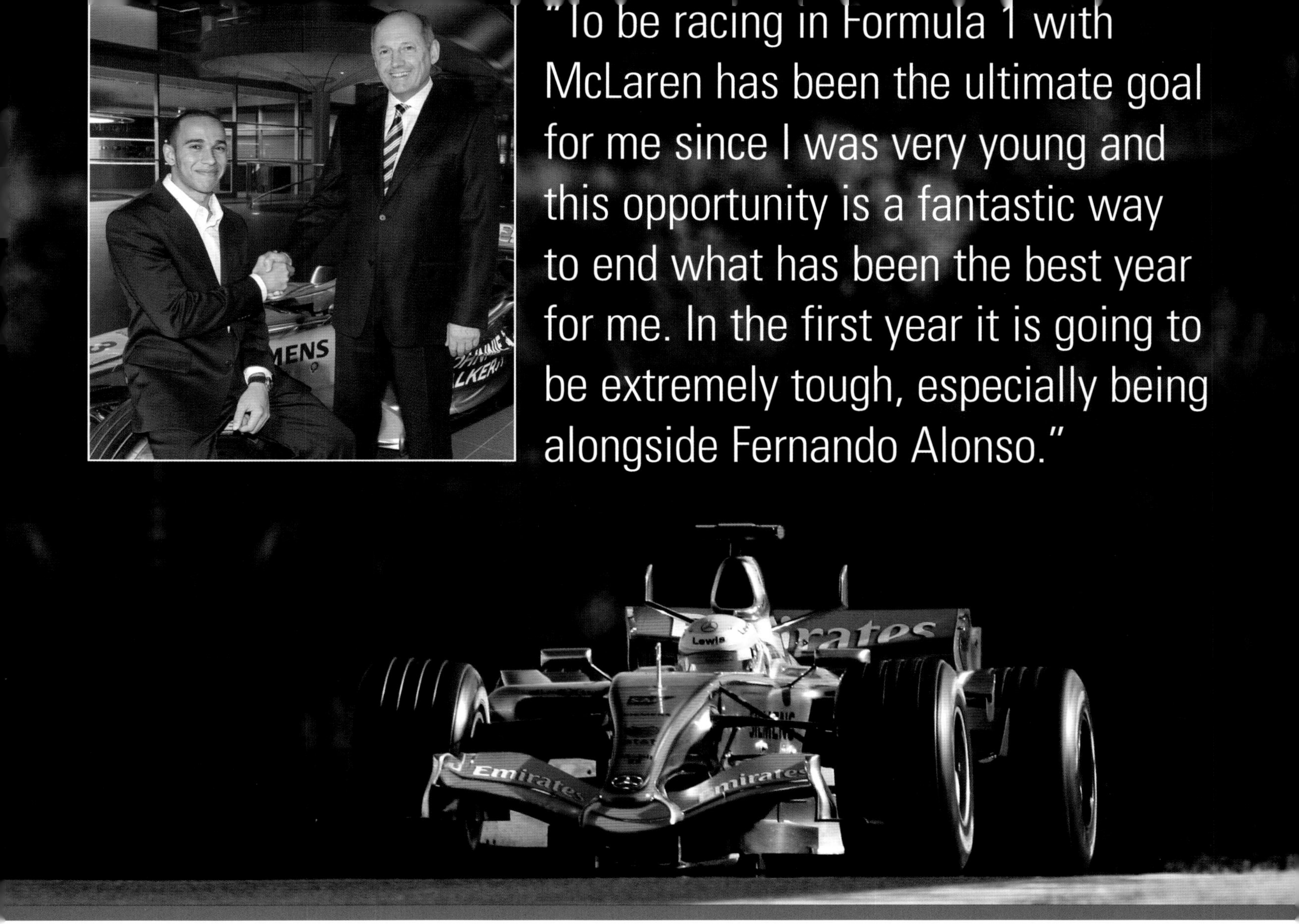

"To be racing in Formula 1 with McLaren has been the ultimate goal for me since I was very young and this opportunity is a fantastic way to end what has been the best year for me. In the first year it is going to be extremely tough, especially being alongside Fernando Alonso."

However, after Silverstone it would be the best part of a month before Lewis would drive an F1 car in anger again, the next test run coming at the Jerez track in southern Spain. The first of his three days of running here was limited to just ten laps, giving him the chance to get a feel for the track. On the second of the three days he did more than a full race distance and in the process recorded a best time less than three-tenths off de la Rosa's. On the final day he set a searing pace, lapping four-tenths faster than de la Rosa to end the test second overall in the times, with only the legendary Michael Schumacher's Ferrari ahead of him.

The next time Lewis would test an F1 car it would be as a fully fledged member of McLaren's 2007 driver line-up. The announcement came on Friday 24 November, but the decision had been reached not long after the conclusion of the Jerez test. "It's a dream come true," said Lewis. "To be racing in Formula 1 with McLaren has been the ultimate goal for me since I was very young and this opportunity is a fantastic way to end what has been the best year for me.

"In the first year it is going to be extremely tough, especially being alongside Fernando Alonso. But I am young, I am here to learn and I am dedicated to doing the best job I can. I will be working as hard as possible on and off track to get up to speed. Having

ABOVE, INSET Twelve years after that famous encounter at the *Autosport* Awards, Lewis poses with Ron Dennis at the official announcement that he would race for McLaren-Mercedes in F1 in 2007.

ABOVE Clocking up more test miles at Jerez in October 2006.

ABOVE "Behind you!" A photocall with Fernando Alonso during the launch of the McLaren-Mercedes MP4-22 at Valencia in January 2007.

OPPOSITE Lewis waves to the crowds whilst smoking the tyres on a Mercedes road car during the McLaren-Mercedes Street Demonstration at the Valencia launch event.

MAIN IMAGE During an intensive pre-season test programme Lewis would complete almost 5,000 miles before the opening race of the 2007 F1 season at Melbourne.

the best driver in the world alongside me is going to be the best position to be in. Having a two-time World Champion, who is very experienced, very talented and a few years older than me is great."

Team boss Ron Dennis had no doubts that he'd made the right choice in picking 21-year-old Lewis as team-mate to Alonso: "It's obviously going to be the biggest challenge of Lewis's career so far, but it's one that we're sure he will be able to meet."

With the contract signed and sealed Lewis headed for the Circuit de Catalunya, near Barcelona in Spain, for his next test outing. Here he had the honour of another double World Champion as his team-mate. After five years away from the F1 cockpit, Mika Häkkinen was keen to experience a modern F1 car, and McLaren gave the Finn a day's running. Unsurprisingly, after such a long gap Häkkinen lacked the raw speed that made him a superstar and he was over two seconds away from Lewis's best time.

It was back to Jerez for the next test, where for the first time in his career Lewis Hamilton's name registered at the top of the timesheets. His best lap from the second of the three test days was almost a second quicker than anybody else. Ripples emanated across the F1 world: could McLaren's rookie be the next wonderkid?

Lewis topped the times on the final day of the next test before the team decamped for a well-earned Christmas break. When testing resumed in January 2007, World Champion Alonso would be part of the programme.

McLaren kicked off the 2007 season with a spectacular launch party in Valencia, where its new drivers were presented to the world along with the striking new MP4-22, resplendent in its new silver and red Vodafone livery. The cars screamed through the packed crowds in the city's impressive America's Cup port and optimism ran high that McLaren could claim its first drivers' title since Häkkinen's second back in 1999. Then, with the festivities over, the team rolled on to the Valencia circuit, where Alonso set a blistering pace, lapping ninth-tenths faster than Lewis on the final day.

A week later McLaren was joined at Valencia by the majority of the rest of the F1 grid and this time it was Lewis who threw down the gauntlet. Although he and Alonso were never on track at the

same time, it was Lewis who ended up with the fastest time, his marker on the final day over half a second quicker than Alonso's best. It was a sign of things to come.

By the time the teams packed up and headed out to Australia for the first race of the season Lewis had completed a packed testing programme, during which time he'd covered almost 5,000 miles around various tracks. He may not have actually started a Grand Prix, but in terms of mileage he already had the equivalent of over 20 races under his belt. "It's been a very, very long winter of testing," he admitted. "We have covered a lot of mileage. There was a lot to do in a short space of time, but I am extremely fit and feel very relaxed about that. I have done a lot of race distances, and honestly I don't feel I could be better prepared."

RBS
RBS
RBS
Santander
JOHNNIE

Formula 1 2007

GRAND PRIX GLORY

aigo
JOHNNIE WALKER
2
SAP
Mobil 1
vodafone

2007 ROUND 1

AUSTRALIAN GRAND PRIX

MELBOURNE

3rd

POINTS TOTAL **6**
POINTS POSITION **3rd**
SEASON WINS **0**

Lap 1 Kimi Räikkönen makes a flying start from pole position. Fernando Alonso, second on the grid, is squeezed by Nick Heidfeld, who moves up to second, while Hamilton moves up to third, ahead of Alonso.

Lap 6 Hamilton runs wide and clips the grass, without losing any places.

Lap 14 Räikkönen continues to lap comfortably faster than the rest of the field. Heidfeld pits, leaving Hamilton in second place, 14.9s behind Räikkönen.

Lap 19 Leader Räikkönen pits, rejoining fourth and leaving Hamilton in the lead from Alonso and Robert Kubica.

Lap 23 On his way to the pits, Hamilton loses time behind Sutil who is given a drive-through penalty for ignoring blue flags. Hamilton rejoins from his stop still in second place.

Lap 31 Räikkönen leads Hamilton by 17.1s, with Alonso third from Kubica.

Lap 37 Kubica suddenly slows and heads to the pits to retire.

Lap 42 Leader Räikkönen pits, leaving Hamilton in the lead from Alonso and Giancarlo Fisichella.

Lap 43 Hamilton makes his final pit stop, rejoining behind Alonso and Räikkönen.

Lap 45 Alonso dives into the pits, leaving Räikkönen in the lead. Alonso makes a perfect stop and rejoins in second place, leap-frogging Hamilton.

Lap 48 Räikkönen leads Alonso by 14.5s with Hamilton third, Heidfeld fourth, Fisichella fifth and Massa sixth. The rest of the field have been lapped by the leader.

Lap 49 David Coulthard tries to pass Alex Wurz for 13th place at Turn 3. The two cars collide, and both retire.

Lap 58 Räikkönen wins his first race for Ferrari, beating Alonso by 7.2s. Hamilton finishes third on his F1 debut, from Heidfeld, Fisichella and Felipe Massa.

ABOVE Into the limelight – Lewis leaves the garage for the opening Friday practice session in Melbourne, his first taste of the pressures of a race weekend as a fully fledged Grand Prix driver.

RIGHT Preparing to enter the inner sanctum – FIA pass in hand, Lewis walks through the turnstile on to the hallowed ground of the Formula 1 paddock.

OPPOSITE Tension mounts as Lewis prepares to step into his waiting McLaren-Mercedes MP4-22 to do battle with the best drivers in the world.

Lewis Hamilton's arrival as a Formula 1 racing driver was announced by blanket coverage on the back pages of Britain's daily newspapers. His podium finish captured the imagination of sports editors, and despite Kimi Räikkönen winning in his first race for Ferrari it was the extraordinary tale of the 22-year-old Brit that grabbed the headlines.

Hamilton's exceptional performances in the junior categories had ensured that his Formula 1 debut would be one of the most eagerly anticipated in history, but, despite his competitive pace in pre-season testing, doubts remained about how he would cope in the glare of the Grand Prix spotlight.

Two hundred metres into the Australian Grand Prix these questions were answered – and how! From fourth on the grid, Lewis found himself boxed in on the inside going into the first corner of Melbourne's Albert Park track. Demonstrating amazing speed of thought and excellent race-craft, he instantly switched to the outside and drove around McLaren-Mercedes team-mate Fernando Alonso and into third place.

For the next 43 laps he stayed ahead of the double World Champion, matching the Spaniard's

"I think this is probably beyond my dreams... I'm loving it... To lead in my first Grand Prix was a fantastic feeling. It's pretty tough when you have a two-times World Champion behind you... It's extremely intense... I'm ecstatic to be here, a podium for my first race, I couldn't be more happy."

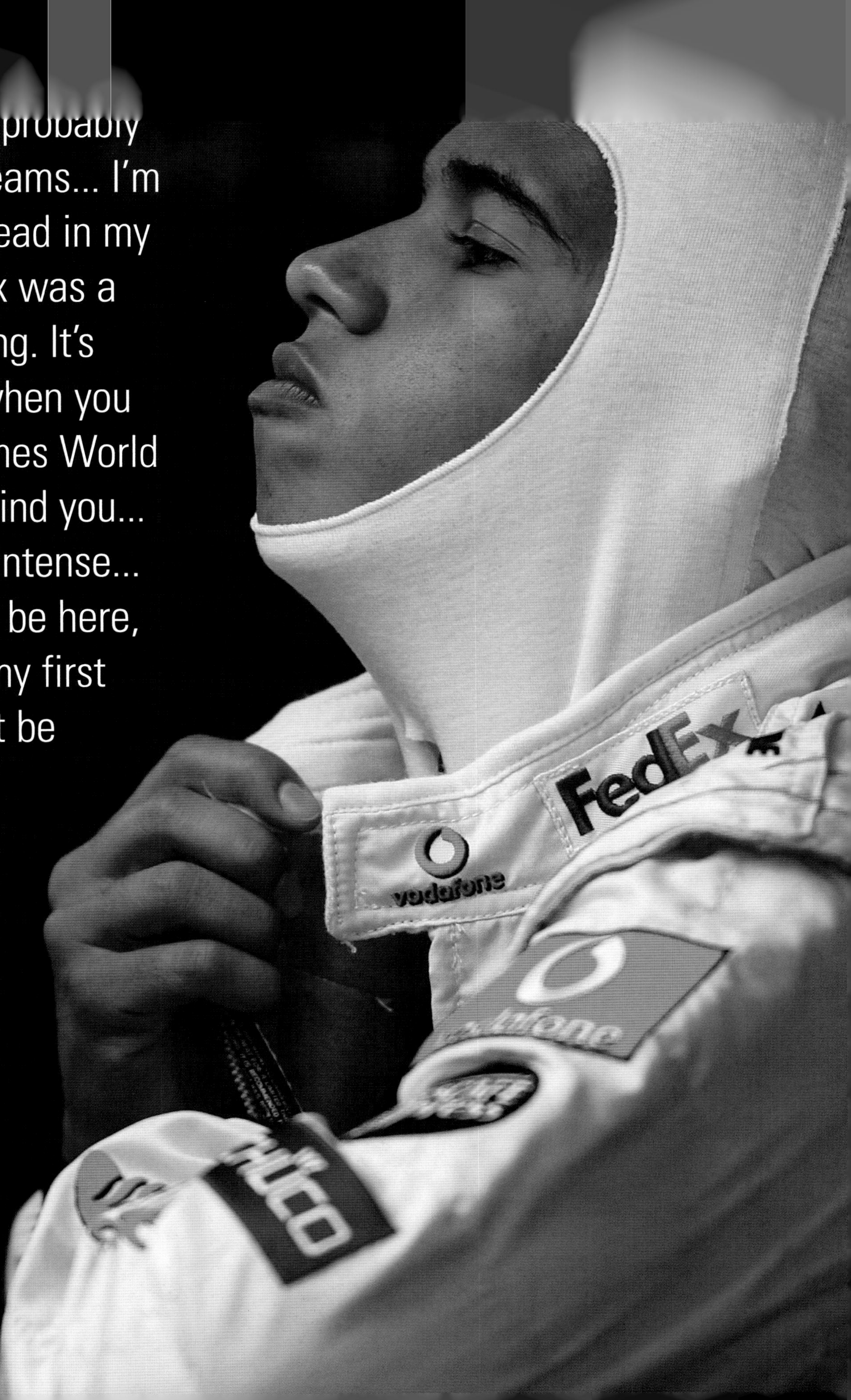

race pace tenth-for-tenth. Third became second when Nick Heidfeld's light-fuelled BMW Sauber pitted, and when Ferrari brought Kimi Räikkönen in for his stop Lewis became the first rookie to lead a Grand Prix since Jacques Villeneuve in 1996.

For four glorious laps Lewis led the race, driving with a calmness and composure that belied his inexperience. He rejoined behind the dominant leading Ferrari of Räikkönen after making his first planned stop, but continued to fend off Alonso for second. Lewis finally relinquished the place only when he was brought in for the second of his two stops two laps before Alonso, when the reigning champion took full advantage of a clear track and a lighter car to leapfrog ahead of him. In the closing stages Lewis backed off to consolidate an unbelievable podium finish in his first-ever Grand Prix.

"I think this is probably beyond my dreams," he said afterwards. "To be in Formula 1 was obviously a dream, but to come into my first race and have such a smooth start is something you don't expect, but something we had been working towards. I'm loving it! To lead in my first Grand Prix was a fantastic feeling. It's pretty tough when you have a two-times World Champion behind you. It's extremely intense, you've got to make sure you make no mistakes. But as I said, I'm ecstatic to be here, a podium for my first race, I couldn't be more happy."

Lewis's performance stunned onlookers, who were amazed at his maturity. Sir Stirling Moss, Britain's first Formula 1 star, said: "Lewis Hamilton is the greatest breath of fresh air we've had since I started following F1. And it's not just his speed – which is necessary – but the way he handles himself, his upbringing, the whole lot. The way he can accept all the titles he's won along the way, and his humility; I find him an extremely refreshing person for the sport. He's incredible. His control of the car is quite stunning."

LEFT, FROM TOP Signing autographs for the enthusiastic Australian fans; Lewis crosses the line for a remarkable podium finish on his Grand Prix debut; a proud father and ecstatic son share their joy after the race, as a dream weekend draws to a close.

RIGHT Into the groove – learning the Albert Park track during Friday practice, against the impressive backdrop of the downtown Melbourne skyline.

AUSTRALIAN GRAND PRIX
MELBOURNE

RACE DATE March 18th 2007
CIRCUIT LENGTH 3.295miles
NO. OF LAPS 58 laps
RACE DISTANCE 191.110 miles
WEATHER Sunny, 22°C
TRACK TEMP 40°C

Practice

Session 1 – Friday

1	Fernando Alonso	McLaren-Mercedes	1m29.214s
2	Felipe Massa	Ferrari	1m30.707s
3	Sebastian Vettel	BMW	1m30.857s
4	**Lewis Hamilton**	**McLaren-Mercedes**	**1m30.878s**

Session 2 – Friday

1	Felipe Massa	Ferrari	1m27.353s
2	Kimi Räikkönen	Ferrari	1m27.750s
3	**Lewis Hamilton**	**McLaren-Mercedes**	**1m27.829s**

Session 3 – Saturday

1	Kimi Räikkönen	Ferrari	1m26.064s
2	Giancarlo Fisichella	Renault	1m26.454s
3	**Lewis Hamilton**	**McLaren-Mercedes**	**1m26.467s**

Qualifying

1	Kimi Räikkönen	Ferrari	1m26.072s
2	Fernando Alonso	McLaren-Mercedes	1m26.493s
3	Nick Heidfeld	BMW	1m26.556s
4	**Lewis Hamilton**	**McLaren-Mercedes**	**1m26.755s**

Race

1	Kimi Räikkönen	Ferrari	1h25m28.770s
2	Fernando Alonso	McLaren-Mercedes	+7.242s
3	**Lewis Hamilton**	**McLaren-Mercedes**	**+18.595s**
4	Nick Heidfeld	BMW	+38.763s
5	Giancarlo Fisichella	Renault	+1m06.469s
6	Felipe Massa	Ferrari	+1m06.805s
7	Nico Rosberg	Williams-Toyota	+1 Lap
8	Ralf Schumacher	Toyota	+1 Lap

Fastest Lap

Kimi Räikkönen	Ferrari	1m25.235s

World Championship Positions

1	Kimi Räikkönen	Ferrari	10 points
2	Fernando Alonso	McLaren-Mercedes	8 points
3	**Lewis Hamilton**	**McLaren-Mercedes**	**6 points**
4	Nick Heidfeld	BMW	5 points
5	Giancarlo Fisichella	Renault	4 points
6	Felipe Massa	Ferrari	3 points
7	Nico Rosberg	Williams-Toyota	2 points
8	Ralf Schumacher	Toyota	1 point

PETRONAS
Henkel
vodafone
Santander
vodafone

2007 ROUND 2
MALAYSIAN GRAND PRIX
SEPANG

2nd
POINTS TOTAL **14**
POINTS POSITION **3rd**
SEASON WINS **0**

Lap 1 Massa, in pole position, is beaten away by Alonso. Hamilton makes a superb start and slices past both Ferraris to claim second ahead of Massa and Räikkönen.

Lap 3 Massa challenges Hamilton at Turn 1, but fails to pass. He then passes briefly at Turn 4 before losing out again, which almost drops him into Räikkönen's clutches.

Lap 6 Massa passes Hamilton at Turn 4, but runs wide onto the grass and drops to fifth, behind Räikkönen and Heidfeld.

Lap 14 After setting a tranche of fastest laps, Alonso laps in 1m36.921s to lead Hamilton by 13.4s.

Lap 18 Alonso pits, as does Räikkönen. Hamilton leads.

Lap 20 Hamilton makes his first pit stop to leave Heidfeld leading, with Alonso second.

Lap 22 Heidfeld pits. Alonso leads again, from Hamilton who sets a new fastest lap of 1m36.701s.

Lap 25 Alonso leads Hamilton by 10.8s, with Räikkönen third, Heidfeld fourth, Massa fifth and Rosberg sixth.

Lap 27 Hamilton is closing on Alonso, and the gap is now down to 8.7s.

Lap 34 Alonso leads Hamilton by 8.1s. Hamilton is 12.7s clear of Räikkönen.

Lap 38 Hamilton makes his second pit stop rejoining in a temporary fifth place, behind Massa.

Lap 40 Alonso pits, leaving Räikkönen in the lead.

Lap 41 Räikkönen pits and Alonso moves back into the lead, 6.1s ahead of Hamilton in second.

Lap 43 With all the stops completed, Alonso leads Hamilton, with Räikkönen 7.7s behind after gaining 1.7s during the lap. Heidfeld is fourth, followed by Massa and Fisichella.

Lap 46 Räikkönen, pushing hard, is gaining rapidly on Hamilton and is now 5.6s behind. Alonso has extended his lead to 18.0s.

Lap 54 Räikkönen has closed the gap to Hamilton to 1.2s. Alonso leads by 22.2s.

Lap 56 Alonso takes his first victory for McLaren, 17.5s ahead of Hamilton, who is just 0.7s ahead of Räikkönen as they cross the line.

After his glorious Grand Prix debut, Lewis Hamilton was well on his way to becoming a superstar back in Britain. But he opted to chill out in Bali ahead of his first visit to the Sepang circuit near Kuala Lumpur, so was blissfully unaware of the impact his Australian Grand Prix performance had created back home.

Pre-race testing gave him a chance to learn the track and he put his experience to good use to head Saturday morning free practice, so for the first time an official Formula 1 timesheet had Hamilton's name at the top. A brief flurry of rain caused Lewis to back off more than he needed to on his qualifying flying lap, so once again he started from fourth on the grid. But just as in Australia, he didn't let this faze him and when the Ferrari drivers up ahead left a gap down the inside of the tight right-hand first turn, Lewis took full advantage and passed two cars in one consummate manoeuvre.

With team-mate Fernando Alonso leading, Lewis played the perfect team role and kept Felipe Massa tucked up behind him for lap after lap, provoking the Brazilian into an over-ambitious move that ended up with the Ferrari in the gravel and the British rookie in a comfortable second place.

On fresh tyres, after the first of two pit stops and with no immediate pressure from behind, Lewis upped his pace, recording his first-ever F1 fastest lap in the process. In fact, such was Hamilton's speed in this part of the race that he halved Alonso's lead to just under eight seconds.

The stifling heat and humidity in Malaysia makes its GP one of the most physically demanding races in the world, and in the final third of the race Lewis was forced to endure extreme dehydration after his drinks bottle malfunctioned. To finish in second place in these circumstances was a stunning achievement. "The last three weeks my trainer and the team doctor have worked very hard to monitor my fluid intake to make sure I was ready for the heat," he said after the race. "When I ran out of water in the car, I could feel myself getting hotter and hotter and it was really difficult to stay concentrated."

LEFT, FROM TOP The Ferraris follow in Lewis's wake after his blinding start; high-fives for a 1–2, celebrating with Fernando Alonso on a perfect result for McLaren.

RIGHT Climbing aboard the company car on the second row of the grid amid the stifling Sepang heat.

MALAYSIAN GRAND PRIX
SEPANG

RACE DATE 8th April 2007
CIRCUIT LENGTH 3.444 miles
NO. OF LAPS 56 laps
RACE DISTANCE 192.887miles
WEATHER Sunny and humid, 36°C
TRACK TEMP 55°C

Practice

Session 1 – Friday

1	Felipe Massa	Ferrari	1m34.972s
2	Fernando Alonso	McLaren-Mercedes	1m35.220s
3	**Lewis Hamilton**	**McLaren-Mercedes**	**1m35.712s**

Session 2 – Friday

1	Felipe Massa	Ferrari	1m35.780s
2	Giancarlo Fisichella	Renault	1m35.910s
3	Heikki Kovalainen	Renault	1m36.106s
9	**Lewis Hamilton**	**McLaren-Mercedes**	**1m36.797s**

Session 3 – Saturday

1	**Lewis Hamilton**	**McLaren-Mercedes**	**1m34.811s**
2	Felipe Massa	Ferrari	1m34.953s
3	Fernando Alonso	McLaren-Mercedes	1m35.311s

Qualifying

1	Felipe Massa	Ferrari	1m35.043s
2	Fernando Alonso	McLaren-Mercedes	1m35.310s
3	Kimi Räikkönen	Ferrari	1m35.479s
4	**Lewis Hamilton**	**McLaren-Mercedes**	**1m36.045s**

Race

1	Fernando Alonso	McLaren-Mercedes	1h32m14.930s
2	**Lewis Hamilton**	**McLaren-Mercedes**	**+17.557s**
3	Kimi Räikkönen	Ferrari	+18.339s
4	Nick Heidfeld	BMW	+33.777s
5	Felipe Massa	Ferrari	+36.705s
6	Giancarlo Fisichella	Renault	+1m05.638s
7	Jarno Trulli	Toyota	+1m10.132s
8	Heikki Kovalainen	Renault	+1m12.015s

Fastest Lap

Lewis Hamilton	**McLaren-Mercedes**	**1m36.701s**

World Championship Positions

1	Fernando Alonso	McLaren-Mercedes	18 points
2	Kimi Räikkönen	Ferrari	16 points
3	**Lewis Hamilton**	**McLaren-Mercedes**	**14 points**
4	Nick Heidfeld	BMW	10 points
5	Felipe Massa	Ferrari	7 points
	Giancarlo Fisichella	Renault	7 points
7	Jarno Trulli	Toyota	2 points
	Nico Rosberg	Williams-Toyota	2 points

Nikon
Nikon
Canon
vodafone
SAP

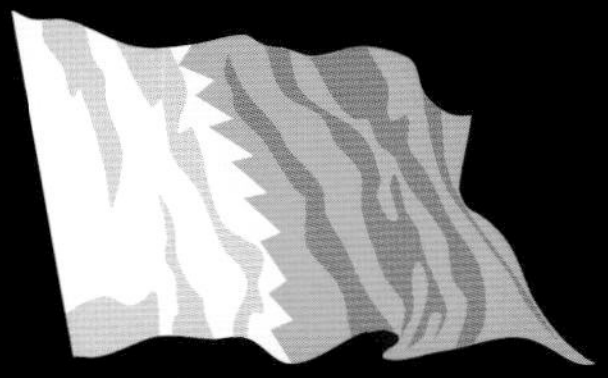

2007 ROUND 3

BAHRAIN GRAND PRIX

SAKHIR

2nd

POINTS TOTAL **22**
POINTS POSITION **=1st**
SEASON WINS **0**

Lap 1 From pole, Massa gets away cleanly to lead Hamilton. The safety car is deployed to allow the debris to be cleared after an incident involving Sutil, Jenson Button and Scott Speed.

Lap 4 The safety car pulls off. Massa leads by 0.6s from Hamilton, Alonso and Räikkönen.

Lap 10 Hamilton sets a fastest lap of 1m34.809s to close to within 0.8s of Massa.

Lap 19 Hamilton pits, rejoining in sixth place behind Kubica.

Lap 21 Massa pits, rejoining ahead of Hamilton. Alonso leads.

Lap 22 Alonso pits, leaving Räikkönen in the lead from Heidfeld.

Lap 23 Räikkönen, Heidfeld and Kubica pit, Räikkönen rejoining ahead of Alonso.

Lap 24 After all leaders have made their first stops, Massa leads Hamilton by 4.6s, with Räikkönen a further 5.9s behind. Alonso is fourth.

Lap 29 Räikkönen closes to within 2.9s of Hamilton.

Lap 32 Heidfeld passes Alonso for fourth.

Lap 40 Massa makes his second stop, leaving Hamilton in the lead.

Lap 41 Räikkönen and Heidfeld pit.

Lap 42 Hamilton leads Alonso by 9.4s, with Massa setting a new fastest lap of 1m34.067s in third.

Lap 43 Alonso makes his second stop.

Lap 44 Hamilton pits, rejoining second between Massa and Räikkönen. Heidfeld is fourth from Alonso.

Lap 45 Massa leads Hamilton by 7.6s with Räikkönen a further 1.8s behind. Alonso is fifth, 2.0s behind Heidfeld, but the McLarens are both gaining ground using the medium compound Bridgestone tyres.

Lap 53 Hamilton has closed within 3.9s of Massa, but traffic is dense, and time is running out.

Lap 57 Massa wins by 2.3s from Hamilton, followed by Räikkönen, Heidfeld and Alonso. Alonso, Räikkönen and Hamilton are level at the top of the championship table on 22 points.

ABOVE **"Is that really you?" Lewis, his brother Nick and step-mum Linda share a joke about the quality of Nick's paddock-pass 'mugshot'.**

OPPOSITE, TOP
A glimpse over Lewis's shoulder into the impressive cockpit of the McLaren-Mercedes MP4-22, as he prepares to head out on to the track during qualifying.

OPPOSITE, BOTTOM
Lewis had raced among the dunes at Bahrain's Sakhir circuit in F3 in 2004, and used his experience to good effect on the way to another podium finish.

The Sakhir circuit, home of the Bahrain Grand Prix, was the first track on the Formula 1 calendar where Lewis Hamilton had raced before – and his record there was outstanding too, having taken an opportunistic win in a one-off Formula 3 event at the end of 2004.

His experience of the track showed itself straight away, and right from the off he was clearly quicker than team-mate Alonso, outpacing the double World Champion in all three practice sessions and repeating this feat in qualifying, with his first-ever front row qualifying position.

For once Lewis didn't make up any positions at the start, but he did hold on to his second place as he and pole-sitter Felipe Massa edged away from the field. It was a great fight between two drivers who had entered the season as the supposed number twos in their respective teams but who were now showing their number ones the way.

For the third race in a row Lewis led during the pit stop phase, but Lewis's McLaren didn't work as well on the softer compound tyre he was fitted with for the middle part of the race, which allowed Massa to build a comfort zone into his lead.

After his second stop, and back on harder tyres, Lewis was flying again. For almost the entire final third of the race he lapped half a second faster than the leader, reducing the gap to just over two seconds by the flag. It had been a sensational effort, and his third podium position in as many races not only set a new F1 record for a rookie but also moved Lewis into the joint lead in the Driver's World Championship alongside team-mate Alonso and Ferrari's Kimi Räikkönen.

"I'm very pleased with this result," Lewis said afterwards. "To have finished on the podium three times out of three is fantastic. We have definitely closed the gap to Ferrari and I know everybody will continue to push hard to improve even more in time for the next race. I was able to keep up with Felipe in the first stint but I really struggled with the balance of the car in the second. I had a lot of understeer and wasn't able to brake as late as I would have liked. However, after the second pit stop when I changed to hard tyres I was able to push again. I really enjoyed the race today and with a few more laps I might have been able to challenge Felipe for the lead."

BAHRAIN GRAND PRIX
SAKHIR

RACE DATE 15th April 2007
CIRCUIT LENGTH 3.363 miles
NO. OF LAPS 57 laps
RACE DISTANCE 191.530 miles
WEATHER Sunny, windy, 31°C
TRACK TEMP 41°C

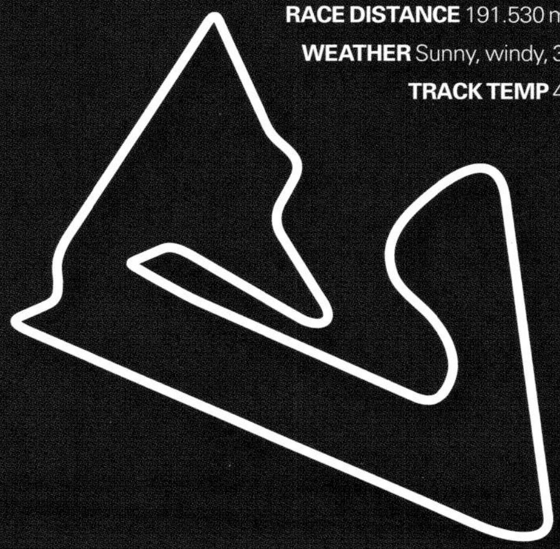

Practice

Session 1 – Friday

1	Kimi Räikkönen	Ferrari	1m33.162s
2	Felipe Massa	Ferrari	1m33.679s
3	**Lewis Hamilton**	**McLaren-Mercedes**	**1m34.110s**

Session 2 – Friday

1	Kimi Räikkönen	Ferrari	1m33.527s
2	**Lewis Hamilton**	**McLaren-Mercedes**	**1m33.540s**
3	Robert Kubica	BMW	1m33.732s

Session 3 – Saturday

1	**Lewis Hamilton**	**McLaren-Mercedes**	**1m32.543s**
2	Kimi Räikkönen	Ferrari	1m32.549s
3	Nick Heidfeld	BMW	1m32.652s

Qualifying

1	Felipe Massa	Ferrari	1m32.652s
2	**Lewis Hamilton**	**McLaren-Mercedes**	**1m32.935s**
3	Kimi Räikkönen	Ferrari	1m33.131s

Race

1	Felipe Massa	Ferrari	1h33m27.515s
2	**Lewis Hamilton**	**McLaren-Mercedes**	**+2.360s**
3	Kimi Räikkönen	Ferrari	+10.839s
4	Nick Heidfeld	BMW	+13.831s
5	Fernando Alonso	McLaren-Mercedes	+14.426s
6	Robert Kubica	BMW	+45.529s
7	Jarno Trulli	Toyota	+1m21.371s
8	Giancarlo Fisichella	Renault	+1m21.701s

Fastest Lap

Felipe Massa	Ferrari	1m34.067s

World Championship Positions

1	Fernando Alonso	McLaren-Mercedes	22 points
	Kimi Räikkönen	Ferrari	22 points
	Lewis Hamilton	**McLaren-Mercedes**	**22 points**
4	Felipe Massa	Ferrari	17 points
5	Nick Heidfeld	BMW	15 points
6	Giancarlo Fisichella	Renault	8 points
7	Jarno Trulli	Toyota	4 points
8	Robert Kubica	BMW	3 points

"To have finished on the podium three times out of three is fantastic... I really enjoyed the race today and with a few more laps I might have been able to challenge Felipe for the lead."

Santander
vodafone
JOHNNIE WALKER
"MM"
BOSS
aigo
爱国者

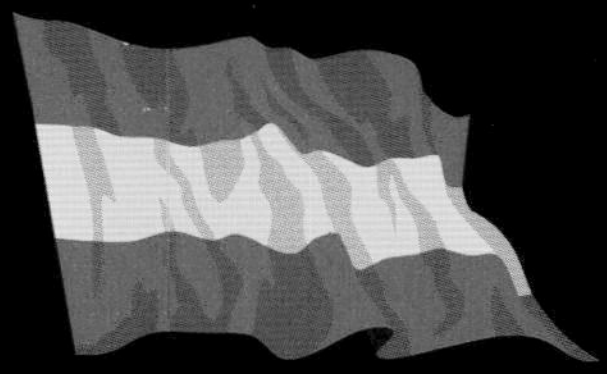

2007 ROUND 4

SPANISH GRAND PRIX
CATALUNYA

2nd

POINTS TOTAL **30**
POINTS POSITION **1st**
SEASON WINS **0**

Pre-start The initial start is aborted when Jarno Trulli stalls. An extra formation lap takes place and Trulli is pushed to the pits.

Lap 1 Alonso tries to pass pole man Massa into Turn 1. Alonso is squeezed wide into the gravel and rejoins in fourth place. Hamilton passes Räikkönen on the run to Turn 1, so the order is Massa, Hamilton, Räikkönen, Alonso, Kubica and Heidfeld.

Lap 3 Massa is 2.5s clear of Hamilton, while Alonso is pushing right behind Räikkönen.

Lap 9 Räikkönen suddenly slows and heads toward the pits at a crawl to retire.

Lap 12 Massa continues to set fastest laps, now leading Hamilton by 7.2s, with Alonso a further 3.9s behind.

Lap 17 Both McLaren drivers set personal best lap times, but Massa remains 8.7s ahead of Hamilton.

Lap 19 Massa pits, as does Alonso, leaving Hamilton in the lead. There is a brief fire at the back of Massa's car due to spilt fuel, but the car suffers no damage.

Lap 22 Hamilton pits and rejoins behind Massa, ahead of Alonso.

Lap 28 Massa leads Hamilton by 11.1s, with Alonso a distant third. Kubica is now fourth from Coulthard and Kovalainen.

Lap 35 Kubica and Coulthard are closing on third-placed Alonso, who is running significantly slower than Hamilton.

Lap 42 Massa, Coulthard and Kovalainen all pit, leaving Hamilton in the lead. Massa rejoins between the two McLarens.

Lap 46 Hamilton leads Massa by 11.5s with Alonso third, 16.0s behind the leader.

Lap 47 Hamilton makes his second stop, as does Kubica.

Lap 48 Alonso makes his second stop.

Lap 49 After the top three have made their second stops, Massa leads Hamilton by 10.5s, with Alonso third.

Lap 52 Alonso, running on the softer Bridgestone tyres, gains slightly on Hamilton, who is running on the harder tyres, and the gap between them is now 14.9s.

Lap 65 Massa wins by 6.7s from new World Championship leader Hamilton, followed by Alonso, Kubica and Coulthard.

After a four-week break Lewis Hamilton's 2007 Formula 1 season sprang back into life at the Spanish Grand Prix in Barcelona. Omitted from the team's pre-race test programme, Lewis's first taste of the revisions made to the McLaren MP4-22 – reckoned by the team to be worth 0.3 seconds a lap – came in free practice. Unfamiliar the car may have been, but it mattered not to Lewis, who headed the timesheets by half a second from McLaren team-mate and local hero Fernando Alonso.

Lewis repeated the trick in final practice, but in qualifying he was weighed down with a heavier fuel load and once again only qualified fourth. But, as was becoming the norm, he made a great start, out-sprinting Kimi Räikkönen into the first corner for third, which soon became second when Alonso's aggressive dive for the lead took him across the gravel and very nearly into Lewis's path.

On a heavier fuel load Lewis couldn't match Felipe Massa's pace in the lead, but he was secure in second place ahead of Räikkönen. He reduced the deficit as his long-running fuel strategy played out, pegging the gap to the leader by just under seven seconds at the finish. His third straight second place took Lewis into a clear points lead in the championship.

"Things just keep getting better and I continue living my dream," he beamed afterwards. "In the early stages I was struggling to get heat into the tyres and had a bit of oversteer, but things improved considerably a few laps into the race – however, the gap to Felipe was already too big. In the second stint I was a bit unlucky with the traffic, but that happens sometimes."

LEFT, FROM TOP McLaren boss Ron Dennis gives Lewis a little friendly advice on the grid; Alonso's attempt to pass Massa into the first corner took him across the gravel and perilously close to Lewis, who moved up to second place as a result; a delighted Lewis gives the thumbs-up at the end of a race which saw him move two points clear of Fernando Alonso at the head of the Drivers' World Championship.

RIGHT It may have been a partisan crowd at Alonso's home race, but Lewis got the better of his team-mate for the second time in four races.

SPANISH GRAND PRIX
CATALUNYA

RACE DATE 27th May 2007
CIRCUIT LENGTH 2.075 miles
NO. OF LAPS 78 laps
RACE DISTANCE 161.850 miles
WEATHER Warm and dry, 24°C
TRACK TEMP 35°C

Practice

Session 1 – Friday

1	**Lewis Hamilton**	**McLaren-Mercedes**	**1m21.880s**
2	Fernando Alonso	McLaren-Mercedes	1m22.268s
3	Kimi Räikkönen	Ferrari	1m22.291s

Session 2 – Friday

1	Fernando Alonso	McLaren-Mercedes	1m21.397s
2	Giancarlo Fisichella	Renault	1m21.684s
3	Heikki Kovalainen	Renault	1m21.966s
5	**Lewis Hamilton**	**McLaren-Mercedes**	**1m22.048s**

Session 3 – Saturday

1	**Lewis Hamilton**	**McLaren-Mercedes**	**1m21.233s**
2	Fernando Alonso	McLaren-Mercedes	1m21.312s
3	Robert Kubica	BMW	1m21.364s

Qualifying

1	Felipe Massa	Ferrari	1m21.421s
2	Fernando Alonso	McLaren-Mercedes	1m21.451s
3	Kimi Räikkönen	Ferrari	1m21.723s
4	**Lewis Hamilton**	**McLaren-Mercedes**	**1m21.785s**

Race

1	Felipe Massa	Ferrari	1h31m36.230s
2	**Lewis Hamilton**	**McLaren-Mercedes**	**+6.790s**
3	Fernando Alonso	McLaren-Mercedes	+17.456s
4	Robert Kubica	BMW	+31.615s
5	David Coulthard	Red Bull-Renault	+58.331s
6	Nico Rosberg	Williams-Toyota	+59.538s
7	Heikki Kovalainen	Renault	+1m02.128s
8	Takuma Sato	Super Aguri-Honda	+1 Lap

Fastest Lap

Felipe Massa	Ferrari	1m22.680s

World Championship Positions

1	**Lewis Hamilton**	**McLaren-Mercedes**	**30 points**
2	Fernando Alonso	McLaren-Mercedes	28 points
3	Felipe Massa	Ferrari	27 points
4	Kimi Räikkönen	Ferrari	22 points
5	Nick Heidfeld	BMW	15 points
6	Giancarlo Fisichella	Renault	8 points
7	Nico Rosberg	Williams-Toyota	5 points
8	David Coulthard	Red Bull-Renault	4 points
	Jarno Trulli	Toyota	4 points

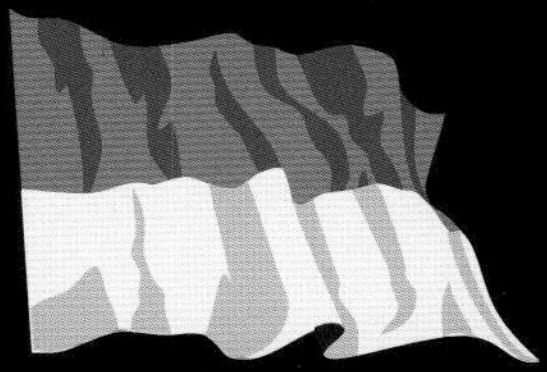

2007 ROUND 5

MONACO GRAND PRIX
MONTE CARLO

2nd

POINTS TOTAL **38**
POINTS POSITION **=1st**
SEASON WINS **0**

Lap 1 Alonso, on pole, leads Hamilton into the first corner; Massa is third ahead of Fisichella, Heidfeld and Nico Rosberg.

Lap 4 Alonso leads Hamilton by 1.8s and is edging away.

Lap 14 Alonso extends his lead to 7.0s.

Lap 20 Alonso gets stuck behind Trulli, while trying to lap him, and his lead over Hamilton is cut to 3.0s.

Lap 21 Hamilton is now stuck behind Trulli, and the gap to Alonso grows to 5.5s.

Lap 24 Hamilton laps in 1m15.833s to reduce the gap to Alonso to 5.2s.

Lap 26 Alonso and Massa make their first pit stops.

Lap 27 Hamilton leads Alonso by 15.2s, but loses time with a mistake at Rascasse.

Lap 29 Hamilton pits, rejoining in second place behind Alonso.

Lap 34 Hamilton has been closing in on Alonso, and the gap is now down to 4.0s.

Lap 39 Alonso leads from Hamilton, Massa, Fisichella, Kubica, Wurz and Button.

Lap 44 Alonso sets a new fastest lap to extend his lead to 9.0s.

Lap 51 Alonso makes his second stop, and Hamilton leads.

Lap 53 Hamilton pits, handing the lead back to Alonso.

Lap 54 Alonso is now 4.0s ahead of Hamilton, with Massa a further 18.9s behind, although Massa pits on the following lap.

Lap 56 Hamilton has closed the gap to Alonso to 2.5s.

Lap 59 Hamilton is now just 0.7s behind Alonso.

Lap 62 The battle at the front continues, but Alonso has managed to extend the gap slightly to 1.1s.

Lap 70 Alonso now leads by 2.9s, with Massa 54.6s behind Hamilton. Fourth-placed Fisichella is next in line to be lapped.

Lap 77 The McLarens are 2.8s apart with one lap to go.

Lap 78 Alonso wins from Hamilton by 4.0s, with Massa a distant third. The rest of the field, headed by Fisichella in fourth place, have been lapped.

ABOVE Lewis climbs out of his car after a brush with the tyre barrier at Ste Devote during Thursday practice, proof that he was not afraid to explore the limits of the car at the most unforgiving circuit on the Grand Prix calendar.

OPPOSITE Celebrating a flawless drive to second place after shadowing Fernando Alonso to the finish. Although there was much anticipation of a maiden Hamilton victory, the fact that Lewis matched Alonso's pace throughout the race proved a point to both the team and the watching world.

Given Lewis Hamilton's stunning record there in Formula 3 and GP2, expectations ran high of a first F1 win on the historic streets of Monaco. But after his failure in front of his adoring home crowd in the previous race, it was Fernando Alonso who stormed to the top of the times in the opening free practice sessions, while for the first time in his career as an F1 racer Lewis felt the ignominy of crashing his car, as a slight error of judgement brought his second session to a premature close at Ste Devote, the tricky first corner.

"Everyone makes mistakes, and I'm only human – these small things happen," he admitted. "I was pushing and right on the limit, which is something you always have to do at Monaco. I then found the limit and found out how unforgiving this track can be. There is just no room for error in Monaco. To be honest, it was a light impact, even if it looked quite quick."

He shrugged off this setback to set an encouraging third quickest time in the wet final session, and going into qualifying he was a contender for pole. All was set as he commenced his final run when he hit traffic going through the fast Swimming Pool section. Forced to back off slightly, his advantage was lost and the crucial position went to Alonso.

While overtaking is all but impossible at Monaco, passing in the pits is on everywhere, and with a heavier fuel load Lewis felt confident he could take the lead during the pit stop phases. However, this didn't take into account McLaren's risk-averse mindset at a track where safety cars are practically inevitable. Rather than let the fuel strategies take their normal course, McLaren chose to pit both drivers in a manner that neutralised the potential impact of a safety car.

With McLaren enjoying a clear advantage over the rest of the field, the race should have been a straight duel, but team orders effectively decided the outcome. Fuelled to run longer than Alonso before the final stop, and running quicker than him at the time, Lewis could have been in a position to leapfrog Alonso for the win, but McLaren called him in for his stop early and his victory hopes were lost.

"At the end of the day, I am a rookie and I finished second in only my first Monaco GP," he said, after missing out on a possible win. "And to see I am of a similar pace to Fernando is a positive for me. But it is something I have to live with. I've got number two on my car. I am the number two driver."

MONACO GRAND PRIX
MONTE CARLO

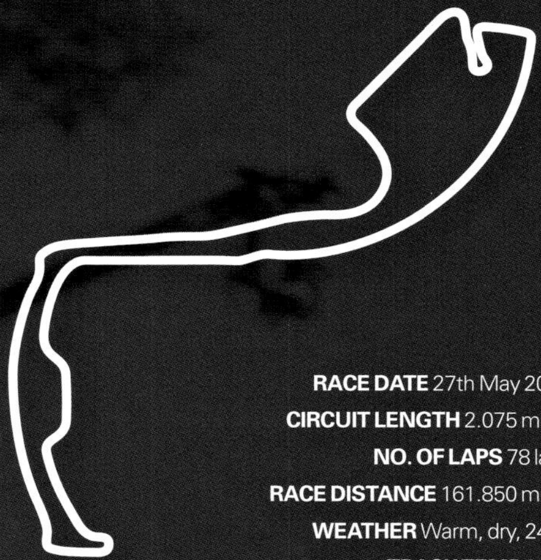

RACE DATE 27th May 2007
CIRCUIT LENGTH 2.075 miles
NO. OF LAPS 78 laps
RACE DISTANCE 161.850 miles
WEATHER Warm, dry, 24°C
TRACK TEMP 35°C

Practice

Session 1 – Thursday

1	Fernando Alonso	McLaren-Mercedes	1m16.973s
2	Lewis Hamilton	McLaren-Mercedes	1m17.601s
3	Nick Heidfeld	BMW	1m17.616s

Session 2 – Thursday

1	Fernando Alonso	McLaren-Mercedes	1m15.940s
2	Kimi Räikkönen	Ferrari	1m16.215s
3	Lewis Hamilton	McLaren-Mercedes	1m16.296s

Session 3 – Saturday

1	Adrian Sutil	Spyker-Ferrari	1m36.612s
2	Kimi Räikkönen	Ferrari	1m36.739s
3	Lewis Hamilton	McLaren-Mercedes	1m36.767s

Qualifying

1	Fernando Alonso	McLaren-Mercedes	1m15.726s
2	Lewis Hamilton	McLaren-Mercedes	1m15.905s
3	Felipe Massa	Ferrari	1m15.967s

Race

1	Fernando Alonso	McLaren-Mercedes	1h40m29.329s
2	Lewis Hamilton	McLaren-Mercedes	+4.095s
3	Felipe Massa	Ferrari	+1m09.114s
4	Giancarlo Fisichella	Renault	+1 Lap
5	Robert Kubica	BMW	+1 Lap
6	Nick Heidfeld	BMW	+1 Lap
7	Alex Wurz	Williams-Toyota	+1 Lap
8	Kimi Räikkönen	Ferrari	+1 Lap

Fastest Lap

Fernando Alonso	McLaren-Mercedes	1m15.284s

World Championship Positions

1	Fernando Alonso	McLaren-Mercedes	38 points
	Lewis Hamilton	McLaren-Mercedes	38 points
3	Felipe Massa	Ferrari	33 points
4	Kimi Räikkönen	Ferrari	23 points
5	Nick Heidfeld	BMW	18 points
6	Giancarlo Fisichella	Renault	13 points
7	Robert Kubica	BMW	12 points
8	Nico Rosberg	Williams-Toyota	5 points

vodafone
BRIDGESTONE
BOSS
SAP
JOHNNIE

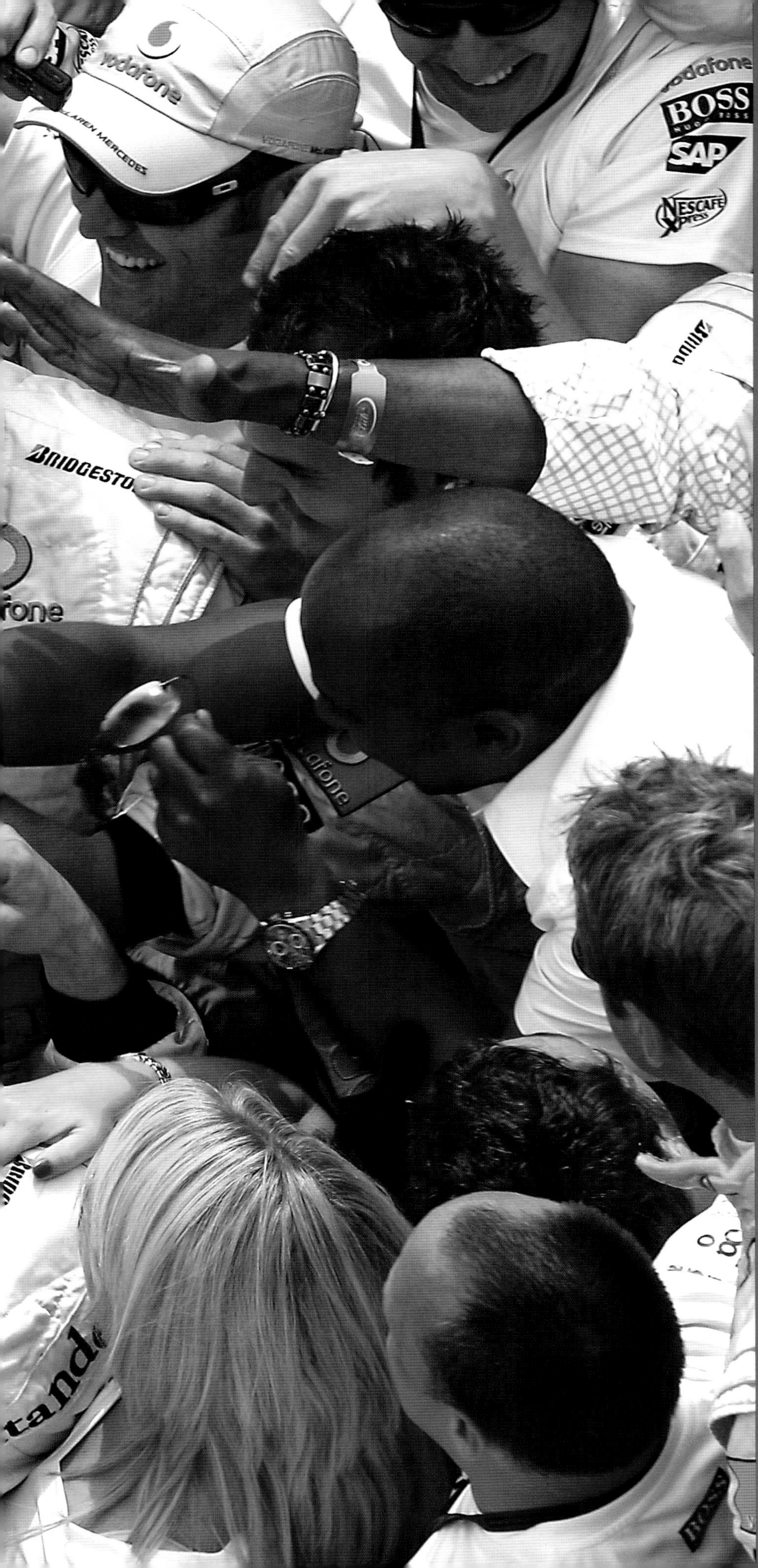

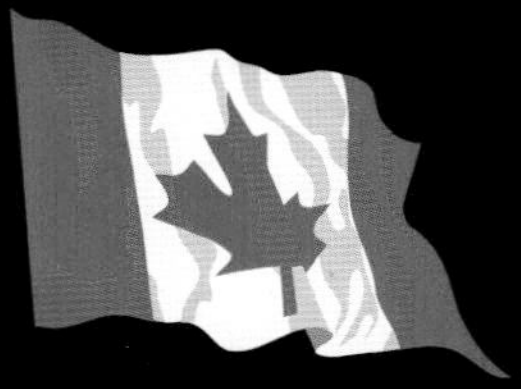

2007 ROUND 6
CANADIAN GRAND PRIX
MONTREAL

1st

POINTS TOTAL **48**
POINTS POSITION **1st**
SEASON WINS **1**

Lap 1 From pole position, Lewis battles with team-mate Fernando Alonso into the first corner. Lewis holds his line and Alonso runs wide, slipping back to third.

Lap 2 Lewis extends his lead over Heidfeld's BMW to 2.1s, with Alonso still third.

Lap 7 Lewis laps in 1m16.744s to extend his lead to 4.6s.

Lap 19 Having run wide on the previous lap, Alonso runs wide again and slips to fourth behind Massa's Ferrari.

Lap 21 Lewis pits. Sutil crashes and comes to rest at the side of the track. The safety car is deployed.

Lap 27 The safety car pulls in and Lewis pulls away to lead Heidfeld, Alonso, Rosberg and Barrichello. Kubica crashes heavily and the safety car is deployed again.

Lap 34 The safety car returns to the pits and Lewis immediately pulls 3.1s clear of Heidfeld.

Lap 36 Lewis laps in 1m16.543s to lead by 4.4s.

Lap 46 Fernando Alonso sets fastest lap of the race, in 1m16.367s, running in fifth place shortly before making his second pit stop.

Lap 48 Lewis makes his second pit stop, rejoining without losing his lead. Christijan Albers runs across the grass, losing the nose from his Spyker and leaving debris on the track.

Lap 50 The safety car is deployed to allow the debris from Albers's mishap to be cleared from the track.

Lap 55 The safety car pulls in and the race restarts, and Lewis pulls 2.2s clear of second-placed Heidfeld. Tonio Liuzzi crashes his Toro Rosso at the final chicane.

Lap 56 The safety car comes out for the fourth time to allow Liuzzi's car to be recovered.

Lap 61 The race restarts, and Lewis pulls 1.3s clear of second-placed Heidfeld.

Lap 70 Lewis crosses the line to win his first Grand Prix, 4.3s ahead of Heidfeld, followed by Wurz, Heikki Kovalainen, Räikkönen, Takuma Sato, Alonso and Ralf Schumacher.

ABOVE In one of the most challenging and incident-packed races for years, Lewis showed astonishing maturity, staying out of trouble and handling with aplomb no fewer than four restarts after safety-car periods, to take a well-deserved maiden Grand Prix victory.

While many F1 pundits had tipped Lewis Hamilton as a potential winner in Monaco, few rated his chances of victory at the ensuing Canadian Grand Prix. After all, it would be his first time at the challenging Circuit Ile Notre Dame, a track reckoned to favour the rival Ferraris. How wrong they were! In one of the most exciting races of the past decade, Lewis produced a brilliant performance. He kept his head while many more experienced drivers were losing theirs, to record an astonishing first win in only his sixth Grand Prix.

His win sparked a mass of publicity not only in Britain but around the world, the like of which Formula 1 had not experienced before. Suddenly the sport had become front-page news again – and there was one man everyone wanted to read about.

And what would ultimately prove to be a defining weekend for Lewis began in typical fashion. On his first visit to the bumpy street track he was a competitive second to Fernando Alonso in the opening free practice session, and followed up with third place in the session held later on. The signs were that McLaren had confounded expectations and had an edge over Ferrari. Lewis confirmed this by setting a scorching pace in final free practice. This sensational form continued into qualifying, where he took full advantage of being on a similar fuel load to team-mate Alonso to claim his first ever F1 pole position. It was a tremendous effort, four-tenths quicker than anyone else.

"The layout looks simple enough but actually it's a real challenge – physical, mental and technical," he revealed. "The key was keeping each sector consistent. Coming into the final chicane I knew the rest of the lap had been fast and in that situation it's tempting to give the chicane a real go – but of course you can end up in the wall. I was approaching faster than I ever had before and I think I got the balance just about right."

With pole in the bag, Lewis's next big challenge was to get his McLaren-Mercedes off the line cleanly and safely through the S-bend at Turn 1 – the scene of countless first-lap pile-ups in the past. With the enormous pressure on him it would have been understandable if he'd made a mistake, but in fact it was Alonso – the reigning World Champion – who made a hash of the first corner. In a bid to pass Lewis round the outside, he ran wide and on to the grass. After a quick piece of rallycross he rejoined, but Hamilton and, crucially, the BMW Sauber of Nick Heidfeld had slipped by.

With his only true rival now compromised, Lewis took full advantage. In the opening stages he was almost a second a lap faster than Heidfeld and a lead of over ten seconds soon opened up. When BMW called their man in for his first pit stop McLaren reacted and brought Lewis in too, even though he could have stayed out for a few more laps. It was a strategy that ensured he won the race.

Almost as Lewis was leaving the pits, his old

TOP Stamping his authority on the race from the start, Lewis sprints from pole position to beat the field into the first corner, as Alonso locks up and slides wide.

ABOVE Lewis received a rapturous reception after the race, and was headline news the next day. Life would never be the same again...

RIGHT Victory in only his sixth Grand Prix and his name at the top of the Drivers' World Championship table – Lewis continued to astound the F1 world.

BELOW Surrounded by photographers, Anthony Hamilton congratulates his son on a remarkable day's work. Lewis Hamilton was about to become an international sporting icon.

OPPOSITE A capacity Canadian crowd took Lewis to their hearts, as he demonstrated remarkable maturity to dominate a challenging race weekend.

F3 team-mate Adrian Sutil was having a sizeable accident in his Spyker. The safety car was required, but under 2007 rules the pit lane remained closed. Alonso was due in that lap, and lacked the fuel to do another tour, so McLaren had no option but to bring him in, despite the fact that it would incur a ten-second stop-go penalty.

Alonso's victory hopes were dashed. All Lewis had to do now was successfully defend his position at the restart and keep the car on the track. Only it wasn't that simple...

Just a minute or so after racing had resumed there was an almighty accident involving Robert Kubica's BMW Sauber. It was one of the biggest crashes seen in F1 for a long time, but miraculously the Pole was unhurt. Still, the track was littered with debris and another lengthy safety-car period followed. Lewis and Kubica have been close since their time in karting, and he was naturally concerned about his friend's condition, but he didn't let it affect his performance and produced a textbook restart to lead comfortably.

Again he opened up a lead and again the safety car brought it back to zero, this time after Christijan Albers crashed his Spyker. The race was doing all it could to knock Lewis off his stride, but he took every hit and came back stronger. There was yet another safety-car period before Lewis could truly relax and run down the final few laps to a hard-fought and emotional first F1 win.

"I could see the pitboard counting down the laps and I was getting slower and slower, telling myself to stay off the kerbs," he admitted. "It's just really hard to grasp everything – it just keeps getting better and better."

CANADIAN GRAND PRIX
MONTREAL

RACE DATE 10th June 2007
CIRCUIT LENGTH 2.710 miles
NO. OF LAPS 70 laps
RACE DISTANCE 189.695 miles
WEATHER Hot, bright, 27°C
TRACK TEMP 50°C

Practice

Session 1 – Friday

1	Fernando Alonso	McLaren-Mercedes	1m17.759s
2	**Lewis Hamilton**	**McLaren-Mercedes**	**1m17.967s**
3	Kimi Räikkönen	Ferrari	1m18.136s

Session 2 – Friday

1	Fernando Alonso	McLaren-Mercedes	1m16.550s
2	Felipe Massa	Ferrari	1m17.090s
3	**Lewis Hamilton**	**McLaren-Mercedes**	**1m17.307s**

Session 3 – Saturday

1	**Lewis Hamilton**	**McLaren-Mercedes**	**1m16.071s**
2	Kimi Räikkönen	Ferrari	1m16.459s
3	Fernando Alonso	McLaren-Mercedes	1m16.465s

Qualifying

1	**Lewis Hamilton**	**McLaren-Mercedes**	**1m15.707s**
2	Fernando Alonso	McLaren-Mercedes	1m16.163s
3	Nick Heidfeld	BMW	1m16.266s

Race

1	**Lewis Hamilton**	**McLaren-Mercedes**	**1h44m11.292s**
2	Nick Heidfeld	BMW	+4.343s
3	Alex Wurz	Williams-Toyota	+5.325s
4	Heikki Kovalainen	Renault	+6.729s
5	Kimi Räikkönen	Ferrari	+13.007s
6	Takuma Sato	Super Aguri-Honda	+16.698s
7	Fernando Alonso	McLaren-Mercedes	+21.936s
8	Ralf Schumacher	Toyota	+22.888s

Fastest Lap

Fernando Alonso	McLaren-Mercedes	1m16.367s

World Championship Positions

1	**Lewis Hamilton**	**McLaren-Mercedes**	**48 points**
2	Fernando Alonso	McLaren-Mercedes	40 points
3	Felipe Massa	Ferrari	33 points
4	Kimi Räikkönen	Ferrari	27 points
5	Nick Heidfeld	BMW	26 points
6	Giancarlo Fisichella	Renault	13 points
7	Robert Kubica	BMW	12 points
8	Heikki Kovalainen	Renault	8 points
	Alex Wurz	Williams-Toyota	8 points

vodafone
2

2007 ROUND 7

US GRAND PRIX

INDIANAPOLIS

1st POINTS TOTAL **58**
POINTS POSITION **1st**
SEASON WINS **2**

Lap 1 From pole position, Hamilton is nearly beaten away by Alonso, but after briefly running side-by-side, Alonso falls into line behind Hamilton. Massa takes third from Heidfeld and Kovalainen as Räikkönen slips to sixth.

Lap 5 After reeling off a series of fastest laps, Hamilton posts a 1m13.681s lap to lead by 1.7s.

Lap 19 Hamilton has extended his lead to 3.4s.

Lap 21 Hamilton, Massa and Heidfeld all pit leaving Alonso in the lead.

Lap 22 Alonso pits and rejoins behind Hamilton and Trulli. Kovalainen leads with Räikkönen second.

Lap 24 Alonso passes Trulli, as Räikkönen pits.

Lap 27 Kovalainen pits, leaving Hamilton back in the lead.

Lap 31 Hamilton leads Alonso by 1.0s, as Trulli pits.

Lap 32 Alonso closes to within 0.6s of Hamilton, with Massa third, ahead of fourth-placed Rosberg who has yet to stop.

Lap 38 Having gained ground over Hamilton in traffic, Alonso attempts a pass on the pit straight, but Hamilton mounts a robust defence, keeping the lead.

Lap 45 Hamilton leads Alonso by 1.1s, with Massa third and Räikkönen closing in fourth.

Lap 47 Hamilton extends his lead to 2.5s.

Lap 50 Alonso makes his second pit stop, rejoining behind Massa.

Lap 51 Hamilton pits, locking his front wheels on the way into the pitlane.

Lap 52 Massa pits from the lead.

Lap 53 After the leaders have all stopped, Hamilton leads Alonso by 1.8s, with Massa defending third place from Räikkönen.

Lap 58 Hamilton leads Alonso by 2.0s, with Massa 15.5s behind the leader, fighting to stay ahead of Räikkönen.

Lap 73 After withstanding intense pressure from Alonso, Hamilton wins by 1.5s from his team-mate, with Massa holding off Räikkönen for third.

Lewis Hamilton didn't have much time to celebrate his fantastic first F1 win, as just a week later he was competing in the United States Grand Prix, run at the majestic setting of the hallowed Indianapolis Motor Speedway.

As in Canada a week earlier, it would be Lewis's first visit to the track, but it didn't take him long to find the groove, and pretty soon he was tackling the flat-out final banked turn with pure aggression, running closer to the concrete outside wall than everyone else. "I'm not everyone else," was his reply when asked why he was doing it!

In free practice he had been competitive, but was usually a couple of tenths shy of team-mate Alonso's pace as McLaren once again held the upper hand. But he transformed this in style in qualifying, pulling an amazing last-minute effort out of the bag to claim his second successive pole position. "I am ecstatic," he said afterwards. "I didn't expect to get pole. Getting my second pole is even better than last week. When I came across the line and they said I had P1 I was screaming in the helmet for the whole lap!"

Alonso lined up alongside Lewis at the start and the two chrome and red McLarens sprinted off at the start, running side-by-side. Lewis bravely defended his line, while Alonso opted for safety first rather than a banzai move and slotted into second.

BELOW Stepping out of the car on the grid after lining up on pole.

OPPOSITE, FROM TOP Lewis makes front-page news again, on the paddock's *Red Bulletin* magazine; keeping a young admirer happy; media interest in Lewis was hitting fever pitch – everyone wanted a sound bite.

The pair proceeded to dominate the race, Lewis opening up a small cushion, but with Alonso running longer before his first stop he was still very much in contention. But a searing sequence of laps prior to Lewis's first stops eked out enough of an advantage to ensure he kept hold of the lead.

By now the leaders were starting to catch the drivers running towards the back of the field, and as the first car to hit this traffic Lewis suffered more of a time loss and this allowed Alonso to close right up.

On lap 37 Lewis lost a chunk of time lapping Vitantonio Liuzzi's Toro Rosso and this gave Alonso his chance. Perfectly placed in the slipstream, he

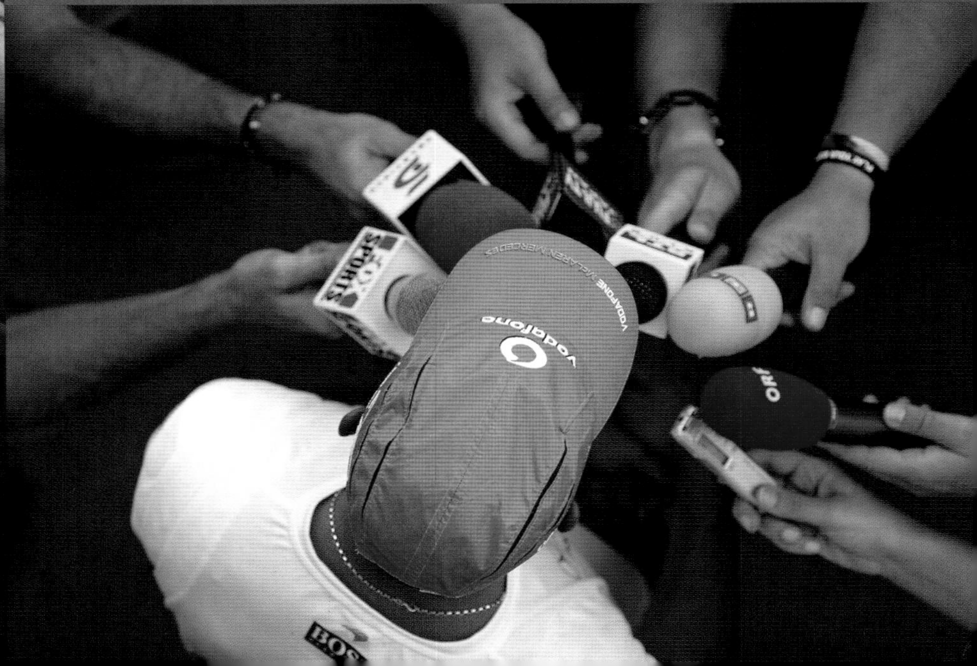

ABOVE Crossing the yard of bricks forming the finish line at the historic Indy circuit.

BELOW Lewis firmly rebuffed his World Champion team-mate's attempts to pass.

OPPOSITE Savouring a second successive win and a ten-point lead in the World Championship.

rocketed out of the final turn and reeled Lewis in down the straight. Lewis instinctively moved to defend the inside line and the two blasted down the main straight just millimetres apart at over 200mph. Alonso had no option but to try the longer outside line, and Lewis kept his cool – and the lead. Alonso's challenge had been rebuffed and Lewis had shown he would not be intimidated by anybody – even his team-mate. His second win in as many weeks took his championship lead to a whopping ten points. The fairytale start to the season was becoming reality...

"We are seven races into a championship and I have to be smart and realise we are running at the front and there is a possibility to win the championship, but it is far, far too early to think about it or get hopes up," he said. "I hoped maybe I would get a podium at some point. I have been on the podium in seven races, it is insane. I find it hard to come to terms with stuff. I am focusing on trying to enjoy it without any of the other stuff, I don't think anyone expected me to do as well as I am doing."

US GRAND PRIX
INDIANAPOLIS

RACE DATE 17th June 2007
CIRCUIT LENGTH 2.605 miles
NO. OF LAPS 73 laps
RACE DISTANCE 190.139 miles
WEATHER Hot, humid, 35°C
TRACK TEMP 45°C

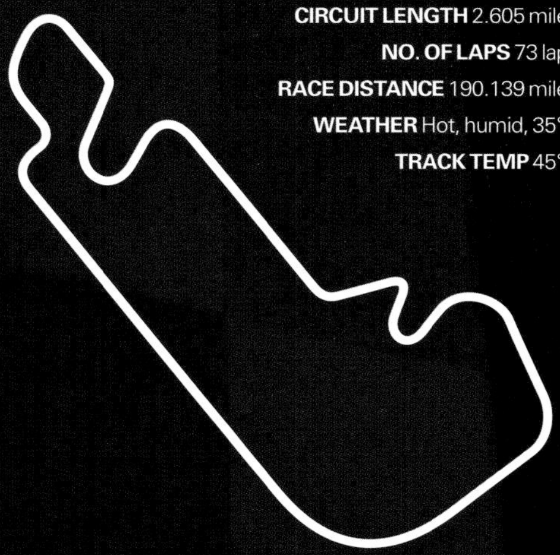

Practice

Session 1 – Friday

1	Fernando Alonso	McLaren-Mercedes	1m11.925s
2	Nick Heidfeld	BMW	1m12.391s
3	**Lewis Hamilton**	**McLaren-Mercedes**	**1m12.628s**

Session 2 – Friday

1	Fernando Alonso	McLaren-Mercedes	1m12.156s
2	**Lewis Hamilton**	**McLaren-Mercedes**	**1m12.209s**
3	Felipe Massa	Ferrari	1m12.435s

Session 3 – Saturday

1	Fernando Alonso	McLaren-Mercedes	1m12.150s
2	Sebastian Vettel	BMW	1m12.321s
3	**Lewis Hamilton**	**McLaren-Mercedes**	**1m12.378s**

Qualifying

1	**Lewis Hamilton**	**McLaren-Mercedes**	**1m12.331s**
2	Fernando Alonso	McLaren-Mercedes	1m12.500s
3	Felipe Massa	Ferrari	1m12.703s

Race

1	**Lewis Hamilton**	**McLaren-Mercedes**	**1h31m09.965s**
2	Fernando Alonso	McLaren-Mercedes	+1.518s
3	Felipe Massa	Ferrari	+12.842s
4	Kimi Räikkönen	Ferrari	+15.422s
5	Heikki Kovalainen	Renault	+41.402s
6	Jarno Trulli	Toyota	+1m06.703s
7	Mark Webber	Red Bull-Renault	+1m07.331s
8	Sebastian Vettel	BMW	+1m07.783s

Fastest Lap

Kimi Räikkönen	Ferrari	1m13.117s

World Championship Positions

1	**Lewis Hamilton**	**McLaren-Mercedes**	**58 points**
2	Fernando Alonso	McLaren-Mercedes	48 points
3	Felipe Massa	Ferrari	39 points
4	Kimi Räikkönen	Ferrari	32 points
5	Nick Heidfeld	BMW	26 points
6	Giancarlo Fisichella	Renault	13 points
7	Robert Kubica	BMW	12 points
8	Heikki Kovalainen	Renault	12 points

"MM"
CARA COAT
Mobil
SAP
BOSS

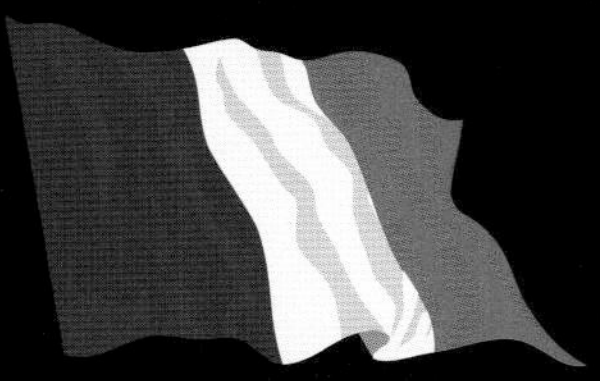

2007 ROUND 8

FRENCH GRAND PRIX

MAGNY-COURS

3rd

POINTS TOTAL **64**
POINTS POSITION **1st**
SEASON WINS **2**

Lap 1 Massa makes a good start from pole position, but Hamilton drops to third behind Räikkönen. Kubica steals fourth from Fisichella, with Heidfeld sixth.

Lap 4 Massa leads Räikkönen by 2.2s.

Lap 12 Massa sets a new fastest lap of 1m16.398s to lead Räikkönen by 4.0s, with Hamilton a further 1.9s behind Räikkönen. Alonso battles for sixth with Heidfeld.

Lap 15 The Ferrari drivers continue to set the pace, Massa lapping in 1m16.229s and Räikkönen in 1m16.524s.

Lap 16 Both McLaren drivers pit, Hamilton ahead of Alonso, Hamilton rejoins in seventh, Alonso ninth.

Lap 19 Massa, Kubica and Fisichella pit, leaving Räikkönen leading from Hamilton.

Lap 22 Räikkönen and Heidfeld pit. Alonso battles with Fisichella but fails to pass. Massa now leads from Räikkönen, with Hamilton still third.

Lap 24 Massa leads Räikkönen by 2.0s, with Hamilton third from Kubica.

Lap 33 Alonso finally passes Heidfeld after several attempts and an enthralling battle.

Lap 35 Massa leads Räikkönen by 1.2s, with Hamilton a further 6.1s adrift.

Lap 37 Hamilton pits, followed by Alonso.

Lap 38 As Hamilton rejoins, Kubica passes, but Hamilton mounts a robust pass back to reclaim third at the hairpin.

Lap 43 Massa pits, leaving Räikkönen leading from Hamilton.

Lap 44 Räikkönen leads Massa, who has rejoined in second place, by 21.6s, with Hamilton 9.3s behind Massa.

Lap 46 Räikkönen pits, and rejoins just ahead of Massa to take the lead.

Lap 51 Hamilton makes his final stop from third place.

Lap 56 Räikkönen leads Massa by 2.8s, with Hamilton third almost 30 seconds behind, well clear of Kubica in fourth place.

Lap 70 Räikkönen wins by 2.4s from Massa, with Hamilton third, maintaining his 100% podium-finish record. Kubica is fourth from Heidfeld, Fisichella, Alonso and Button.

ABOVE Running wheel-to-wheel with ex-F3 team-mate Robert Kubica during a daring passing manoeuvre on the Pole.

BELOW On Formula 1's return to Europe, and with his home race the next weekend, Lewis again proved to be the faster McLaren driver.

OPPOSITE A trademark thumbs-up, and a confident smile, during the pre-race drivers' parade around the circuit on Sunday morning.

The Formula 1 circus returned to Europe for the French Grand Prix with Lewis Hamilton still at the top of the standings – the first British driver to be there at this stage of the season since Damon Hill in his 1996 title-winning season.

In the break since the North American races Ferrari had been busy honing the design of its F2007, and it soon became apparent in the free practice sessions that the red cars would be the ones to beat at Magny-Cours, especially as the McLarens were running with reduced rpm on their Mercedes-Benz engines after the flat-out battle for the lead last time out at Indianapolis.

Lewis gave McLaren cause for optimism by setting the pace in the final Saturday practice session, and then going quickest in the opening two parts of qualifying. The final qualifying session would be a four-way shoot-out for pole position between the two Ferraris and the two McLarens, but this soon became a three-way tussle after gearbox failure took Fernando Alonso out of the reckoning. In the end it was Felipe Massa's Ferrari on pole, just 0.007 of a second faster than Lewis, who had been on a quicker lap until he made a slight error when pushing too hard. "It was great fun fighting it out with Felipe like that," he reckoned.

Come race day it would be a different story. Beaten off the line by Kimi Räikkönen, Lewis was powerless to match the pace of the Ferraris and they pulled away at half-a-second a lap in the opening part of the race. Third was now the best he could do, and while he had a comfortable gap to Robert Kubica's fourth-placed BMW Sauber the Pole was on a two-stop strategy, while Lewis would be stopping three times.

As Lewis emerged from his second stop Kubica flashed by. It was almost certain that Lewis would regain the place when Kubica stopped again, but he couldn't bank on that, as he needed another stop too. So as they headed into the Adelaide hairpin two corners later, Lewis dived down the inside in a stunning late-braking moment reminiscent of his GP2 race-winning moves. Kubica didn't give in though, and they ran wheel-to-wheel through to the next corner, where he finally had to concede.

Third was now secure, and with Alonso only able to fight his way back to seventh, Lewis headed into his home Grand Prix at Silverstone with a significant 14-point lead in the championship.

"At the end, when I came out of my third pit stop I knew that I was 20 seconds behind already so there was no point in wrenching the neck out of the engine. I just relaxed and kept that position," he said.

FRENCH GRAND PRIX
MAGNY-COURS

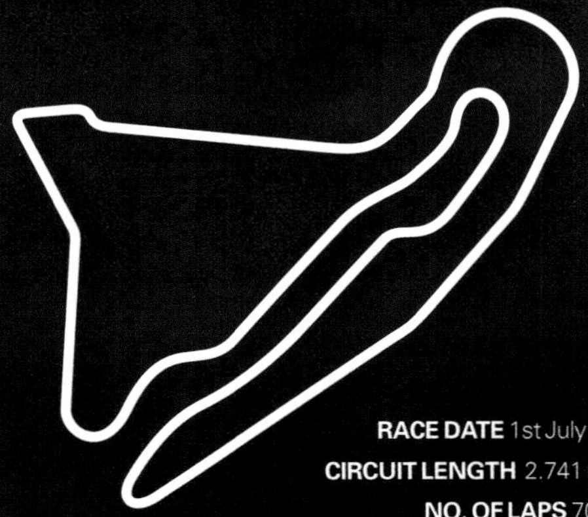

RACE DATE 1st July 2007
CIRCUIT LENGTH 2.741 miles
NO. OF LAPS 70 laps
RACE DISTANCE 191.870 miles
WEATHER Bright, humid, 25°C
TRACK TEMP 40°C

Practice

Session 1 – Friday

1	Kimi Räikkönen	Ferrari	1m15.382s
2	Felipe Massa	Ferrari	1m15.447s
3	Fernando Alonso	McLaren-Mercedes	1m16.154s
6	**Lewis Hamilton**	**McLaren-Mercedes**	**1m16.277s**

Session 2 – Friday

1	Felipe Massa	Ferrari	1m15.453s
2	Kimi Räikkönen	Ferrari	1m15.488s
3	Scott Speed	Toro Rosso-Ferrari	1m15.773s
4	**Lewis Hamilton**	**McLaren-Mercedes**	**1m15.780s**

Session 3 – Saturday

1	**Lewis Hamilton**	**McLaren-Mercedes**	**1m14.843s**
2	Felipe Massa	Ferrari	1m14.906s
3	Kimi Räikkönen	Ferrari	1m15.276s

Qualifying

1	Felipe Massa	Ferrari	1m15.034s
2	**Lewis Hamilton**	**McLaren-Mercedes**	**1m15.104s**
3	Kimi Räikkönen	Ferrari	1m15.257s

Race

1	Kimi Räikkönen	Ferrari	1h30m11.292s
2	Felipe Massa	Ferrari	+2.414s
3	**Lewis Hamilton**	**McLaren-Mercedes**	**+32.153s**
4	Robert Kubica	BMW	+41.727s
5	Nick Heidfeld	BMW	+48.801s
6	Giancarlo Fisichella	Renault	+52.210s
7	Fernando Alonso	McLaren-Mercedes	+56.516s
8	Jenson Button	Honda	+58.885s

Fastest Lap

Felipe Massa	Ferrari	1m16.099s

World Championship Positions

1	**Lewis Hamilton**	**McLaren-Mercedes**	**64 points**
2	Fernando Alonso	McLaren-Mercedes	50 points
3	Felipe Massa	Ferrari	47 points
4	Kimi Räikkönen	Ferrari	42 points
5	Nick Heidfeld	BMW	30 points
6	Robert Kubica	BMW	17 points
7	Giancarlo Fisichella	Renault	16 points
8	Heikki Kovalainen	Renault	12 points

VODAFONE McLAREN MERCEDES
vodafone

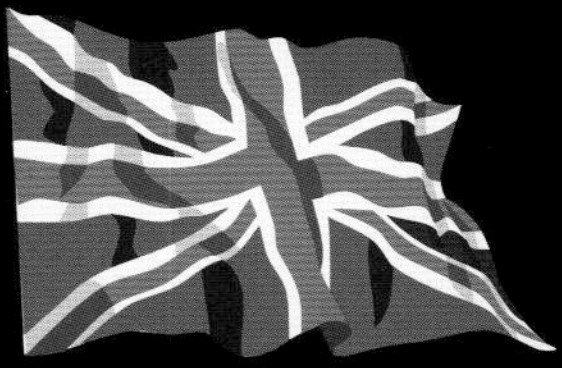

2007 ROUND 9

BRITISH GRAND PRIX

SILVERSTONE

3rd POINTS TOTAL **70**
POINTS POSITION **1st**
SEASON WINS **2**

Pre-start The initial start is aborted when Massa stalls. An extra formation lap takes place and Massa is pushed to the pits.

Lap 1 Hamilton makes a good start from pole and holds off Räikkönen. Alonso stays third, ahead of Kubica, Kovalainen, Fisichella and Heidfeld. Massa starts from the pitlane and lies 19th at the end of the lap.

Lap 2 Hamilton leads Räikkönen by 0.6s. Massa passes three cars during the lap.

Lap 4 Hamilton leads by 1.0s. Massa now lies 14th.

Lap 5 Räikkönen cuts Hamilton's lead by 0.2s. Massa moves up to 13th.

Lap 11 Hamilton laps in 1m21.675s to lead by 1.0s. Alonso is third, 1.7s behind Räikkönen. Massa passes Trulli for 9th.

Lap 12 Räikkönen sets a new fastest lap of 1m21.511s, then Massa laps in 1m21.450s.

Lap 14 Räikkönen tries to pass Hamilton at Brooklands, but the leader holds position.

Lap 16 Hamilton pits, but almost sets off before the fuel nozzle is released. Räikkönen leads, while Massa laps in 1m21.165s.

Lap 17 Räikkönen sets a new fastest lap of 1m20.658s.

Lap 18 Räikkönen pits, rejoining ahead of Hamilton. Alonso now leads.

Lap 20 Alonso pits, making a short stop, and rejoins ahead of Räikkönen.

Lap 21 Alonso leads Räikkönen by 2.4s with Hamilton 5.0s behind, followed by Kubica, Heidfeld, Fisichella and Massa.

Lap 28 Alonso has been extending his lead and now leads Räikkönen by 4.4s. Hamilton is falling further behind in third.

Lap 37 Alonso pits, followed by Hamilton a lap later.

Lap 40 Räikkönen leads Alonso by 25.9s, and is pulling away significantly on his lighter fuel load.

Lap 43 Räikkönen pits and rejoins in the lead.

Lap 48 Räikkönen leads Alonso by 4.0s, with Hamilton third.

Lap 59 Räikkönen eases up to win by 2.4s from Alonso. Hamilton is a distant third from Kubica, Massa and Heidfeld.

ABOVE Focusing on the task ahead before the final qualifying session.

OPPOSITE A resurgent Ferrari proved more than a match for McLaren at its home track, but the sell-out crowd willed on their man to yet another podium finish.

A capacity crowd at Silverstone greeted Lewis for his first-ever home Grand Prix. And he gave them exactly what they came to see, with a stellar qualifying performance.

Having been generally a fraction slower than McLaren team-mate Fernando Alonso and the Ferraris in free practice and the first two qualifying sessions, Lewis pulled out all the stops in the dying seconds of Q3 to take his third career F1 pole. "Coming into the final sector I could see from my readout that I was well up and that pole was possible," he said. As he slowly toured around on his way back to the pits the 80,000-strong crowd gave him a standing ovation.

His qualifying efforts had raised expectations, but in truth Lewis was battling with an ill-handling car that lacked the overall speed of both Alonso's sister machine and, especially, the two Ferraris. But he was dealt a lucky hand as the cars lined up for the start and the engine of Felipe Massa's Ferrari died. This meant the Brazilian had to start from the pits and was effectively out of contention.

Lewis chopped in front of Kimi Räikkönen's fast-starting Ferrari to lead into the first corner. The crowd erupted as if he'd won the race, but in truth Lewis's hopes of winning were on borrowed time. In order to grab pole he had gone for a light-fuel strategy, which meant he would be stopping well before Räikkönen, who stuck to his tail no matter how hard Lewis pushed.

But, as is often the way in modern F1, Kimi waited for the pit stops, knowing he had a greater fuel load than Lewis. After the first round of pit stops Lewis was third, having lost out to Alonso as well as Räikkönen. He also lost a fraction of time in the pits when, in his desire to get back out to defend his lead, he misinterpreted the turning of the pit lollipop as a sign to go. Lewis realised his error straight away, and as refuelling was still under way a potentially nasty incident was avoided.

Lewis was really struggling at this stage of the race with the balance of his car and the wear of his tyres. He was losing a second a lap to the leaders, although he still had a comfortable advantage over Robert Kubica's fourth-placed BMW Sauber. "I was struggling to get the car balance I needed all weekend," he admitted.

On the softer of the two tyre options Lewis's relative performance improved in the final stint, and he duly came in third for his ninth podium in a row.

BRITISH GRAND PRIX
SILVERSTONE

RACE DATE 8th July 2007
CIRCUIT LENGTH 3.194 miles
NO. OF LAPS 59 laps
RACE DISTANCE 188.446 miles
WEATHER Sunny, dry, 20°C
TRACK TEMP 32°C

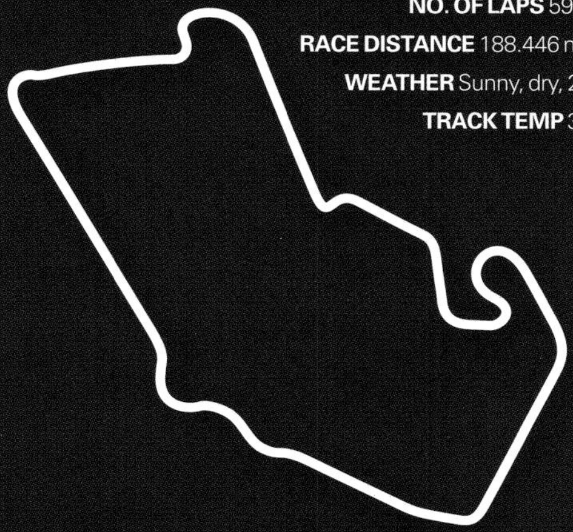

Practice

Session 1 – Friday

1	**Lewis Hamilton**	**McLaren-Mercedes**	**1m21.100s**
2	Kimi Räikkönen	Ferrari	1m21.211s
3	Felipe Massa	Ferrari	1m21.285s

Session 2 – Friday

1	Kimi Räikkönen	Ferrari	1m20.639s
2	Felipe Massa	Ferrari	1m21.138s
3	Ralf Schumacher	Toyota	1m21.381s
4	**Lewis Hamilton**	**McLaren-Mercedes**	**1m21.381s**

Session 3 – Saturday

1	Kimi Räikkönen	Ferrari	1m19.751s
2	Fernando Alonso	McLaren-Mercedes	1m19.920s
3	Felipe Massa	Ferrari	1m19.969s
4	**Lewis Hamilton**	**McLaren-Mercedes**	**1m20.344s**

Qualifying

1	**Lewis Hamilton**	**McLaren-Mercedes**	**1m19.997s**
2	Kimi Räikkönen	Ferrari	1m20.099s
3	Fernando Alonso	McLaren-Mercedes	1m20.147s

Race

1	Kimi Räikkönen	Ferrari	1h21m43.074s
2	Fernando Alonso	McLaren-Mercedes	+2.459s
3	**Lewis Hamilton**	**McLaren-Mercedes**	**+39.373s**
4	Robert Kubica	BMW	+53.319s
5	Felipe Massa	Ferrari	+54.063s
6	Nick Heidfeld	BMW	+56.336s
7	Heikki Kovalainen	Renault	+1 Lap
8	Giancarlo Fisichella	Renault	+1 Lap

Fastest Lap

Kimi Räikkönen	Ferrari	1m20.638s

World Championship Positions

1	**Lewis Hamilton**	**McLaren-Mercedes**	**70 points**
2	Fernando Alonso	McLaren-Mercedes	58 points
3	Kimi Räikkönen	Ferrari	52 points
4	Felipe Massa	Ferrari	51 points
5	Nick Heidfeld	BMW	33 points
6	Robert Kubica	BMW	22 points
7	Giancarlo Fisichella	Renault	17 points
8	Heikki Kovalainen	Renault	14 points

"Coming into the final sector I could see from my readout that I was well up and that pole was possible... I really felt the pressure at that moment."

Mobil 1

2007 ROUND 10
EUROPEAN GRAND PRIX
NÜRBURGRING

9th POINTS TOTAL **70** POINTS POSITION **1st** SEASON WINS **2**

Lap 1 Räikkönen leads away from pole, followed by Massa and Alonso. Hamilton moves up to sixth from tenth, but then suffers a puncture as he is clipped when the two BMWs collide. He limps to the pits for intermediates, as rain starts to fall and several cars run wide. Markus Winkelhock, debuting for Spyker, started on wets, and so stays out.

Lap 2 Winkelhock leads, as the dry-tyre runners pit for wets.

Lap 3 Button, Hamilton, Rosberg, Sutil, Speed and Liuzzi all slide off into the gravel. Hamilton stays in his car, and is lifted back on to the track with a crane. Winkelhock pits and rejoins at the head of the field. The safety car is deployed.

Lap 4 The race is red-flagged. Winkelhock leads, from Massa, Alonso, Webber and Coulthard. Hamilton is at the back of the field, 17th. The race is suspended, pending a safety-car restart.

Lap 5 The rain has stopped as the restart takes place.

Lap 6 As the field runs behind the safety car, Hamilton – a lap down – is instructed to pass all the other cars and reclaim his missing lap. Once he has made up his lap, he pits for dry tyres.

Lap 8 The safety car pulls in. Massa and Alonso immediately pass Winkelhock. Hamilton is at the back of the field, a lap down again, due to his extra stop and being on slower dry tyres in the still-wet conditions.

Lap 10 Hamilton ploughs through the gravel at Turn 7.

Lap 11 Hamilton is suddenly the fastest man on the track.

Lap 12 The leaders pit for dry tyres.

Lap 29 Hamilton has been setting a succession of fastest laps, but is still at the back of the field in 14th place.

Lap 33 Hamilton passes Fisichella, then pits on the next lap.

Lap 40 Massa is 7.2s clear of Alonso. Hamilton is 11th.

Lap 52 Heavy rain begins to fall again.

Lap 54 Hamilton pits for wet tyres.

Lap 56 After a battle, Alonso passes Massa for the lead.

Lap 58 Hamilton passes Fisichella for ninth place.

Lap 60 Alonso wins by 8.1s from Massa, Mark Webber and Wurz. Hamilton finishes ninth, his first non-podium finish of 2007.

TOP Lewis is stretchered to the waiting medical helicopter after his accident on Saturday.

ABOVE Lewis joins the first-corner parking lot and is then craned back on the track.

BELOW Torrential rain caused a chaotic race, which caught out many experienced drivers.

Lewis had just set the fastest first-sector time in final qualifying at the Nürburgring. As he approached the 'Schumacher S', his car veered out of control and he crashed head-on into the tyres.

As he clambered from the car it was clear all was not 100 per cent, and he was dramatically stretchered off to an ambulance, which took him to the medical centre, where he was kept under observation for a few hours.

The cause of the accident was a malfunctioning wheelgun which had failed to tighten the right-front wheelnut properly. The wheel fouled against the brake ducts, which caused the tyre to deflate spectacularly.

Thankfully he was unhurt, and he duly lined up on Sunday morning tenth – his worst-ever starting slot.

He nevertheless rocketed off the line and was challenging for sixth when his left-rear wheel was clipped by a spinning BMW Sauber, puncturing the tyre. He limped back to the pits, but by now the race was descending into chaos as heavy rain hit part of the circuit. McLaren fitted Lewis with intermediates, but the rain had worsened, and the first corner had become a lagoon. Button and Sutil had already spun out here. Arriving next, Lewis skipped over the gravel and came to a halt just inches from the barrier.

He kept the engine running and waited to be retrieved. Conditions continued to worsen, and as yet more cars spun off, the race was stopped. The ability of the Mercedes engine to idle meant that when Lewis was craned back on to the track he was able to select first and drive off!

There was mass confusion as to the actual order now, with McLaren convinced Lewis was on the lead lap, the race officials that he was a lap down. By the time the race restarted the rain had stopped and the track was drying rapidly. As the field lined up behind the safety car Lewis was waved by and allowed back on to the lead lap. He took this opportunity to dive into the pits for dry-weather tyres, but it was a premature decision and he went off twice on the slippery surface, going a lap down in the process, before conditions finally started to favour his tyres.

He eventually caught and passed the remaining tailenders, coming home pointless in ninth. With Alonso pulling a daring passing move on Massa to take the win, Lewis's title lead was slashed to just two points.

EUROPEAN GRAND PRIX
NÜRBURGRING

RACE DATE 22nd July 2007
CIRCUIT LENGTH 3.199 miles
NO. OF LAPS 60 laps
RACE DISTANCE 191.938 miles
WEATHER Wet, dry, then wet, 20°C
TRACK TEMP 30°C

Practice

Session 1 – Friday

1	**Lewis Hamilton**	**McLaren-Mercedes**	**1m32.515s**
2	Kimi Räikkönen	Ferrari	1m32.751s
3	Fernando Alonso	McLaren-Mercedes	1m32.932s

Session 2 – Friday

1	Kimi Räikkönen	Ferrari	1m33.339s
2	**Lewis Hamilton**	**McLaren-Mercedes**	**1m33.478s**
3	Felipe Massa	Ferrari	1m33.590s

Session 3 – Saturday

1	Kimi Räikkönen	Ferrari	1m31.396s
2	**Lewis Hamilton**	**McLaren-Mercedes**	**1m31.627s**
3	Fernando Alonso	McLaren-Mercedes	1m32.039s

Qualifying

1	Kimi Räikkönen	Ferrari	1m31.450s
2	Fernando Alonso	McLaren-Mercedes	1m31.741s
3	Felipe Massa	Ferrari	1m31.778s
10	**Lewis Hamilton**	**McLaren-Mercedes**	**1m33.833s**

Race

1	Fernando Alonso	McLaren-Mercedes	2h06m26.358s
2	Felipe Massa	Ferrari	+8.155s
3	Mark Webber	Red Bull-Renault	+1m05.674s
4	Alexander Wurz	Williams-Toyota	+1m05.937s
5	David Coulthard	Red Bull-Renault	+1m.13.656s
6	Nick Heidfeld	BMW	+1m20.298s
7	Robert Kubica	BMW	+1m22.415s
8	Heikki Kovalainen	Renault	+1 Lap
9	**Lewis Hamilton**	**McLaren-Mercedes**	**+1 Lap**

Fastest Lap

Felipe Massa	Ferrari	1m32.853s

World Championship Positions

1	**Lewis Hamilton**	**McLaren-Mercedes**	**70 points**
2	Fernando Alonso	McLaren-Mercedes	68 points
3	Felipe Massa	Ferrari	59 points
4	Kimi Räikkönen	Ferrari	52 points
5	Nick Heidfeld	BMW	36 points
6	Robert Kubica	BMW	24 points
7	Giancarlo Fisichella	Renault	17 points
8	Heikki Kovalainen	Renault	15 points

aigo
aigo
SAP
Mobil
vodafone
vodafone

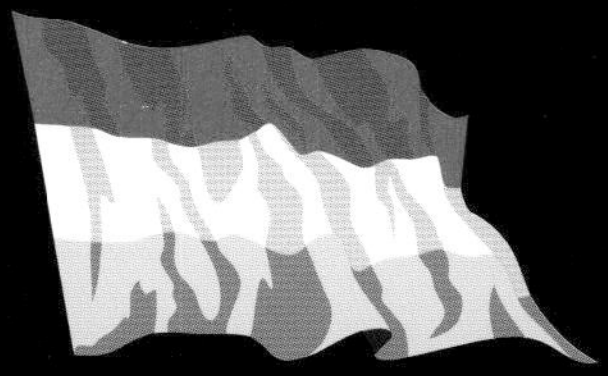

2007 ROUND 11

HUNGARIAN GRAND PRIX

BUDAPEST

1st

POINTS TOTAL **80**
POINTS POSITION **1st**
SEASON WINS **3**

Lap 1 Pole-sitter Hamilton leads away, but Räikkönen passes Heidfeld into the first corner, with Rosberg, Schumacher and Kubica in pursuit. Alonso, starting from seventh, gets on to the dirt in the first corner and drops to eighth.

Lap 2 Hamilton extends his lead to 2.4s.

Lap 4 Hamilton laps in 1m21.529s to lead by 3.3s. Alonso has now passed Webber and Kubica to lie sixth.

Lap 5 The top two set personal bests with a 1m21.444s for Hamilton and 1m21.307s for Räikkönen.

Lap 13 After trading fastest laps with Räikkönen for several laps, Hamilton leads by 4.5s.

Lap 19 The two leaders pit, along with Kubica and Fisichella. Hamilton rejoins still leading, by 2.0s from Räikkönen.

Lap 28 Räikkönen has been gaining on Hamilton for several laps, and the gap has reduced to 0.8s.

Lap 30 Hamilton pulls 1.5s clear of Räikkönen.

Lap 32 Sato makes his first stop and almost trips up Hamilton at Turn One as he rejoins.

Lap 37 Hamilton and Räikkönen are separated by 0.9s.

Lap 46 Räikkönen makes his second stop, rejoining still in second place.

Lap 50 Hamilton, Alonso and Massa pit. Hamilton emerges more than 4s clear of Räikkönen.

Lap 53 Räikkönen closes the gap to 3.1s.

Lap 55 Räikkönen closes still further, to within 2.2s of Hamilton.

Lap 56 The gap between the leaders has reduced to 1.2s.

Lap 57 The two leaders are now 0.5s apart. Alonso is pushing Heidfeld for third, with Kubica, Schumacher, Rosberg and Kovalainen following.

Lap 61 The gap at the front is 0.7s.

Lap 68 Hamilton leads by 1.2s – his biggest margin for a while.

Lap 70 Hamilton takes the third F1 win of his career, 0.7s ahead of Räikkönen. Heidfeld is third from Alonso, Kubica, Schumacher, Rosberg and Kovalainen.

RIGHT Lewis helps to recover his stricken car during the second practice session on Friday, after spinning trying to avoid the slow Spyker of Yamamoto.

BELOW Lewis is held in the pit lane behind team-mate Alonso, who has apparently completed his stop for tyres, in the dying seconds of final qualifying – an incident which would have serious repercussions.

OPPOSITE At the post-qualifying press conference, the atmosphere between the two McLaren drivers was somewhat frosty. Their relationship would never be quite the same again.

After his no-score result in the European Grand Prix, Hamilton responded in style in Hungary. But his superb lights-to-flag win, after a race-long battle with Kimi Räikkönen's Ferrari, was overshadowed by the events of qualifying, where his team rivalry with Fernando Alonso – and his relationship with the McLaren management – hit the rocks in spectacular fashion.

Rumours of discontent had surrounded McLaren since the early part of the season, but McLaren had been at pains to play them down. However, the team was unable to put a positive spin on the events surrounding final qualifying at the Hungaroring.

The problems started when, in order to maintain an advantageous track position, Lewis decided to ignore a team order for him to move over for team-mate Alonso during the fuel-burn phase of the session. Alonso felt this cost him a potential extra lap of running, which is crucial in determining the level of fuel the drivers start with. The Spaniard chose to exact his revenge by holding on in the pits for a good ten seconds after being waved out for his final qualifying run. This left Lewis queued up in the pit lane, and when he was finally able to slot in for a fresh set of tyres it left him too little time to complete his out-lap and make his final qualifying effort.

Lewis was fuming as he crossed the line just seconds after the flag fell, and there was an angry exchange of words with Ron Dennis on the pit-to-car radio. Alonso snatched pole position from Lewis with his final effort, but the race stewards took exception to his block on Lewis and penalised him five grid spaces, while McLaren was prevented from scoring Constructors' Championship points for its role in the farrago.

MERCEDES
FedEx

"I really don't understand why I was held back," Lewis admitted. "It definitely needs a good explanation. I'm not angry. I'm curious as to what's gone on and I find it quite interesting and amusing."

Succeeding to pole position following Alonso's penalty, Lewis made full use of it to lead the fast-starting Räikkönen into the first corner. He soon established a comfortable lead but found it impossible to stretch the advantage past 3.5 seconds. In fact, as both drivers headed towards the first of their two pit stops the gap had reduced to a little over a second, as they exchanged fastest laps in a classic duel. Lewis narrowly managed to hold on to his lead, as he did after the second pit stops too. Although Räikkönen was never close enough to attempt a pass, Lewis was never far enough ahead to relax either.

Hamilton's third GP win opened up his championship lead to seven points. "It's been an eventful weekend and quite emotional for all the team," he said. "I had a problem with my steering and it made it quite difficult to keep the pace. I was quite nervous that something was going to break but thank God it didn't. It was probably one of the hardest races I've had to do, and even more satisfying that I had to push that bit extra to keep Kimi behind me."

ABOVE Catch! Lewis drops his champagne from the podium to the waiting team below.

BELOW After an eventful weekend, Lewis's family and crew had something to celebrate.

OPPOSITE Speeding towards the third victory of his burgeoning Formula 1 career.

HUNGARIAN GRAND PRIX
BUDAPEST

RACE DATE 5th August 2007
CIRCUIT LENGTH 2.722miles
NO. OF LAPS 70 laps
RACE DISTANCE 190.551 miles
WEATHER Bright, dry, 31°C
TRACK TEMP 43°C

Practice

Session 1 – Friday

1	Robert Kubica	BMW	1m22.390s
2	Felipe Massa	Ferrari	1m22.519s
3	Kimi Räikkönen	Ferrari	1m22.540s
5	**Lewis Hamilton**	**McLaren-Mercedes**	**1m22.654s**

Session 2 – Friday

1	Fernando Alonso	McLaren-Mercedes	1m20.919s
2	Heikki Kovalainen	Renault	1m21.283s
3	**Lewis Hamilton**	**McLaren-Mercedes**	**1m21.338s**

Session 3 – Saturday

1	Felipe Massa	Ferrari	1m20.183s
2	Fernando Alonso	McLaren-Mercedes	1m20.414s
3	**Lewis Hamilton**	**McLaren-Mercedes**	**1m20.461s**

Qualifying

1	Fernando Alonso	McLaren-Mercedes	1m19.674s
2	**Lewis Hamilton**	**McLaren-Mercedes**	**1m19.781s**
3	Nick Heidfeld	BMW	1m20.259s

Race

1	**Lewis Hamilton**	**McLaren-Mercedes**	**1h35m52.991s**
2	Kimi Räikkönen	Ferrari	+0.715s
3	Nick Heidfeld	BMW	+43.129s
4	Fernando Alonso	McLaren-Mercedes	+44.858s
5	Robert Kubica	BMW	+47.616s
6	Ralf Schumacher	Toyota	+50.669s
7	Nico Rosberg	Williams-Toyota	+59.139s
8	Heikki Kovalainen	Renault	+1m08.104s

Fastest Lap

Kimi Räikkönen	Ferrari	1m20.047s

World Championship Positions

1	**Lewis Hamilton**	**McLaren-Mercedes**	**80 points**
2	Fernando Alonso	McLaren-Mercedes	73 points
3	Kimi Räikkönen	Ferrari	60 points
4	Felipe Massa	Ferrari	59 points
5	Nick Heidfeld	BMW	42 points
6	Robert Kubica	BMW	28 points
7	Giancarlo Fisichella	Renault	17 points
8	Heikki Kovalainen	Renault	16 points

2007 ROUND 12

TURKISH GRAND PRIX

ISTANBUL

5th POINTS TOTAL **84**
POINTS POSITION **1st**
SEASON WINS **3**

Lap 1 Felipe Massa sprints away from pole to lead into Turn One. Fellow front-row starter Hamilton is passed by Räikkönen, while Kubica and Heidfeld pass Alonso for fourth and fifth. Trulli spins at Turn One following a nudge from Fisichella.

Lap 4 Massa leads Räikkönen by 1.2s, with Hamilton a further 1.5s behind in third.

Lap 6 Räikkönen laps in 1m28.698s to close the gap to Massa to 1.0s.

Lap 11 Räikkönen laps in 1m28.457s to close to within 0.8s of Massa.

Lap 18 After trading successive fastest laps with Räikkönen, Massa laps in 1m27.922s. Räikkönen pits.

Lap 19 Massa pits and rejoins comfortably clear of Räikkönen.

Lap 20 Hamilton pits, rejoining without losing third place.

Lap 21 Temporary leader Kovalainen pits.

Lap 23 Massa leads Räikkönen from Hamilton, Alonso, Heidfeld, Kovalainen, Kubica and Rosberg.

Lap 38 After closing on Massa through traffic, Räikkönen is right with the leader. Hamilton still lies third.

Lap 41 Räikkönen and Heidfeld pit.

Lap 42 Massa pits and rejoins ahead of Räikkönen.

Lap 43 Hamilton sustains a front right puncture and limps to the pits. Alonso and Fisichella pit.

Lap 44 Massa leads from Räikkönen, Alonso and Heidfeld. Hamilton has rejoined in fifth after pitting for fuel and tyres, but with a damaged front wing.

Lap 57 Räikkönen sets a fastest lap of 1m27.295s, although he is still 4.5s behind Masssa.

Lap 58 Massa scores his third win of 2007, 2.2s clear of Räikkönen. Alonso takes third from Heidfeld, with Hamilton fifth followed by Kovalainen, Rosberg and Kubica.

TOP **Shiny, happy person, after setting the fastest time in Saturday's free practice session.**

ABOVE **Lewis does his best to fend off a fast-starting Felipe Massa into the first corner.**

OPPOSITE **Lewis chats to his race engineer, Phil Prew, in the garage during practice.**

Lady luck can be a fickle mistress and Lewis Hamilton experienced both sides of her charms in the Turkish Grand Prix.

The flowing high-speed corners of the fabulous Istanbul Park circuit – in particular the crucial four-apex Turn 8 – were expected to suit Ferrari's long-wheelbase F2007 chassis over McLaren's agile MP4-22; but while Kimi Räikkönen shot to the top of the times in the opening free practice session, Lewis was quickest for McLaren in the next two sessions, so qualifying was again set to be a four-way shoot-out. He wasn't a factor to begin with, but a stunning late effort moved him on to provisional pole – only for Felipe Massa to steal it away with just seconds left on the clock.

At the start of the race the two Ferraris made better getaways: Lewis was demoted to third, while team-mate Fernando Alonso was back in sixth, swamped by the BMW Saubers. The Ferraris pulled away initially, but the gap soon stabilised at around five seconds, and as Lewis was carrying a heavier fuel load he halved that gap after the first round of pit stops. As he would again be pitting later than the Ferraris for his second and final stop, he held an outside chance of leap-frogging one, or even both, of the red cars in the pits. But this was where luck intervened and a punctured right-front tyre ended any thoughts of victory.

"As I exited the fast left-hander at Turn 8 I saw some bits fly off the tyre and as soon as I braked into Turn 9 the tyre just exploded. I went off and almost hit the barrier. The wheel just locked up and I was very lucky not to hit the barrier." He limped back to the pits, dropping behind Alonso and BMW's Nick Heidfeld. Though the McLaren's front wing had been damaged by the flaying rubber, compromising the car's handling, Lewis nevertheless kept Heikki Kovalainen's charging Renault behind for four valuable points.

A certain podium had been lost – and worse, Alonso had been gifted an extra place. But had the puncture happened a corner earlier, Lewis would almost certainly have failed to score at all. Bridgestone cited 'chunking' – the process of picking up discarded pieces of old rubber on the tyre from the surface of the circuit – as the cause for its failure. The effect was to cut Lewis's championship lead over his team-mate, Fernando Alonso, to just five points.

TURKISH GRAND PRIX
ISTANBUL

RACE DATE 26th August 2007
CIRCUIT LENGTH 3.317 miles
NO. OF LAPS 58laps
RACE DISTANCE 192.388 miles
WEATHER Dry, bright, 33°C
TRACK TEMP 48°C

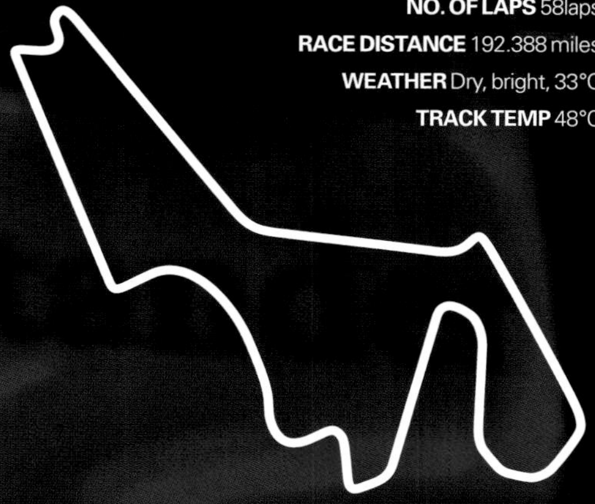

Practice

Session 1 – Friday

1	Kimi Räikkönen	Ferrari	1m27.988s
2	Felipe Massa	Ferrari	1m28.391s
3	Fernando Alonso	McLaren-Mercedes	1m29.222s
5	**Lewis Hamilton**	**McLaren-Mercedes**	**1m29.261s**

Session 2 – Friday

1	**Lewis Hamilton**	**McLaren-Mercedes**	**1m28.469s**
2	Kimi Räikkönen	Ferrari	1m28.762s
3	Ralf Schumacher	Toyota	1m28.773s

Session 3 – Saturday

1	**Lewis Hamilton**	**McLaren-Mercedes**	**1m27.325s**
2	Felipe Massa	Ferrari	1m27.366s
3	Kimi Räikkönen	Ferrari	1m27.506s

Qualifying

1	Felipe Massa	Ferrari	1m27.329s
2	**Lewis Hamilton**	**McLaren-Mercedes**	**1m27.373s**
3	Kimi Räikkönen	Ferrari	1m27.546s

Race

1	Felipe Massa	Ferrari	1h26m42.161s
2	Kimi Räikkönen	Ferrari	+2.275s
3	Fernando Alonso	McLaren-Mercedes	+26.181s
4	Nick Heidfeld	BMW	+39.674s
5	**Lewis Hamilton**	**McLaren-Mercedes**	**+45.085s**
6	Heikki Kovalainen	Renault	+46.169s
7	Nico Rosberg	Williams-Toyota	+55.778s
8	Robert Kubica	BMW	+56.707s

Fastest Lap

Kimi Räikkönen	Ferrari	1m27.295s

World Championship Positions

1	**Lewis Hamilton**	**McLaren-Mercedes**	**84 points**
2	Fernando Alonso	McLaren-Mercedes	79 points
3	Felipe Massa	Ferrari	69 points
3	Kimi Räikkönen	Ferrari	68 points
5	Nick Heidfeld	BMW	47 points
6	Robert Kubica	BMW	29 points
7	Heikki Kovalainen	Renault	19 points
8	Giancarlo Fisichella	Renault	17 points

"As I exited the fast left-hander at Turn 8 I saw some bits fly off the tyre and as soon as I braked into Turn 9 the tyre just exploded... I went off and almost hit the barrier."

vodafone
vodafone

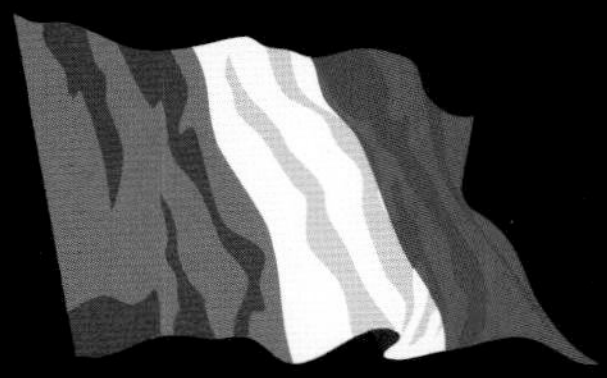

2007 ROUND 13

ITALIAN GRAND PRIX

MONZA

2nd

POINTS TOTAL **92**
POINTS POSITION **1st**
SEASON WINS **3**

Lap 1 Pole-sitter Alonso beats Hamilton in the drag to Turn 1. Hamilton is swamped by the Ferraris and gets sideways at the first chicane, but holds on to second from Massa, Räikkönen, Heidfeld, Kubica and Kovalainen.

Lap 2 The safety car is deployed after Coulthard crashes at the Curve Grande due to his front wing breaking.

Lap 7 The race restarts and Alonso holds off Hamilton to lead by 0.6s.

Lap 10 Alonso leads by 1.3s, while Räikkönen is an increasingly distant third. Massa pits to retire.

Lap 18 Hamilton makes his first stop, rejoining in sixth place.

Lap 19 Alonso leads Räikkönen by 12.7s.

Lap 20 Alonso pits, leaving Räikkönen in the lead.

Lap 25 Räikkönen pits and slips back to third behind the two McLarens.

Lap 27 Alonso leads Hamilton by 2.2s, with Räikkönen a further 14.1s behind.

Lap 38 Alonso leads Hamilton by 5.9s and Räikkönen by 29.9s. The Finn's pace suggests that he is one-stopping.

Lap 40 Hamilton pits and rejoins behind Räikkönen.

Lap 43 Alonso pits. Hamilton passes Räikkönen with a breathtaking outbraking manoeuvre at Turn 1.

Lap 53 Alonso wins by a margin of 6.0s from Hamilton, followed by Räikkönen, Heidfeld, Kubica, Rosberg, Kovalainen and Button.

A year earlier Lewis Hamilton had wrapped up the GP2 title at Monza: now he arrived at the legendary circuit at the top of the Formula 1 World Championship. But ahead of the race, McLaren was reeling from the news that it would have to appear before the World Motorsport Council to face charges that it had used data leaked from Ferrari to its chief designer, Mike Coughlan.

Following the bombshell news that 'smoking gun' evidence had come from correspondence between Fernando Alonso and test driver Pedro de la Rosa on the eve of the event, it was no surprise that Lewis was in third place in opening free practice as the team struggled to keep its focus on the on-track action.

Lewis was a solid second quickest behind a fired-up Alonso in the second session. The Spaniard was in excellent form, and with the title battle entering a crucial phase Lewis knew he had to try to prevent the World Champion from gaining an advantage. He therefore tried an aggressive low-fuel strategy in qualifying, but in spite of running lighter missed out on pole position – by just three hundredths of a second. This put him on the dirty side of the track, from where he was beaten off the line by Felipe Massa's Ferrari. But rather than settle for third, Lewis darted to the outside and went around Massa into the first turn. Such was his pace that he very nearly had a shot at passing Alonso for the lead, until a light wheel bang with Massa sent him across the run-off area.

Now up to second, Lewis was in Alonso's wheel-tracks but just couldn't quite match his team-mate's pace. With Massa retiring early on, the McLarens – both on a two-stop strategy – pulled well clear of Kimi Räikkönen in third; but it soon became clear that the Finn was only stopping once.

As Lewis neared his second and final stop, he pushed hard to open up enough of an advantage so that he could emerge from the pits ahead of the Ferrari. However, it wasn't quite enough, and the Ferrari streamed by into second.

Next time around, under heavy braking for the tight first chicane, Lewis pulled off an unbelievable pass, coming from more than two car's lengths back to dive under the Ferrari into a crucial second place.

"I knew I had two laps at most on the softer tyres before they started to go off," he explained, "and I knew that with Kimi on his harder, worn tyres, I would be a lot quicker. I pulled out some really great laps, the tyres and car were great. I had an opportunity and made sure I stuck it in there and got it."

The reward for his bravery was an extra two points, giving him a three-point lead in the championship.

BELOW After his second pit stop, Lewis dropped briefly behind Kimi Räikkönen's Ferrari, but he reclaimed second position with an astonishing pass into the first chicane, claiming two invaluable extra points in his championship battle with team-mate Alonso.

ITALIAN GRAND PRIX
MONZA

RACE DATE 9th September 2007
CIRCUIT LENGTH 3.600 miles
NO. OF LAPS 53 laps
RACE DISTANCE 190.587 miles
WEATHER Dry, bright, 25°C
TRACK TEMP 35°C

Practice

Session 1 – Friday

1	Kimi Räikkönen	Ferrari	1m22.446s
2	Felipe Massa	Ferrari	1m22.590s
3	**Lewis Hamilton**	**McLaren-Mercedes**	**1m22.618s**

Session 2 – Friday

1	Fernando Alonso	McLaren-Mercedes	1m22.386s
2	**Lewis Hamilton**	**McLaren-Mercedes**	**1m23.209s**
3	Giancarlo Fisichella	Renault	1m23.584s

Session 3 – Saturday

1	Fernando Alonso	McLaren-Mercedes	1m22.054s
2	**Lewis Hamilton**	**McLaren-Mercedes**	**1m22.200s**
3	Felipe Massa	Ferrari	1m22.615s

Qualifying

1	Fernando Alonso	McLaren-Mercedes	1m21.997s
2	**Lewis Hamilton**	**McLaren-Mercedes**	**1m22.034s**
3	Felipe Massa	Ferrari	1m22.549s

Race

1	Fernando Alonso	McLaren-Mercedes	1h18m37.806s
2	**Lewis Hamilton**	**McLaren-Mercedes**	**+6.062s**
3	Kimi Räikkönen	Ferrari	+27.325s
4	Nick Heidfeld	BMW	+56.562s
5	Robert Kubica	BMW	+1m00.558s
6	Nico Rosberg	Williams-Toyota	+1m05.810s
7	Heikki Kovalainen	Renault	+1m06.751s
8	Jenson Buton	Honda	+1m12.168s

Fastest Lap

Fernando Alonso	McLaren-Mercedes	1m22.871s

World Championship Positions

1	**Lewis Hamilton**	**McLaren-Mercedes**	**92 points**
2	Fernando Alonso	McLaren-Mercedes	89 points
3	Kimi Räikkönen	Ferrari	74 points
3	Felipe Massa	Ferrari	69 points
5	Nick Heidfeld	BMW	52 points
6	Robert Kubica	BMW	33 points
7	Heikki Kovalainen	Renault	21 points
8	Giancarlo Fisichella	Renault	17 points

ABOVE Friends and rivals. Lewis shares a joke with Ferrari's Felipe Massa after Saturday's final qualifying session.

BELOW Even the passionately pro-Ferrari *tifosi* were enthralled by the daring of Lewis Hamilton.

vodafone
vodafone
vodafone
vodafone
vodafone
vodafone

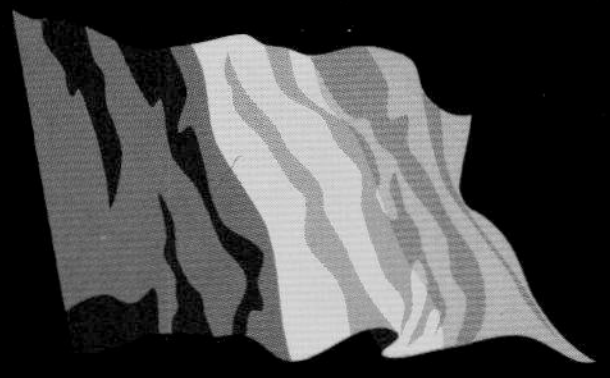

2007 ROUND 14

BELGIAN GRAND PRIX
SPA-FRANCORCHAMPS

4th POINTS TOTAL **97**
POINTS POSITION **1st**
SEASON WINS **3**

Lap 1 Räikkönen sprints away from pole, beating Massa into the first corner. Alonso swerves to defend against Hamilton, forcing him wide at La Source. The two McLarens run side-by-side up to and through La Source before Alonso finally claims third ahead of his team-mate.

Lap 4 Räikkönen has extended his lead over Massa to 1.7s, with Alonso a further 1.9s back, closely followed by Hamilton.

Lap 7 Räikkönen continues to up the pace, lapping in 1m48.498s.

Lap 10 Räikkönen leads Massa by 3.7s and Alonso by 7.9s.

Lap 12 Räikkönen continues to increase the pace, while Hamilton has been slowly closing on Alonso.

Lap 13 Alonso begins to edge away from Hamilton again.

Lap 15 Räikkönen and Alonso pit. Massa leads from Hamilton.

Lap 16 Massa and Hamilton pit, rejoining behind their respective team-mates, with Heidfeld third separating the Ferraris and McLarens.

Lap 18 Heidfeld pits.

Lap 20 Räikkönen leads Massa by 4.5s, with Alonso a further 10.5s back. Hamilton is 2.5s behind Alonso.

Lap 27 After all the leaders have pitted, Räikkönen leads Massa from Alonso, Hamilton, Heidfeld, Rosberg, Webber and Kubica.

Lap 31 Räikkönen makes his second stop, leaving team-mate Massa in the lead.

Lap 32 Massa pits. Alonso leads temporarily from Hamilton.

Lap 33 Alonso pits, leaving Hamilton in the lead.

Lap 37 Hamilton pits, rejoining fourth behind Alonso.

Lap 38 Räikkönen leads Massa by 3.1s, Alonso by 17.2s and Hamilton by 23.6s.

Lap 43 Hamilton runs wide at Pouhon and loses three seconds.

Lap 44 Räikkönen wins by 4.6s from Massa, Alonso, Hamilton, Heidfeld, Rosberg, Webber and Kovalainen.

ABOVE Lewis takes to the run-off area at the La Source hairpin on the opening lap, after being forced wide by team-mate Fernando Alonso.

OPPOSITE, TOP Putting the hammer down on the way to fourth place behind the two Ferraris and Alonso. Lewis would leave Europe for the final three 'fly-away' races with a slender two-point championship advantage.

OPPOSITE, MAIN Lewis gives the photographer a few handy tips on his close-up technique.

Ahead of the Belgian Grand Prix all attention was focused on the World Motorsport Council's extraordinary meeting in Paris, where McLaren's fate in the on-going 'spy scandal' was decided.

Lewis Hamilton showed up at the hearing, in a show of solidarity with the team that had supported him for almost his entire career and now faced possible expulsion from the Formula 1 World Championship. In the end, McLaren received an unprecedented fine of $100 million and had all of its constructors' championship points for 2007 nullified. The drivers, however, escaped sanction, which left Lewis and Fernando Alonso free to continue their epic title battle at one of F1's most daunting venues – Spa-Francorchamps.

When the talk of the implications of the punishment made way for motor racing, it soon became clear that Spa was a Ferrari track. Lewis and Alonso headed the times in the second free practice session, but that would be the only time they would be on top, and, for the first time in 2007, qualifying produced a Ferrari lock-out of the front row. Lewis qualified fourth, a few tenths off Alonso, but with slightly more fuel on board.

In a race that offered little in the way of on-track action, most of the fireworks took place at the start. The tight La Source first-corner hairpin always has the potential to create trouble, and when Lewis got a good run around the outside of team-mate Alonso they very nearly collided as the Spaniard aggressively defended his position. Lewis was forced to take evasive action and took to the asphalt run-off. This gave him a good run into the awesome Eau Rouge compression, and the McLaren drivers were practically wheel-to-wheel as they approached the 170mph flat-out corner.

Something had to give, and wisely Lewis decided to back off and let Alonso have the corner, but he was unimpressed by his team-mate's actions. "He pushed me wide quite deliberately," said Lewis. "The last few years I have been watching F1, and Alonso has always been complaining about people being unfair.

"I had out-braked him through Turn One. There was room for us both to get round but suddenly I didn't have any room. I was just really lucky that there was a run-off area so I could take that."

Ferrari ran away with the race, with Kimi Räikkönen's fourth win of the season moving him right into the thick of the title battle. Fourth place ensured that Lewis kept his title lead, but the margin was now down to just two points and the fight was beginning to get ugly.

BELGIAN GRAND PRIX
SPA-FRANCORCHAMPS

RACE DATE 16th September 2007
CIRCUIT LENGTH 4.352 miles
NO. OF LAPS 44 laps
RACE DISTANCE 191.491 miles
WEATHER Dry, cloudy, 21°C
TRACK TEMP 31°C

Practice

Session 1 – Friday

1	Kimi Räikkönen	Ferrari	1m47.339s
2	**Lewis Hamilton**	**McLaren-Mercedes**	**1m47.881s**
3	Fernando Alonso	McLaren-Mercedes	1m47.994s

Session 2 – Friday

1	Fernando Alonso	McLaren-Mercedes	1m46.654s
2	**Lewis Hamilton**	**McLaren-Mercedes**	**1m46.765s**
3	Felipe Massa	Ferrari	1m46.953s

Session 3 – Saturday

1	Kimi Räikkönen	Ferrari	1m46.137s
2	Felipe Massa	Ferrari	1m46.388s
3	Fernando Alonso	McLaren-Mercedes	1m46.507s
4	**Lewis Hamilton**	**McLaren-Mercedes**	**1m46.782s**

Qualifying

1	Kimi Räikkönen	Ferrari	1m45.994s
2	Felipe Massa	Ferrari	1m46.011s
3	Fernando Alonso	McLaren-Mercedes	1m46.091s
4	**Lewis Hamilton**	**McLaren-Mercedes**	**1m46.406s**

Race

1	Kimi Räikkönen	Ferrari	1h20m39.066s
2	Felipe Massa	Ferrari	+4.695s
3	Fernando Alonso	McLaren-Mercedes	+14.343s
4	**Lewis Hamilton**	**McLaren-Mercedes**	**+23.615s**
5	Nick Heidfeld	BMW	+51.879s
6	Nico Rosberg	Williams-Toyota	+1m.16.876s
7	Mark Webber	Red Bull-Renault	+1m20.639s
8	Heikki Kovalainen	Renault	+1m25.106s

Fastest Lap

Felipe Massa	Ferrari	1m48.036s

World Championship Positions

1	**Lewis Hamilton**	**McLaren-Mercedes**	**97 points**
2	Fernando Alonso	McLaren-Mercedes	95 points
3	Kimi Räikkönen	Ferrari	84 points
3	Felipe Massa	Ferrari	77 points
5	Nick Heidfeld	BMW	56 points
6	Robert Kubica	BMW	33 points
7	Heikki Kovalainen	Renault	22 points
8	Giancarlo Fisichella	Renault	17 points

vodafone
aigo
aigo
vodafone
vodafone

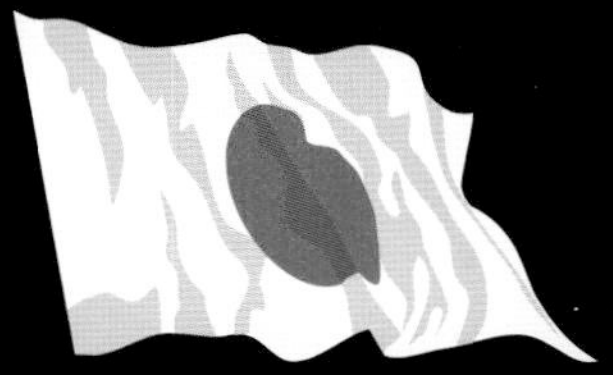

2007 ROUND 15

JAPANESE GRAND PRIX
FUJI SPEEDWAY

1st

POINTS TOTAL **107**
POINTS POSITION **1st**
SEASON WINS **4**

Pre-race Persistent rain stops 15 minutes before the start. Most cars come to the grid with extreme-wet tyres, but the Ferraris opt for 'standard' wets. A safety-car start is declared.

Lap 1 The race starts behind the safety car, with pole-sitter Hamilton leading.

Lap 2 Fourth-placed Massa spins and pits at the end of the lap to change from wets to extreme wets.

Lap 3 Räikkönen, also running on wets, pits for extreme wets, rejoining in 21st place behind team-mate Massa.

Lap 6 Räikkönen spins, as spray continues to cause a serious problem around the circuit.

Lap 14 Räikkönen pits followed by Massa on the next lap.

Lap 19 The safety car comes in. Hamilton pulls 1.9s clear of Alonso, and Vettel moves up to third as Button pushes Heidfeld sideways. Massa pits for a drive-through penalty for overtaking behind the safety car.

Lap 27 Alonso pits, followed by Hamilton on the next lap.

Lap 29 Vettel leads from Webber and Hamilton. Alonso is eighth, behind Coulthard.

Lap 32 Vettel pits, leaving Webber in the lead.

Lap 34 Kubica taps Hamilton into a spin. They drop to third and fourth. Heidfeld passes Alonso.

Lap 35 Vettel nudges Alonso into a spin and the Spaniard drops behind Vettel and Räikkönen.

Lap 38 Kubica is handed a drive-through penalty for causing an avoidable collision.

Lap 42 Alonso crashes at Turn Five. The safety car is deployed.

Lap 46 Running in third place behind the safety car, Vettel hits Webber. Both drivers retire.

Lap 49 The safety car comes in, as Hamilton pulls 2.6s clear of Kovalainen, with Massa third and Coulthard fourth.

Lap 67 Hamilton wins. Kovalainen beats Räikkönen for second, with Coulthard fourth, Fisichella fifth and Massa and Kubica battling to the line, Massa finishing ahead in sixth.

For the first time in 30 years the Japanese Grand Prix took place at the Fuji circuit near Tokyo. After two previous Grands Prix, the track had become most famous for the sodden 1976 event in which James Hunt captured the world title for McLaren after Ferrari's Niki Lauda decided that conditions were too dangerous to race and withdrew.

Following significant investment from Toyota, the track had been substantially altered from the Fuji that hosted those races three decades earlier. But, as the 22 F1 cars took to the grid for the 2007 Japanese GP, the conditions were pretty much the same as they had been on that fateful day back in 1976.

Given that the track was new to all the teams and drivers it was unclear who it would favour, and this

was reflected in free practice as the Ferraris of Kimi Räikkönen and Felipe Massa and the McLarens of Lewis Hamilton and Fernando Alonso traded places at the head of the timesheet. Torrential rain caused the final session to be abandoned, and qualifying would be held on a tricky damp track.

In very trying conditions, Lewis produced another sublime qualifying effort to grab pole position from Alonso in the dying seconds of the session. It was sweet revenge for Lewis after their clash at the previous race in Spa, and it was an important psychological victory too, as the tension mounted between the two team-mates.

Pole position also meant Lewis headed the field as the race started under the safety car, as the extremely wet conditions were deemed too dangerous for racing. Unbelievably, both Ferraris were soon running at the back of the pack, having been brought in for unplanned pit stops after the team failed to heed a notice instructing all cars to start on extreme-wet tyres.

The race finally got going after 18 slow laps behind the safety car, and with a clear track ahead of him, and the best visibility, Lewis started to build up a comfortable lead. But the number of laps run slowly under full-course yellow flags meant that rather than rejoin on a clear track after the first of his two planned pit stops, as is usually the case, Lewis didn't have time to pull sufficiently far ahead of the pack, and had to blend back into the heat of the fight for points.

OPPOSITE, TOP
Mount Fuji provides an impressive backdrop during Friday afternoon's sunny practice session.

OPPOSITE, BOTTOM
Lewis shrugged off Saturday morning's torrential rain to take pole in the damp final qualifying session...

ABOVE ...to the delight of his father, Anthony.

ABOVE F1 supremo Bernie Ecclestone has a word in Lewis's ear.

BELOW Passing Alonso's stricken sister car.

OPPOSITE Leaving all in his wake, Lewis takes another stunning victory.

In fact, he came out just in front of the BMW of Robert Kubica, who fancied his chances of making a place up at Lewis's expense. He dived for a gap as Lewis ran wide at Turn 13, and as Lewis turned in there was contact, sending both cars spinning.

The same thing happened to Alonso after his first stop, with Sebastian Vettel in the Toro Rosso tagging the McLaren into a quick pirouette. Lewis had escaped from his assault without injury; Alonso, however, sustained some bodywork damage, which was a contributing factor when he subsequently crashed out in spectacular style.

With the Ferraris still working their way back up the order and Alonso out, everything was conspiring to boost Lewis's title hopes. And it got better still when Mark Webber in second and Vettel in third clashed and retired under the safety car – which had been deployed following Alonso's crash – effectively removing Lewis's last remaining challengers for victory.

Lewis produced a flawless drive after the restart to claim his fourth win of the season and his first in the wet. His points lead over Alonso was back up to 12, while Räikkönen was 17 adrift with just 20 to play for. If the results went the right way, Lewis could wrap up the championship a week later at the Chinese GP...

"It was the longest race of my life," said Lewis. "It seemed to go on and on and on. Now I'll just attack 100 per cent, go out with all guns blazing. I'll keep pushing and trying to do the best job I can without making mistakes.

"The World Championship sits at the back of my mind. I do think about it a little bit, but the key for me is just to focus on the next race and make sure my preparations are done properly."

JAPANESE GRAND PRIX
FUJI SPEEDWAY

RACE DATE 30th September 2007
CIRCUIT LENGTH 2.835 miles
NO. OF LAPS 67 laps
RACE DISTANCE 191.488 miles
WEATHER Heavy rain, 17°C
TRACK TEMP 20°C

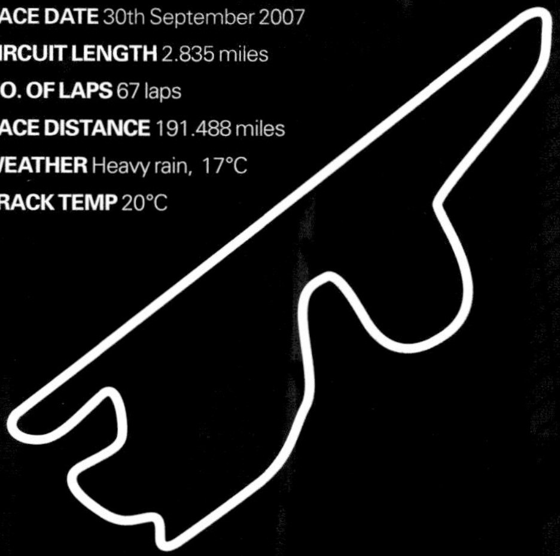

Practice

Session 1 – Friday

1	Kimi Räikkönen	Ferrari	1m19.119s
2	Felipe Massa	Ferrari	1m19.498s
3	Fernando Alonso	McLaren-Mercedes	1m19.667s
4	**Lewis Hamilton**	**McLaren-Mercedes**	**1m19.807s**

Session 2 – Friday

1	**Lewis Hamilton**	**McLaren-Mercedes**	**1m18.734s**
2	Fernando Alonso	McLaren-Mercedes	1m18.498s
3	Felipe Massa	Ferrari	1m19.483s

Session 3 – Saturday

1	Alexander Wurz	Williams-Toyota	1m32.746s
2	Nico Rosberg	Williams-Toyota	1m34.758s
3	Jarno Trulli	Toyota	1m36.150s
20	**Lewis Hamilton**	**McLaren-Mercedes**	**No time**

Qualifying

1	**Lewis Hamilton**	**McLaren-Mercedes**	**1m25.368s**
2	Fernando Alonso	McLaren-Mercedes	1m25.438s
3	Kimi Räikkönen	Ferrari	1m25.516s

Race

1	**Lewis Hamilton**	**McLaren-Mercedes**	**2h00m34.579s**
2	Heikki Kovalainen	Renault	+8.377s
3	Kimi Räikkönen	Ferrari	+9.478s
4	David Coulthard	Red Bull-Renault	+20.297s
5	Giancarlo Fisichella	Renault	+38.864s
6	Felipe Massa	Ferrari	+49.042s
7	Robert Kubica	BMW	+49.285s
8	Adrian Sutil	Spyker-Ferrari	+1m00.129s

Fastest Lap

Lewis Hamilton	**McLaren-Mercedes**	**1m28.193s**

World Championship Positions

1	**Lewis Hamilton**	**McLaren-Mercedes**	**107 points**
2	Fernando Alonso	McLaren-Mercedes	95 points
3	Kimi Räikkönen	Ferrari	90 points
4	Felipe Massa	Ferrari	80 points
5	Nick Heidfeld	BMW	56 points
6	Robert Kubica	BMW	35 points
7	Heikki Kovalainen	Renault	30 points
8	Giancarlo Fisichella	Renault	21 points

"It was the longest race of my life... Now I'll just attack 100 per cent, go out with all guns blazing. I'll keep pushing and trying to do the best job I can..."

vodafone
Santander
Mobil 1
vodafone
SAP
SAP
Mobil 1
BOSS

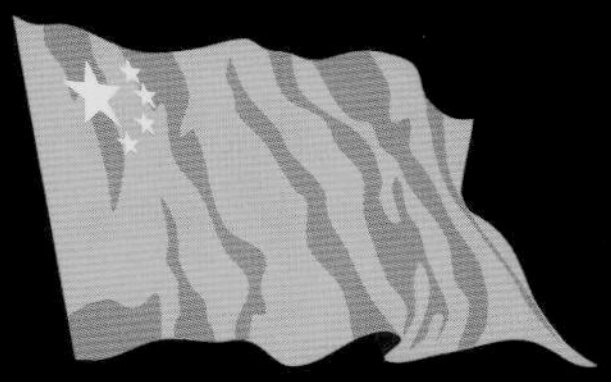

2007 ROUND 16

CHINESE GRAND PRIX
SHANGHAI

Rtd POINTS TOTAL **107**
POINTS POSITION **1st**
SEASON WINS **4**

Pre-start With rain falling on an already damp track, a wet race is declared, with all runners starting the race on wets.

Lap 1 Hamilton makes a good start from pole to beat Räikkönen into Turn One.

Lap 2 Hamilton leads Räikkönen by 1.5s.

Lap 4 Hamilton continues to pull away and is now 2.7s clear.

Lap 8 After a succession of fastest laps, Hamilton leads by 5.2s.

Lap 14 Hamilton has extended his lead over Räikkönen to 8.6s, with Massa a further 5.3s adrift in third, and Alonso 2.0s behind him in fourth.

Lap 15 As the track begins to dry slightly, Hamilton makes his first stop for fuel, rejoining in fourth place, still on wet tyres. Räikkönen now leads.

Lap 19 After setting a series of fastest laps, Räikkönen pits, rejoining in second place behind Hamilton.

Lap 22 Hamilton sets a new fastest lap to lead by 5.3s.

Lap 27 More rain begins to fall and Hamilton slows significantly.

Lap 29 After battling for several corners, Räikkönen passes Hamilton. Several cars run wide as the rain worsens.

Lap 30 Hamilton's pace continues to slow, and it appears that his tyres have worn down to the canvas.

Lap 31 Hamilton peels off into the pitlane and slides into the gravel trap at the pit entry. He climbs out of the car for his first retirement of the season.

Lap 32 Räikkönen makes his second stop. Kubica leads.

Lap 34 Leader Kubica pulls off to retire.

Lap 41 Second-placed Alonso trails Räikkönen by 7.9s.

Lap 43 Räikkönen leads Alonso by 8.5s, with third-placed Massa a further 6.7s behind.

Lap 56 Räikkönen wins by 9.8s from Alonso, Massa, Vettel, Button, Liuzzi, Heidfeld and Coulthard. Hamilton now leads the championship table by four points from Alonso, with Räikkönen a further three points behind, ensuring a three-way fight for the drivers' title at the season's final race in Brazil.

ABOVE As the McLaren's tyres begin to lose grip, Lewis tries to fend off Kimi Räikkönen's Ferrari.

BELOW Despite his obvious frustration, Lewis put his retirement down to experience and vowed to fight on at the season's finale in Brazil.

OPPOSITE The condition of Lewis's right-rear tyre leaves no doubt as to the cause of his retirement.

Lewis Hamilton went to the Chinese Grand Prix knowing that if he finished ahead of Fernando Alonso and Kimi Räikkönen he would be crowned 2007 Formula 1 World Champion.

Of course, it wasn't that simple. Firstly, it would be Lewis's debut at the Shanghai circuit. Secondly, an approaching typhoon made another wet race a distinct possibility. And finally, his pre-race preparations were disrupted by an investigation into his driving whilst behind the safety car in the Japanese GP. Forced to defend himself against allegations of erratic driving, leading to the collision between Mark Webber and Sebastian Vettel, Hamilton robustly denied the charge.

Lewis was cleared of any wrongdoing ahead of qualifying, and duly produced arguably his best lap of the season so far to take a sensational pole position.

The race started on a damp track, with the threat of more rain hanging in the air. Lewis made a perfect start and comfortably pulled away from Räikkönen and the rest of the pack in a stunning opening stint.

The track began to dry after the first of his two pit stops but remained damp, and McLaren opted to leave him on the same set of intermediate tyres with which he'd started the race. However, his early pace was taking its toll, and as his tyres became more and more worn so Räikkönen ate into his lead.

Lewis initially fended off the Ferrari, but it was clear that he was running short of grip and the Finn eventually found a way past. Still, second place, with Alonso back in third, would be enough for the title.

The track was getting drier, and Lewis's tyres were taking a real beating, but with his second planned stop still a few laps away and the prediction of more rain to come, McLaren chose not to call him in for new tyres.

By the time the call to pit finally came, his tyres were so badly worn that the canvas of the right rear was showing through. It was all he could do to keep the car on the track, and as he turned into the tight pit entry he slid wide and into the gravel run-off.

The car became beached and, agonisingly, Lewis was forced to switch off the engine and retire in the most ignominious fashion imaginable. Still, despite his obvious frustration, Lewis took the time to go back to the McLaren garage and show his thanks to his team of mechanics and engineers.

"When I was out of the car I was just gutted because it was my first mistake all year and to do it on the way into the pits was not something I usually do," he admitted. "You can't go through life without making mistakes. But I'm over it and we look forward to Brazil. The team will be working hard to make sure the car is quick enough there, and we still have points in the bag."

Martin Whitmarsh, McLaren's Chief Operating Officer, said the team had to take the blame for the incident. "Quite simply we didn't call him in," he said. "The weather was pretty changeable at that time and we wanted to make sure that we weren't taking any risks and that we covered Kimi. In the end it was decided we had to come in, but at that stage it was frankly a lap too late."

The result was that with one race to go Lewis held a four-point lead over Alonso, with Kimi three points further behind. And for the first time since 1986, there would be a three-way shoot-out for the title...

CHINESE GRAND PRIX
SHANGHAI

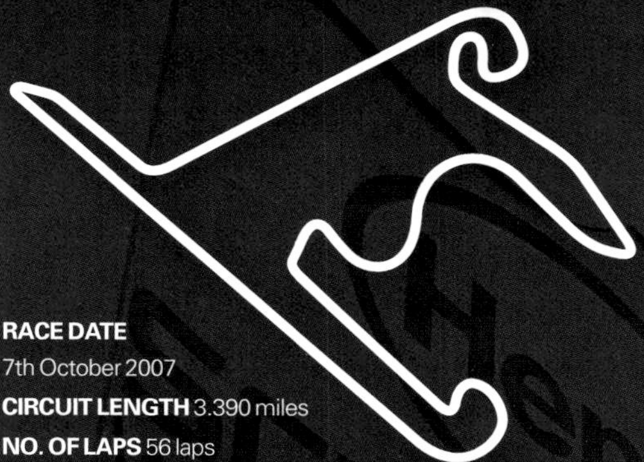

RACE DATE
7th October 2007
CIRCUIT LENGTH 3.390 miles
NO. OF LAPS 56 laps
RACE DISTANCE 189.680 miles
WEATHER Overcast, then wet, 28°C
TRACK TEMP 27°C

Practice

Session 1 – Friday

1	Kimi Räikkönen	Ferrari	1m37.024s
2	Fernando Alonso	McLaren-Mercedes	1m37.108s
3	Felipe Massa	Ferrari	1m37.128s
4	Lewis Hamilton	McLaren-Mercedes	1m37.210s

Session 2 – Friday

1	Kimi Räikkönen	Ferrari	1m36.607s
2	Fernando Alonso	McLaren-Mercedes	1m36.613s
3	Felipe Massa	Ferrari	1m36.630s
4	Lewis Hamilton	McLaren-Mercedes	1m36.876s

Session 3 – Saturday

1	Kimi Räikkönen	Ferrari	1m36.100s
2	Fernando Alonso	McLaren-Mercedes	1m36.126s
3	Lewis Hamilton	McLaren-Mercedes	1m36.227s

Qualifying

1	Lewis Hamilton	McLaren-Mercedes	1m35.908s
2	Kimi Räikkönen	Ferrari	1m36.044s
3	Felipe Massa	Ferrari	1m36.221s

Race

1	Kimi Räikkönen	Ferrari	1h37m58.395s
2	Fernando Alonso	McLaren-Mercedes	+12.891s
3	Felipe Massa	Ferrari	+9.478s
4	Sebastian Vettel	Toro Rosso-Ferrari	+53.509s
5	Jenson Button	Honda	+1m08.666s
6	Vitantonio Liuzzi	Toro Rosso-Ferrari	+1m13.673s
7	Nick Heidfeld	BMW	+1m14.224s
8	David Coulthard	Red Bull-Renault	+1m20.750s
R	Lewis Hamilton	McLaren-Mercedes	

Fastest Lap

Felipe Massa	Ferrari	1m37.454s

World Championship Positions

1	Lewis Hamilton	McLaren-Mercedes	107 points
2	Fernando Alonso	McLaren-Mercedes	103 points
3	Kimi Räikkönen	Ferrari	100 points
4	Felipe Massa	Ferrari	86 points
5	Nick Heidfeld	BMW	58 points
6	Robert Kubica	BMW	35 points
7	Heikki Kovalainen	Renault	30 points
8	Giancarlo Fisichella	Renault	21 points

"You can't go through life without making mistakes. But I'm over it and we look forward to Brazil. The team will be working hard to make sure the car is quick enough there, and we still have points in the bag."

vodafone
vodafone
aigo
vodafone
vodafone
SAP
vodafone

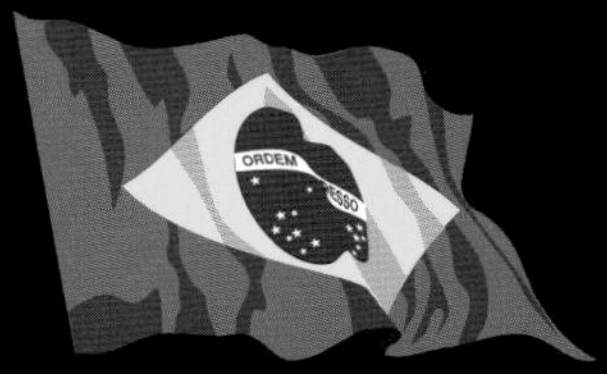

2007 ROUND 17

BRAZILIAN GRAND PRIX
SÃO PAULO

7th POINTS TOTAL **109**
POINTS POSITION **2nd**
SEASON WINS **4**

Lap 1 Massa leads away from pole, but Räikkönen passes Hamilton, as does Alonso at the bottom of the Senna S. Hamilton attempts to re-pass Alonso at Turn Four, but runs wide and drops to eighth. The order at the end of the first lap is Massa, Räikkönen, Alonso, Webber, Kubica, Heidfeld, Trulli and Hamilton.

Lap 2 Massa leads by 0.6s. Hamilton passes Trulli.

Lap 7 Hamilton passes Heidfeld as the German runs wide on the entry to Turn One.

Lap 8 Hamilton slows to a crawl, then picks up speed again. He drops to 18th place.

Lap 11 Massa now leads by 1.8s. Hamilton passes Barrichello.

Lap 12 Hamilton passes Sutil.

Lap 15 The Ferraris are now 0.7s apart. Hamilton passes Schumacher.

Lap 17 Hamilton passes Nakajima, and is now 11th.

Lap 22 Alonso, Trulli, Vettel, Hamilton, Anthony Davidson and Sutil pit. Hamilton is the only one to opt for super-soft tyres.

Lap 29 Hamilton passes Barrichello to take 12th.

Lap 33 Kubica passes Alonso, and Hamilton passes Vettel.

Lap 36 Hamilton makes his second stop and fits soft tyres.

Lap 42 Coulthard pits. Hamilton is now eighth.

Lap 48 Massa leads Räikkönen by 1.5s, with Alonso almost 40s adrift in third.

Lap 50 Massa pits, leaving Räikkönen in the lead.

Lap 53 Räikkönen pits, and rejoins still in the lead.

Lap 56 Hamilton pits.

Lap 58 Hamilton laps in 1m12.506s – the race's fastest lap so far.

Lap 61 Hamilton is around 22s away from the fifth place he needs to take the championship.

Lap 63 Trulli pits and Hamilton moves up to seventh.

Lap 71 Räikkönen wins the race by 1.4s – and with it the championship. Massa finishes second, with Alonso a distant third. Rosberg and Kubica finish fourth and fifth after an intense battle in the dying laps, with Heidfeld sixth. Hamilton finishes seventh – and second in the Drivers' World Championship.

Going into the final race of the 2007 season, the simplist equation for Lewis to be crowned World Champion was that if he finished ahead of Räikkönen and Alonso, the title would be his.

Lewis underlined his intention to win the championship from the front by bagging the quickest time in second practice. Only Massa in the Ferrari was quicker in the final session, and it was the Brazilian who again denied Lewis in the vital qualifying shoot-out. Nevertheless, championship rivals Räikkönen and Alonso lined up behind Lewis third and fourth.

Although Lewis got off the line well, Räikkönen shot away behind him and went around his outside into the tight first corner. Lewis had to back off slightly to avoid hitting the rear of Räikkönen's car, which gave Alonso the chance to draw alongside as into the Turn 3 left-hander. Alonso forced his way through, but Lewis was still alongside as they braked for Turn 4.

Lewis locked up and ran wide, falling to eighth. With 70 laps left to pass the two BMW Saubers and Mark Webber's Red Bull ahead of him it was still all to play for.

Worse was to follow, however, as without warning his car selected neutral. Lewis coasted along as the field blasted by. Then, his transmission returned to life. By now he was back in 18th place, and with the Ferraris cruising at the head of the pack, Lewis would have to fight his way up to fifth to win the championship.

Just as he had in GP2 the year before, he started to carve his way through the field. With the aid of a couple of retirements ahead, in no time Lewis was back in the top ten and on the verge of the points.

His head didn't drop, and he put in a superb fastest lap in his forlorn chase. When Jarno Trulli made a late third stop, Lewis moved up to seventh, but with Räikkönen passing Massa for the win during the second bout of pit stops his two points would not be enough.

Agonisingly he missed the title by just two points. With the top three championship places covered by a single point, the 2007 season was the closest in F1 history.

LEFT, FROM TOP **Lewis shows his support for England's Rugby World Cup team; all smiles for the press on Thursday; sliding wide after trying to re-pass Alonso at Turn Four.**

OPPOSITE **No regrets. With a philosophical smile, Lewis looks ahead to a bright future, and no doubt many more seasons challenging for the World Championship.**

BRAZILIAN GRAND PRIX
INTERLAGOS

RACE DATE 21st October 2007
CIRCUIT LENGTH 2.677 miles
NO. OF LAPS 71laps
RACE DISTANCE 190.067 miles
WEATHER Sunny, dry, 36°C
TRACK TEMP 63°C

Practice

Session 1 – Friday

1	Kimi Räikkönen	Ferrari	1m19.580s
2	Felipe Massa	Ferrari	1m20.062s
3	Heikki Kovalainen	Renault	1m20.829s
5	**Lewis Hamilton**	**McLaren-Mercedes**	**1m21.121s**

Session 2 – Friday

1	**Lewis Hamilton**	**McLaren-Mercedes**	**1m12.787s**
2	Fernando Alonso	McLaren-Mercedes	1m12.889s
3	Felipe Massa	Ferrari	1m13.075s

Session 3 – Saturday

1	Felipe Massa	Ferrari	1m11.810s
2	**Lewis Hamilton**	**McLaren-Mercedes**	**1m11.934s**
3	Kimi Räikkönen	Ferrari	1m11.942s

Qualifying

1	Felipe Massa	Ferrari	1m11.931s
2	**Lewis Hamilton**	**McLaren-Mercedes**	**1m12.082s**
3	Kimi Räikkönen	Ferrari	1m12.322s

Race

1	Kimi Räikkönen	Ferrari	1h28m15.270s
2	Felipe Massa	Ferrari	+1.493s
3	Fernando Alonso	McLaren-Mercedes	+57.019s
4	Nico Rosberg	Williams	+1m02.848s
5	Robert Kubica	BMW	+1m10.957s
6	Nick Heidfeld	BMW	+1m11.317s
7	**Lewis Hamilton**	**McLaren-Mercedes**	**+1 lap**
8	Jarno Trulli	Toyota	+1 lap

Fastest Lap

Kimi Räikkönen	Ferrari	1m12.445s

World Championship Positions

1	Kimi Räikkönen	Ferrari	110 points
2	**Lewis Hamilton**	**McLaren-Mercedes**	**109 points**
3	Fernando Alonso	McLaren-Mercedes	109 points
4	Felipe Massa	Ferrari	94 points
5	Nick Heidfeld	BMW	61 points
6	Robert Kubica	BMW	39 points
7	Heikki Kovalainen	Renault	30 points
8	Giancarlo Fisichella	Renault	21 points

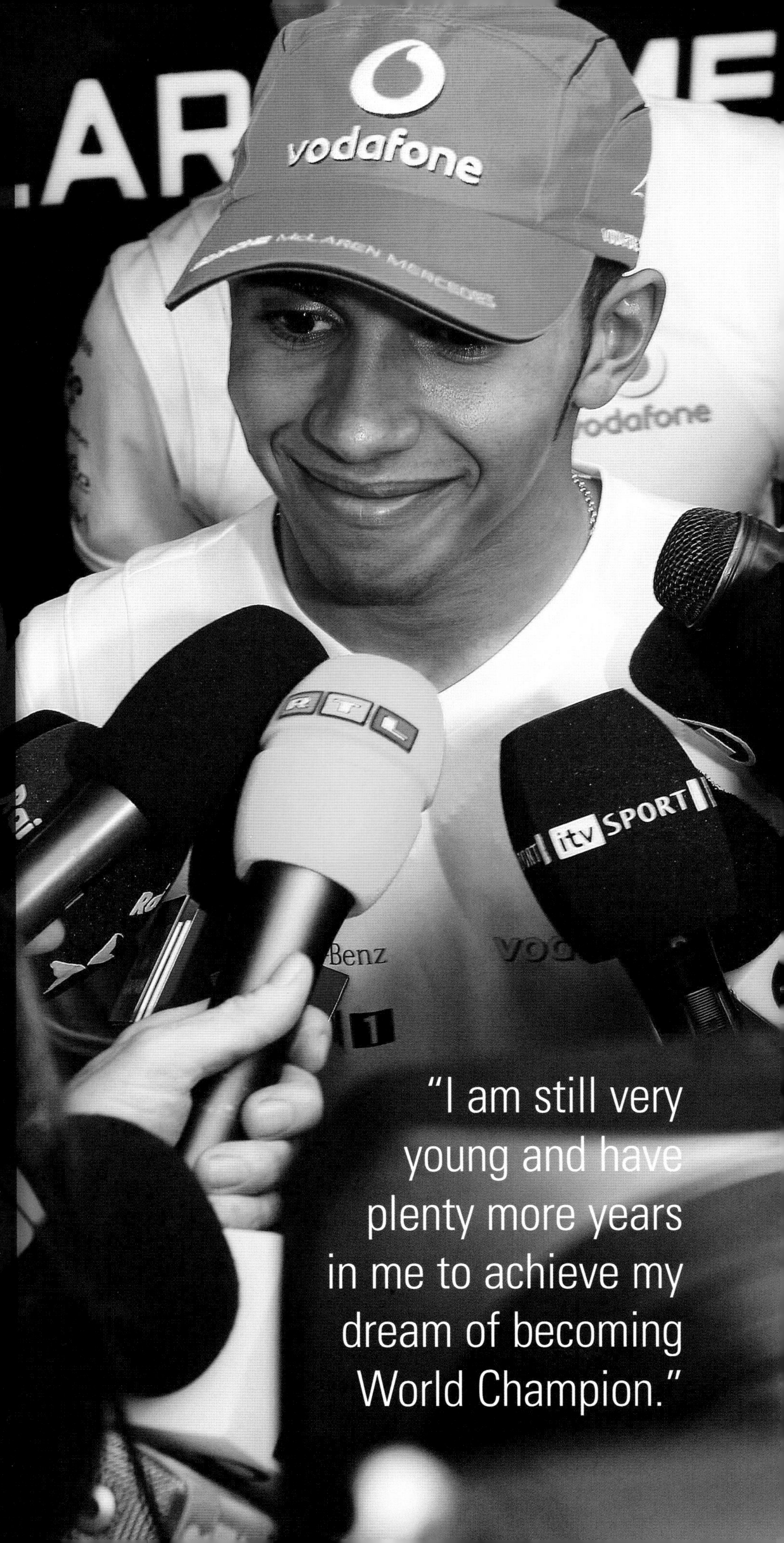

"I am still very young and have plenty more years in me to achieve my dream of becoming World Champion."

LEWIS
SAP
aigo 爱国者

Formula 1
2 0 0 8
WORLD CHAMPION

ING

2008 ROUND 1

AUSTRALIAN GRAND PRIX
MELBOURNE

1st

POINTS TOTAL **10**
POINTS POSITION **1st**
SEASON WINS **1**

Lap 1 From pole, Hamilton leads Kubica and Kovalainen. Massa spins and hits the wall, pitting at the end of the lap. Rosberg is fourth, from Heidfeld, Trulli, Barrichello and Räikkönen (who qualified 15th). Several midfielders sustain damage in incidents during the lap. The safety car is deployed.

Lap 3 The safety car pulls in. Hamilton maintains his lead.

Lap 10 Hamilton leads Kubica by 7.6s. Kovalainen is third, from Rosberg, Heidfeld, Trulli, Barrichello and Räikkönen.

Lap 16 Hamilton continues to extend his lead. Kubica pits.

Lap 17 Hamilton now leads Kovalainen by 14.7s.

Lap 18 Hamilton pits and rejoins fourth, behind Heidfeld. Kovalainen leads.

Lap 21 Rosberg and Heidfeld pit from second and third. Heidfeld rejoins second, ahead of Alonso and Rosberg.

Lap 22 Kovalainen pits. Hamilton leads again.

Lap 23 Hamilton leads Kovalainen by 11.7s.

Lap 26 Massa and Coulthard collide at Turn One. The Scot retires. With debris on the track, the safety car is deployed.

Lap 31 The safety car pulls off and the race restarts.

Lap 39 Hamilton sets a new fastest lap to lead by 6.4s.

Lap 43 Hamilton and Rosberg pit. Kovalainen leads.

Lap 44 Heidfeld pits. Glock crashes heavily. The safety car is deployed for a third time.

Lap 47 Kovalainen and Alonso pit. Hamilton leads from Heidfeld, Barrichello, Rosberg, Bourdais, Kubica, Nakajima and Räikkönen.

Lap 49 Restart. Hamilton continues in the lead. Kovalainen passes Räikkönen and Alonso passes both of them.

Lap 58 Hamilton wins by 5.4s, with Heidfeld second from Rosberg, Alonso, Kovalainen, Barrichello (subsequently excluded for exiting the pitlane when the pit exit lights were red), Nakajima and Bourdais.

TOP **A smile and a pat on the back for former McLaren team-mate Fernando Alonso as he signs autographs for the fans in the Melbourne paddock.**

ABOVE **Lewis leads from Kubica, as Massa gets sideways after selecting the wrong gear while battling with Kovalainen.**

After his troubled end to the 2007 season, Lewis Hamilton began 2008 in perfect fashion, leading from start to finish to win the Australian Grand Prix in Melbourne.

Winter testing had suggested that, once again, the championship would boil down to a fight between Ferrari and McLaren, and so it proved during the opening day of free practice, with first Kimi Räikkönen and then Lewis setting the pace at the head of the times.

Given the different strategies employed by the teams, few considered Robert Kubica's pace-setting effort in practice three to be representative, yet it was the BMW Sauber driver who proved to be Lewis's closest challenger in qualifying and the race.

In spite of producing a lap he considered to be "less than perfect" Lewis clinched his seventh career pole, while a broken fuel pump left 2007 World Champion Räikkönen back in 16th and facing the prospect of a difficult race.

Lewis knew that the biggest threat to a race win was conceding the lead at the start, so he robustly defended from the fast-starting Kubica into the first corner before setting off at the head of the field. Behind him Ferrari's Felipe Massa dropped a gear too far as he battled with Lewis's new McLaren team-mate Heikki Kovalainen

and spun into the retaining wall, knocking the front wing off his car. This indirectly led to a multi-car pile-up further back and the first of three safety-car periods.

Lewis made an excellent restart and duly pulled well clear of Kubica, who had his mirrors full of Kovalainen.

"If I'd needed to push more, I could have," said Lewis, "but I just kept a comfortable pace and the team were telling me I had half a second per lap on the field, so I just looked after my tyres and paced myself."

With a comfortable advantage over the rest, Lewis extended his lead past 10 seconds, but he had it all to do again after David Coulthard was sent crashing out of the race when he tangled with Massa, resulting in the second appearance of the safety car.

With Kovalainen now up into second, Lewis found himself in the perfect situation to rebuild his advantage, and he pulled out a comfortable cushion on his team-mate, who had a charging Räikkönen right behind him.

Barring disaster, the race was now in the bag for Lewis, and with this in mind he was brought in for his final pit stop a couple of laps early. It was an inspired decision, as almost as soon as Lewis rejoined, Timo Glock suffered a huge accident and brought on a third safety-car period.

While the timing worked perfectly for Lewis, it hit Kovalainen hard, and Lewis went into the final restart

ABOVE Lewis exits his pit after a perfectly timed final pit stop, just before Timo Glock's accident brought the safety car out for a third time.

ABOVE Third-placed Nico Rosberg and Lewis taste the spoils on the podium.

BELOW Ready to hit the loud pedal with Kiss.

OPPOSITE Lewis checks the Friday practice times.

without the comfort of his wingman. But BMW's Nick Heidfeld lacked the pace to trouble Lewis, who again scorched off into the distance for his fifth F1 race win.

The result was made even better by the troubled race endured by the Ferrari drivers. Massa eventually retired with an engine problem, and while a spin dented Räikkönen's fightback, he too eventually stopped with a broken engine. But such was the attrition rate that he picked up the final point for eighth.

Hamilton was joined on the podium by his old karting team-mate Nico Rosberg, who bagged third place for Williams after his most competitive F1 showing to date.

"It is the perfect way to begin the season," said Hamilton. "I was saying to Nico it was eight years since we were on the podium together back in karting, so it's great to be here again. We need to continue with the momentum we have. We could have gone quicker, so I am not particularly bothered by the Ferrari pace. BMW and Williams have great pace, so we need to keep on pushing, and I hope we can get a good result again.

"It was a super race which I controlled from the beginning. I was able to drive at a steady pace without feeling any pressure, which is always the ideal situation when you are leading. The three safety-car periods meant there was never time to relax, and the whole situation was a bit like Canada last year when I claimed my first victory.

"We constantly had to change our strategy and the strategists were on the ball throughout which was super. The car is fantastic to drive and the team has done a superb job. I have prepared much better this year than last, and it's important that myself and the team continue to push hard in the months to come."

AUSTRALIAN GRAND PRIX
MELBOURNE

RACE DATE 16th March 2008
CIRCUIT LENGTH 3.295miles
NO. OF LAPS 58 laps
RACE DISTANCE 191.110 miles
WEATHER Dry and bright, 40°C
TRACK TEMP 51°C

Practice

Session 1 – Friday

1	Kimi Räikkönen	Ferrari	1m26.461s
2	**Lewis Hamilton**	**McLaren-Mercedes**	**1m26.948s**
3	Felipe Massa	Ferrari	1m26.958s

Session 2 – Friday

1	**Lewis Hamilton**	**McLaren-Mercedes**	**1m26.559s**
2	Mark Webber	Red Bull-Renault	1m27.473s
3	Felipe Massa	Ferrari	1m27.640s

Session 3 – Saturday

1	Robert Kubica	BMW Sauber	1m25.613s
2	Nick Heidfeld	BMW Sauber	1m25.950s
3	Fernando Alonso	Renault	1m26.082s
12	**Lewis Hamilton**	**McLaren-Mercedes**	**1m27.084s**

Qualifying

1	**Lewis Hamilton**	**McLaren-Mercedes**	**1m26.714s**
2	Robert Kubica	BMW Sauber	1m26.869s
3	Heikki Kovalainen	McLaren-Mercedes	1m27.079s

Race

1	**Lewis Hamilton**	**McLaren-Mercedes**	**1h34m50.616s**
2	Nick Heidfeld	BMW Sauber	+5.478s
3	Nico Rosberg	Williams-Toyota	+8.163s
4	Fernando Alonso	Renault	+17.181
5	Heikki Kovalainen	McLaren-Mercedes	+18.014s
DQ	Rubens Barrichello	Honda	+52.453s
6	Kazuki Nakajima	Williams-Toyota	1 Lap
7	Sebastien Bourdais	Toro Rosso-Ferrari	3 Laps
8	Kimi Räikkönen	Ferrari	5 Laps

Fastest Lap

Heikki Kovalainen	McLaren-Mercedes	1m27.418s

World Championship Positions

1	**Lewis Hamilton**	**McLaren-Mercedes**	**10 points**
2	Nick Heidfeld	BMW Sauber	8 points
3	Nico Rosberg	Williams-Toyota	6 points
4	Fernando Alonso	Renault	5 points
5	Heikki Kovalainen	McLaren-Mercedes	4 points
6	Kazuki Nakajima	Williams-Toyota	3 points
7	Sebastien Bourdais	Toro Rosso-Ferrari	2 points
8	Kimi Räikkönen	Ferrari	1 point

vodafone
vodafone
vodafone
vodafone

2008 ROUND 2

MALAYSIAN GRAND PRIX

SEPANG

5th

POINTS TOTAL **14**
POINTS POSITION **1st**
SEASON WINS **1**

Lap 1 From pole, Massa holds off a Räikkönen challenge to lead into Turn One. Kubica grabs third as Trulli edges Heidfeld wide. Webber seizes fourth and Hamilton swiftly leaps from ninth to fifth to lead Trulli, Kovalainen and Coulthard.

Lap 3 Massa leads by 1.6s. Kubica is 4.5s behind Räikkönen. Hamilton is pushing Webber for fourth.

Lap 6 Massa leads by 2.0s. Kubica is now 7.2s adrift of Räikkönen.

Lap 14 The gap between the Ferraris has been seesawing for several laps and Massa now leads Räikkönen by 1.9s.

Lap 17 Massa, Trulli and Heidfeld pit.

Lap 18 Räikkönen pits, and emerges ahead of Massa on the road. Kubica leads.

Lap 19 Hamilton pits and loses time with a jammed front-right wheel. He drops to 11th.

Lap 21 Kubica pits. Räikkönen leads.

Lap 22 Räikkönen heads Massa by 3.5s.

Lap 25 With all the drivers having stopped once, Räikkönen leads from Massa, Kubica, Kovalainen, Trulli, Webber, Hamilton and Heidfeld.

Lap 31 Massa spins off at Turn Eight. He's out. Räikkönen leads Kubica by 22.4s, with Kovalainen third.

Lap 38 Räikkönen pits, Kubica leads – but only just. The Finn rejoins just behind him.

Lap 46 With everybody now having stopped twice, Räikkönen leads by 19.9s from Kubica, Kovalainen, Trulli, Hamilton, Heidfeld, Webber and Alonso.

Lap 55 With one lap to go, Hamilton is only 0.6s behind Trulli.

Lap 56 Räikkönen wins by 19.5s from Kubica, Kovalainen, Trulli, Hamilton, Heidfeld, Webber and Alonso.

ABOVE Lewis is the focus of attention as he faces the press.

BELOW Speeding towards the top of the timesheets on Friday.

OPPOSITE A five-place grid penalty gave Lewis reason to look pensive.

Following the ease with which he won in Australia, Lewis Hamilton found the going much tougher a week later at the Malaysian Grand Prix.

The Ferraris of Felipe Massa and Kimi Räikkönen were quick from the off in the heat of Sepang. And while Lewis struggled to find a perfect handling balance on his McLaren MP4-23, he appeared well set to be the best of the rest. His hopes of joining the Ferraris on the podium were undone, however, when he picked up a five-place grid penalty for blocking the BMW Sauber of Nick Heidfeld and the Renault of ex-team-mate Fernando Alonso while he was in fuel-save mode having completed his qualifying effort.

This was the difference between starting fourth and ninth, although Lewis produced one of his trademark fantastic opening laps to vault up to fifth place with some demon overtaking moves. But now he was boxed in behind the defensively driven Red Bull of Mark Webber. His best hope of leap-frogging the Australian was during the first round of pit stops, but there was a delay in changing the right-front wheel of his McLaren, which cost him around 10 seconds and any hope of passing Webber. Not only that, he also lost a place to team-mate Heikki Kovalainen and the Toyota of Jarno Trulli.

During the second round of stops, Lewis finally got ahead of the Red Bull, and set a series of fastest laps as he closed in on Trulli. With Massa having earlier spun out of a comfortable second place, Lewis came home a frustrated fifth. Räikkönen won the race for Ferrari, and in doing so reduced Lewis's points lead over him from nine to just three.

"I got a really good start and was pretty happy as we jumped five positions from ninth to fifth," said Lewis. "I was pushing Webber for a very long time, but being behind someone, no matter how quick you are, it is really difficult to get past. We were in a good position for a shot at third place at least, but then I had the problem in my first pit stop which lost me a lot of time."

MALAYSIAN GRAND PRIX
SEPANG

RACE DATE 23rd March 2008
CIRCUIT LENGTH 3.444 miles
NO. OF LAPS 56 laps
RACE DISTANCE 192.887miles
WEATHER Sunny and humid, 30°C
TRACK TEMP 45°C

Practice

Session 1 – Friday

1	Felipe Massa	Ferrari	1m35.392s
2	Kimi Räikkönen	Ferrari	1m36.459s
3	Heikki Kovalainen	McLaren-Mercedes	1m36.556s
5	**Lewis Hamilton**	**McLaren-Mercedes**	**1m36.626s**

Session 2 – Friday

1	**Lewis Hamilton**	**McLaren-Mercedes**	**1m35.055s**
2	Felipe Massa	Ferrari	1m35.206s
3	Kimi Räikkönen	Ferrari	1m35.428s

Session 3 – Saturday

1	Nick Heidfeld	BMW Sauber	1m35.019s
2	Kimi Räikkönen	Ferrari	1m35.262s
3	Felipe Massa	Ferrari	1m35.388s
11	**Lewis Hamilton**	**McLaren-Mercedes**	**1m35.927s**

Qualifying

1	Felipe Massa	Ferrari	1m35.748s
2	Kimi Räikkönen	Ferrari	1m36.230s
3	Jarno Trulli	Toyota	1m36.711s
9*	**Lewis Hamilton**	**McLaren-Mercedes**	**1m36.709s**

* PENALISED FIVE POSITIONS FOR IMPEDING RIVAL DRIVERS IN Q3

Race

1	Kimi Räikkönen	Ferrari	1h31m18.555s
2	Robert Kubica	BMW Sauber	+19.570s
3	Heikki Kovalainen	McLaren-Mercedes	+38.450s
4	Jarno Trulli	Toyota	+45.832s
5	**Lewis Hamilton**	**McLaren-Mercedes**	**+46.548s**
6	Nick Heidfeld	BMW Sauber	+49.833s
7	Mark Webber	Red Bull-Renault	+1m08.130s
8	Fernando Alonso	Renault	+1m10.041s

Fastest Lap

Nick Heidfeld	BMW Sauber	1m35.366s

World Championship Positions

1	**Lewis Hamilton**	**McLaren-Mercedes**	**14 points**
2	Kimi Räikkönen	Ferrari	11 points
	Nick Heidfeld	BMW Sauber	11 points
4	Heikki Kovalainen	McLaren-Mercedes	10 points
5	Robert Kubica	BMW Sauber	8 points
6	Nico Rosberg	Williams-Toyota	6 points
	Fernando Alonso	Renault	6 points
8	Jarno Trulli	Toyota	5 points

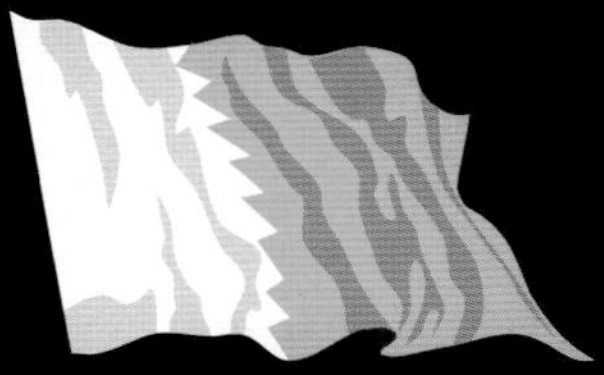

2008 ROUND 3

BAHRAIN GRAND PRIX

SAKHIR

13th

POINTS TOTAL **14**
POINTS POSITION **=3rd**
SEASON WINS **1**

Lap 1 On pole position for the first time in Formula One, Kubica is beaten to Turn One by fellow front-row starter Massa. Hamilton briefly stalls in third place and is subsequently swamped. Räikkönen grabs third from Kovalainen, Trulli, Heidfeld, Rosberg, Alonso, Hamilton and Webber.

Lap 2 Hamilton runs into Alonso and loses his nose. He pits at the end of the lap.

Lap 3 Räikkönen passes Kubica and Heidfeld passes Kovalainen.

Lap 10 Massa leads Räikkönen by 4.4s, with Kubica a further 1.5s adrift and Heidfeld fourth.

Lap 18 Kubica runs wide at Turn 11 shortly after rejoining from his pit stop.

Lap 20 Räikkönen, Trulli and Alonso pit. Massa leads.

Lap 23 Massa, Heidfeld and Kovalainen pit.

Lap 24 Massa leads Räikkönen by 5.4s.

Lap 28 Approaching half-distance, Massa leads Räikkönen, Kubica, Heidfeld, Kovalainen, Trulli, Webber, Rosberg, Glock, Alonso, Nakajima (yet to stop), Barrichello, Fisichella and Hamilton.

Lap 31 Räikkönen reduces his deficit to 4.0s. Hamilton passes Fisichella, but then pits at the end of the lap.

Lap 38 Räikkönen pits, followed by Massa on the next lap.

Lap 47 Kovalainen is the last of the leading drivers to make his second stop.

Lap 53 Hamilton passes Nakajima for 13th.

Lap 57 Massa scores his first victory of the season, winning by 3.3s from Räikkönen. Kubica is third ahead of Heidfeld, Kovalainen, Trulli, Webber and Rosberg. Hamilton finishes 13th, behind Fisichella.

ABOVE The aftermath of Lewis's Friday crash; 'Just one tiny tweak...'

BELOW Minus front wing after the second collision with Alonso.

OPPOSITE The heat's on for Lewis as he struggles home to 13th place.

After trailing home 13th in the Bahrain Grand Prix, Lewis Hamilton stated: "I'm as disappointed as can be."

The worst result of his F1 career to date capped a difficult weekend for Lewis. His problems started in second practice, where he suffered a huge crash, which meant he required a new tub for qualifying. He used this to line up third behind the Ferraris of Räikkönen and Massa, but in the build-up to the start he left the priming of his launch-control software a fraction too late, and he was swamped by the field while his car struggled to get up to pace as the race got under way.

"I hadn't hit the switch early enough," Lewis admitted.

In a bid to claw back as many places as quickly as possible, he tagged the rear of Alonso's Renault on the opening lap, damaging his front wing in the process. A lap later, when a piece flew off his broken wing acting like a boost button in his McLaren, he smashed into the back of Alonso again, causing considerable damage to his front wing and suspension. This forced Lewis in for an early pit stop, and a switch to a one-stop strategy. And with Lewis's Mercedes-Benz engine also having to be used for the following Spanish GP, the wick was turned down and he was left to struggle home a lap behind race winner Massa's Ferrari.

"A poor result was inevitable because I've had such a good run in Formula 1, but there's still a long way to go," said Lewis, who dropped to third place in the World Championship points table behind Ferrari's defending World Champion Räikkönen and BMW Sauber's Nick Heidfeld. "It was a very poor performance. I sort of let the team down today."

BAHRAIN GRAND PRIX
SAKHIR

RACE DATE 6th April 2008
CIRCUIT LENGTH 3.363 miles
NO. OF LAPS 57 laps
RACE DISTANCE 191.530 miles
WEATHER Sunny, 31°C
TRACK TEMP 35°C

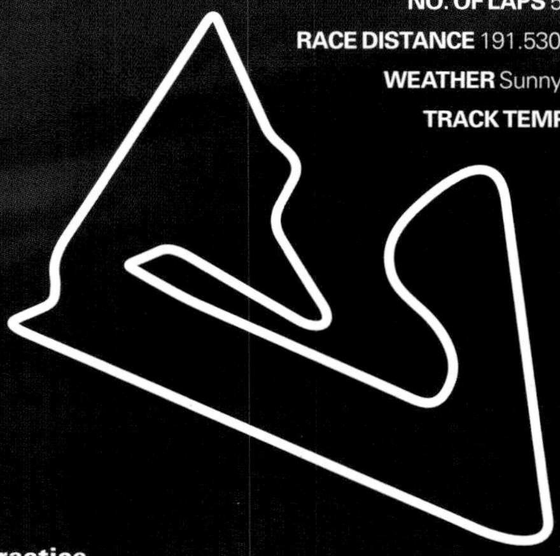

Practice

Session 1 – Friday

1	Felipe Massa	Ferrari	1m32.233s
2	Kimi Räikkönen	Ferrari	1m32.350s
3	Nico Rosberg	Williams-Toyota	1m32.415s
4	**Lewis Hamilton**	**McLaren-Mercedes**	**1m32.705s**

Session 2 – Friday

1	Felipe Massa	Ferrari	1m31.420s
2	Kimi Räikkönen	Ferrari	1m32.327s
3	Heikki Kovalainen	McLaren-Mercedes	1m32.752s
4	**Lewis Hamilton**	**McLaren-Mercedes**	**1m32.487s**

Session 3 – Saturday

1	Nico Rosberg	Williams-Toyota	1m32.521s
2	Felipe Massa	Ferrari	1m32.726s
3	Mark Webber	Red Bull-Renault	1m32.742s
18	**Lewis Hamilton**	**McLaren-Mercedes**	**1m33.659s**

Qualifying

1	Robert Kubica	BMW Sauber	1m33.096s
2	Felipe Massa	Ferrari	1m33.123s
3	**Lewis Hamilton**	**McLaren-Mercedes**	**1m33.292s**

Race

1	Felipe Massa	Ferrari	1h31m06.970s
2	Kimi Räikkönen	Ferrari	+3.339s
3	Robert Kubica	BMW Sauber	+4.998s
4	Nick Heidfeld	BMW Sauber	+8.409s
5	Heikki Kovalainen	McLaren-Mercedes	+26.789s
6	Jarno Trulli	Toyota	+41.314s
7	Mark Webber	Red Bull-Renault	+45.473s
8	Nico Rosberg	Williams-Toyota	+55.889s
13	**Lewis Hamilton**	**McLaren-Mercedes**	**+1 lap**

Fastest Lap

Heikki Kovalainen	McLaren-Mercedes	1m33.193s

World Championship Positions

1	Kimi Räikkönen	Ferrari	19 points
2	Nick Heidfeld	BMW Sauber	16 points
3	**Lewis Hamilton**	**McLaren-Mercedes**	**14 points**
	Robert Kubica	BMW Sauber	14 points
	Heikki Kovalainen	McLaren-Mercedes	14 points
6	Felipe Massa	Ferrari	10 points
7	Jarno Trulli	Toyota	8 points
8	Nico Rosberg	Williams-Toyota	7 points

"I'm as disappointed as can be... A poor result was inevitable because I've had such a good run in Formula 1, but there's still a long way to go."

vodafone

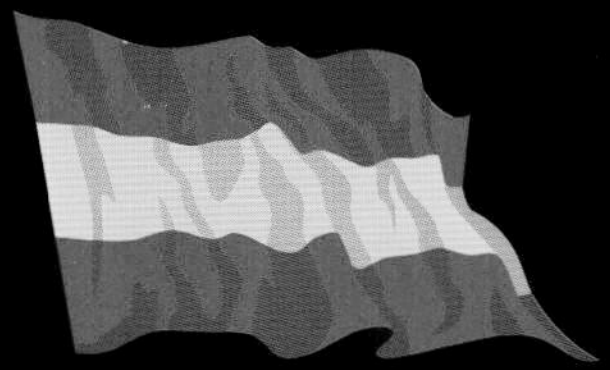

2008 ROUND 4

SPANISH GRAND PRIX
CATALUNYA

3rd POINTS TOTAL **20**
POINTS POSITION **2nd**
SEASON WINS **1**

Lap 1 Räikkönen leads cleanly into the first corner from pole. Local hero Alonso is beaten away by Massa, who lies second. Hamilton takes fourth from Kubica. Kovalainen lies sixth ahead of Heidfeld, Webber, Trulli and Piquet. Sutil spins at Turn Four and collects Vettel who is then rammed by Sato. The safety car is deployed.

Lap 4 As the race restarts, Räikkönen leads Massa by 1.3s.

Lap 10 The leader is getting quicker, extending his lead over Massa. Alonso leads fourth-placed Hamilton by 1.2s.

Lap 16 Alonso pits for fuel and drops to 11th.

Lap 19 Massa pits.

Lap 20 Räikkönen, Webber, Trulli and Sato pit. Hamilton leads.

Lap 21 Hamilton and Kubica pit.

Lap 22 Kovalainen crashes heavily at Turn Nine. The safety car is deployed, and the race is neutralised with Heidfeld leading.

Lap 24 Heidfeld comes in for fuel, although the pits are not yet open.

Lap 27 Released from his wrecked car, Kovalainen gives the crowd a thumbs-up sign.

Lap 29 The race restarts with Räikkönen leading Massa, Hamilton, Kubica, Heidfeld, Alonso, Webber and Trulli.

Lap 30 Heidfeld is handed a 10s stop-go penalty for refuelling before the pitlane had opened.

Lap 31 Räikkönen leads Massa by 1.8s. Hamilton is third, a further 1.0s back.

Lap 35 Alonso pulls off at Turn Four, trailing engine smoke.

Lap 46 Massa, Webber and Trulli pit.

Lap 47 Räikkönen, Hamilton and Kubica pit. Räikkönen retains the lead, from Massa and Hamilton.

Lap 49 Räikkönen leads Massa by 1.9s and Hamilton by 5.0s.

Lap 55 Heidfeld passes Fisichella at Turn One – the first on-track change of position since the opening lap.

Lap 66 Räikkönen wins by 3.2s from Massa, Hamilton, Kubica, Webber, Button, Nakajima and Trulli.

ABOVE Lewis makes a rapid exit at the end of his first pit stop, just before team-mate Kovalainen's accident.

BELOW Larger than life, Lewis and local hero Alonso meet the fans.

Lewis Hamilton bounced back from his no-score in Bahrain with a solid podium finish in the Spanish Grand Prix. But while Lewis was only four seconds behind winner Kimi Räikkönen at the finish, in truth it was a race dominated by the Ferraris.

Lewis's best chance of upsetting the Ferrari 1–2 at the head of the field followed a mid-race safety-car period brought on by an enormous crash for his team-mate Heikki Kovalainen. With Lewis's McLaren able to generate heat in its front tyres quicker than Felipe Massa's Ferrari, he used his temporary extra grip to get a run on the Brazilian, but while he had a look down the inside of Massa on one occasion, he was never close enough to make a move stick. From there on to the finish he ran close behind the leading Ferraris, while at the same time protecting his precious podium spot from BMW Sauber's Robert Kubica.

Third place meant Lewis dropped to nine points behind Räikkönen in the title fight, but post-race he admitted his concern for his team-mate's well-being was more important than the result.

"First of all I am really happy to hear that Heikki is OK. During the race I saw a car had gone into the barriers and was told it was Heikki. As soon as the team knew he was OK, Ron came on the radio and told me, which was a great relief.

"It's good to be back on the podium. After qualifying, we knew it would be a difficult, so I am actually pleased to be third. I pushed extremely hard, particularly in the second and third stints, and tried to keep up with the Ferraris. We did a good job today, but there are areas where we definitely need to improve, but it's comforting to know that we are relatively close to Ferrari."

ABOVE Lewis looks satisfied with his first podium finish since Melbourne.

BELOW The McLarens struggled in qualifying, a lack of grip resulting in Lewis lining up fifth.

SPANISH GRAND PRIX
CATALUNYA

RACE DATE 27th April 2008
CIRCUIT LENGTH 2.075 miles
NO. OF LAPS 78 laps
RACE DISTANCE 161.850 miles
WEATHER Dry and bright, 24°C
TRACK TEMP 38°C

Practice

Session 1 – Friday

1	Kimi Räikkönen	Ferrari	1m20.649s
2	Felipe Massa	Ferrari	1m20.699s
3	**Lewis Hamilton**	**McLaren-Mercedes**	**1m21.192s**

Session 2 – Friday

1	Kimi Räikkönen	Ferrari	1m21.935s
2	Nelson Piquet Jnr	Renault	1m22.019s
3	Fernando Alonso	Renault	1m22.032s
11	**Lewis Hamilton**	**McLaren-Mercedes**	**1m22.685s**

Session 3 – Saturday

1	Nick Heidfeld	BMW Sauber	1m21.269s
2	David Coulthard	Red Bull-Renault	1m21.465s
3	Fernando Alonso	Renault	1m21.599s
11	**Lewis Hamilton**	**McLaren-Mercedes**	**1m22.094s**

Qualifying

1	Kimi Räikkönen	Ferrari	1m21.813s
2	Fernando Alonso	Renault	1m21.904s
3	Felipe Massa	Ferrari	1m22.058s
5	**Lewis Hamilton**	**McLaren-Mercedes**	**1m22.096s**

Race

1	Kimi Räikkönen	Ferrari	1h38m19.051s
2	Felipe Massa	Ferrari	+3.228s
3	**Lewis Hamilton**	**McLaren-Mercedes**	**+4.187s**
4	Robert Kubica	BMW Sauber	+5.694s
5	Mark Webber	Red Bull-Renault	+35.938s
6	Jenson Button	Honda	+53.010s
7	Kazuki Nakajima	Williams-Toyota	+58.244s
8	Jarno Trulli	Toyota	+59.435s

Fastest Lap

Kimi Räikkönen	Ferrari	1m21.670s

World Championship Positions

1	Kimi Räikkönen	Ferrari	29 points
2	**Lewis Hamilton**	**McLaren-Mercedes**	**20 points**
3	Robert Kubica	BMW Sauber	19 points
4	Felipe Massa	Ferrari	18 points
5	Nick Heidfeld	BMW Sauber	16 points
6	Heikki Kovalainen	McLaren-Mercedes	14 points
7	Jarno Trulli	Toyota	9 points
8	Mark Webber	Red Bull-Renault	8 points

vodafone

2008 ROUND 5

TURKISH GRAND PRIX
ISTANBUL

2nd

POINTS TOTAL **28**
POINTS POSITION **=2nd**
SEASON WINS **1**

Lap 1 From pole, Massa leads Hamilton. Kubica lies third, ahead of Kovalainen, and Räikkönen drops to sixth, between Alonso and Webber. Fisichella and Nakajima clash at Turn One, resulting in the safety car being deployed.

Lap 2 Kovalainen pits for repairs after sustaining a puncture.

Lap 3 Restart. Massa leads Hamilton by 0.6s. Räikkönen passes Alonso for fourth.

Lap 15 Hamilton moves to within 0.7s of Massa. Alonso pits.

Lap 16 Hamilton pits and drops, temporarily, to sixth.

Lap 19 Massa and Kubica pit.

Lap 21 Räikkönen pits, as does second-placed Heidfeld.

Lap 22 Massa leads from Hamilton, Räikkönen and Kubica.

Lap 24 Hamilton passes Massa at Turn 12 to lead.

Lap 27 Hamilton leads Massa by 3.8s.

Lap 28 Hamilton pulls another second clear. Behind Massa, Räikkönen, Kubica, Heidfeld, Alonso, Webber and Button (yet to stop) complete the top eight.

Lap 32 Hamilton makes his second stop. He sticks with the prime tyres – a three-stop strategy beckons.

Lap 34 Massa leads Räikkönen by 2.7s. Hamilton is third, a further 2.6s in arrears.

Lap 40 Massa pits, as does Kubica. Räikkönen leads.

Lap 41 Räikkönen leads Hamilton by 1.6s. Massa lies third.

Lap 43 Räikkönen and Rosberg pit. Hamilton leads.

Lap 45 Hamilton pits. He rejoins second, ahead of Räikkönen.

Lap 46 Massa leads Hamilton by 5.2s. Räikkönen is third from Kubica, Heidfeld, Alonso, Trulli and Webber.

Lap 52 Räikkönen is applying pressure to Hamilton. The gap is about half a second.

Lap 58 Massa wins from Hamilton by 3.7s. Räikkönen is a close third. Kubica, Heidfeld, Alonso, Webber and Rosberg complete the scorers.

ABOVE **Sprinting away from Massa after pulling off a stunning pass.**

BELOW **Reason to smile after one of the best drives of Lewis's career.**

OPPOSITE **Powering round the scenic Istanbul circuit during Friday.**

Lewis Hamilton produced a fantastic against-the-odds charge to second in the Turkish Grand Prix to reignite his title campaign.

Lewis's aggressive turn-in driving style means he puts a lot of stress on the front tyres, and combined with Turkey's super-fast, four-apex Turn 8, there were concerns of a repeat of his 2007 race, where a punctured right-front robbed him of valuable championship points. On the advice of tyre supplier Bridgestone, to combat this the team opted for an unusual three-stop pit strategy, but to make this work Lewis would have to produce one of his finest performances behind the wheel of a racing car. And he duly delivered.

"I probably drove the best race I have ever done," he revealed. "I strongly feel we couldn't have done a better job. I just feel my race pace is getting stronger and stronger at each race."

From third on the grid, Lewis was instantly up into second after out-dragging team-mate Heikki Kovalainen off the line. Lewis and Ferrari's Felipe Massa quickly pulled away from the field, with the Brazilian holding a small, but comfortable lead over the McLaren. But as the first of Lewis's three pit stops approached, he put on a charge and reduced the lead to under a second.

On fresh tyres and a relatively light fuel load, Lewis was dynamite in this phase of the race, and was right on the tail of Massa, following his first (of two) scheduled stops. Knowing that he would have to pit once more than his rival, Lewis could not afford to be delayed in the Ferrari's wake, and on lap 23 he produced one of his trademark demon overtaking moves, selling Massa a dummy to the outside with a crafty feint down the back straight, before diving down the inside and into the lead.

Lewis sprinted away at around a second a lap and when he rejoined after his second stop, he was just 2.5 secs off Kimi Räikkönen's second-placed Ferrari. With all three of the leaders now having to stop once more, Lewis again had to pull out all the stops, and leapfrogged Kimi to take second after they both pitted for the final time.

For his final stint, Lewis was on the softer of the tyre compounds – the one that Bridgestone was worried he was over-using. And although Massa was in his sights initially, Lewis had no answer to the Ferrari's pace at this stage, but instead found himself having to fend off Räikkönen for second.

This he did, to narrow Kimi's points lead by two. But Massa's second win of the season meant that things were getting very tight at the top of the table.

"Before the race our prediction was that all being well I would finish fifth, so second is such a bonus," said Lewis. "We knew that we would have to use a three-stop strategy as a precaution, as we had some issues with our tyres. The team did a fantastic job, the pit stops were great, and the balance of the car was superb, and we all kept our spirits up. There were no problems with the tyres in the race. I managed to overtake Felipe at one point, and I really think we have closed the gap to Ferrari."

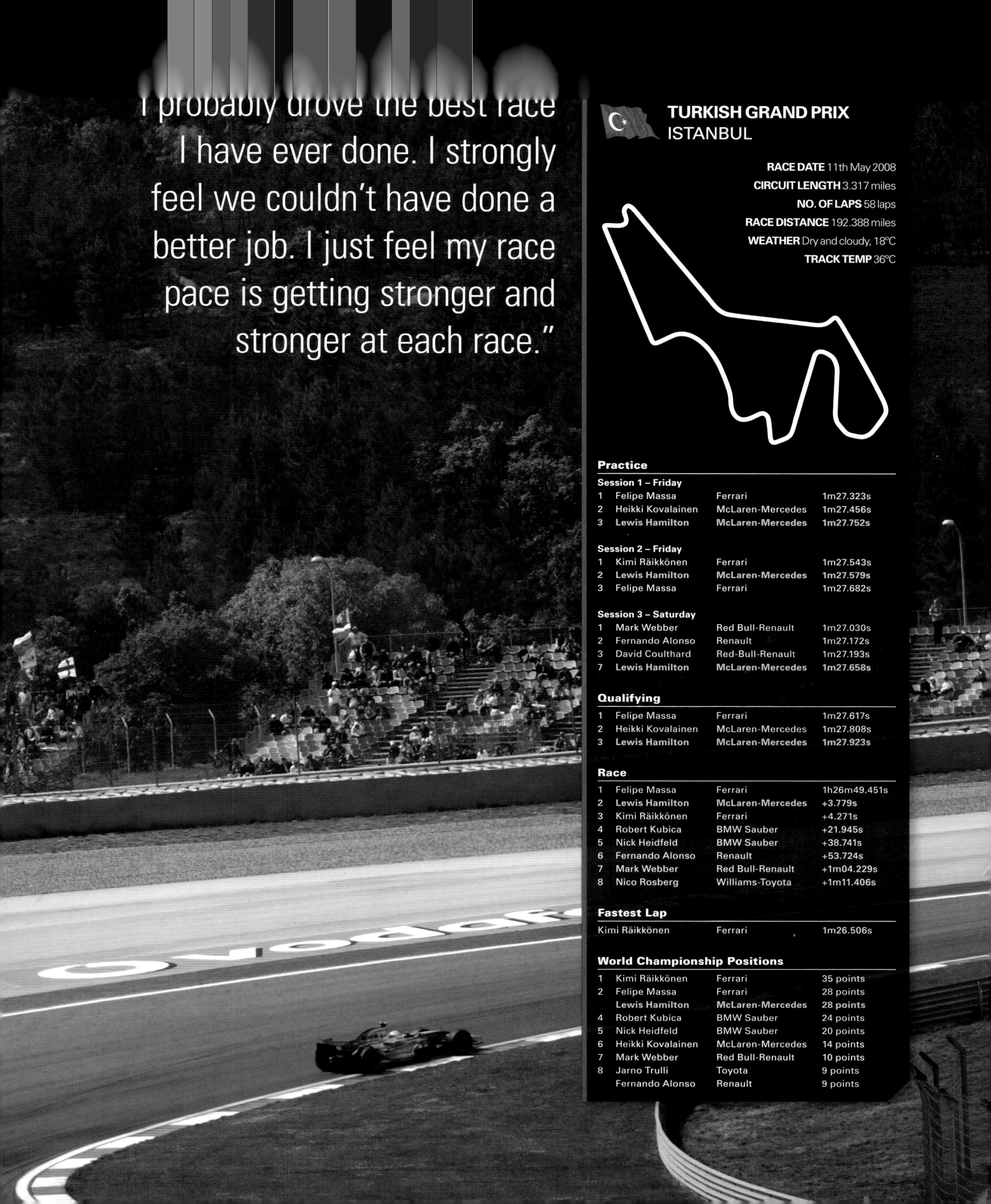

I probably drove the best race I have ever done. I strongly feel we couldn't have done a better job. I just feel my race pace is getting stronger and stronger at each race."

TURKISH GRAND PRIX
ISTANBUL

RACE DATE 11th May 2008
CIRCUIT LENGTH 3.317 miles
NO. OF LAPS 58 laps
RACE DISTANCE 192.388 miles
WEATHER Dry and cloudy, 18°C
TRACK TEMP 36°C

Practice

Session 1 – Friday

1	Felipe Massa	Ferrari	1m27.323s
2	Heikki Kovalainen	McLaren-Mercedes	1m27.456s
3	**Lewis Hamilton**	**McLaren-Mercedes**	**1m27.752s**

Session 2 – Friday

1	Kimi Räikkönen	Ferrari	1m27.543s
2	**Lewis Hamilton**	**McLaren-Mercedes**	**1m27.579s**
3	Felipe Massa	Ferrari	1m27.682s

Session 3 – Saturday

1	Mark Webber	Red Bull-Renault	1m27.030s
2	Fernando Alonso	Renault	1m27.172s
3	David Coulthard	Red-Bull-Renault	1m27.193s
7	**Lewis Hamilton**	**McLaren-Mercedes**	**1m27.658s**

Qualifying

1	Felipe Massa	Ferrari	1m27.617s
2	Heikki Kovalainen	McLaren-Mercedes	1m27.808s
3	**Lewis Hamilton**	**McLaren-Mercedes**	**1m27.923s**

Race

1	Felipe Massa	Ferrari	1h26m49.451s
2	**Lewis Hamilton**	**McLaren-Mercedes**	**+3.779s**
3	Kimi Räikkönen	Ferrari	+4.271s
4	Robert Kubica	BMW Sauber	+21.945s
5	Nick Heidfeld	BMW Sauber	+38.741s
6	Fernando Alonso	Renault	+53.724s
7	Mark Webber	Red Bull-Renault	+1m04.229s
8	Nico Rosberg	Williams-Toyota	+1m11.406s

Fastest Lap

Kimi Räikkönen	Ferrari	1m26.506s

World Championship Positions

1	Kimi Räikkönen	Ferrari	35 points
2	Felipe Massa	Ferrari	28 points
	Lewis Hamilton	**McLaren-Mercedes**	**28 points**
4	Robert Kubica	BMW Sauber	24 points
5	Nick Heidfeld	BMW Sauber	20 points
6	Heikki Kovalainen	McLaren-Mercedes	14 points
7	Mark Webber	Red Bull-Renault	10 points
8	Jarno Trulli	Toyota	9 points
	Fernando Alonso	Renault	9 points

BRIDGESTONE
BOSS
aigo
Santander
vodafone
MUMM
MUMM

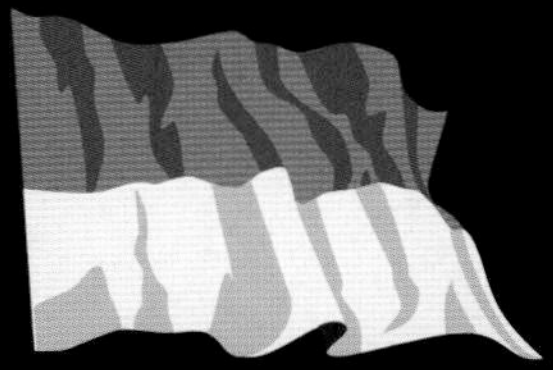

2008 ROUND 6

MONACO GRAND PRIX

MONTE CARLO

1st POINTS TOTAL **38**
POINTS POSITION **1st**
SEASON WINS **2**

Lap 1 Massa leads from pole on a damp track. Hamilton beats Räikkönen into second, from Kubica, Alonso and Rosberg.

Lap 6 Hamilton clips the barriers at Tabac and pits with a damaged right-rear wheel, rejoining fifth.

Lap 8 Alonso pits after sliding off at Massenet. Coulthard and Bourdais go off to end their races. The safety car is deployed.

Lap 11 Restart. Räikkönen is handed a drive-through penalty for a rule infringement on the grid. Massa leads by 3.0s from Räikkönen, Kubica, Hamilton, Heidfeld, Webber and Alonso.

Lap 13 Räikkönen serves his penalty.

Lap 14 Alonso pushes Heidfeld into a spin at the hairpin. Webber rams Alonso and most of the midfield comes to a halt. Alonso and Rosberg pit. Sutil vaults from 11th to seventh.

Lap 16 Massa spins at Ste Dévote. Kubica leads.

Lap 22 Massa is now 1.9s behind leader Kubica.

Lap 26 Kubica pits.

Lap 27 Räikkönen goes straight on at Ste Dévote: his front wing is damaged and he pits. Massa leads Hamilton by 16.5s.

Lap 33 Massa pits and rejoins second, ahead of Kubica.

Lap 43 Hamilton has extended his lead over Massa to 24.9s. Kubica is another 6.1s back in third. Webber lies fourth, followed by Sutil and Räikkönen.

Lap 44 Webber is catching Kubica. Alonso pits for dry tyres.

Lap 53 Hamilton leads Massa by 37.6s. Alonso sets fastest lap.

Lap 54 Hamilton pits: he rejoins, in the lead, on dries.

Lap 56 Hamilton leads by 15.4s. Massa pits, almost going off as he rejoins behind Kubica on super-soft dries.

Lap 57 Hamilton leads Kubica and Massa. Räikkönen pits from fourth and loses a place to Sutil.

Lap 62 Rosberg crashes heavily. The safety car is deployed. Hamilton leads Kubica, Massa, Sutil, Räikkönen and Webber.

Lap 68 Restart. Räikkönen rams Sutil at the chicane.

Lap 76 The race ends two laps early due to the two-hour time limit. Hamilton wins by 3.064s from Kubica, Massa, Webber, Vettel, Barrichello, Nakajima and Kovalainen (who started from the pitlane).

Of the moment that defined the Monaco Grand Prix, Lewis Hamilton recalled: "There was a river running across the track at Tabac and I just hit it and oversteered into the barrier." With his wheel rim and tyre damaged, Lewis had no option but to head for an early pit stop, where great strategic thinking from his McLaren team – fuelling him for a one-stop race – laid the foundations for his second GP victory of the season.

But it wasn't strategy alone that accounted for Lewis's win. Lady Luck also played a significant part, but nothing should take away from a tremendous drive in very difficult conditions.

The race started on a wet track, and Lewis, the

two Ferraris and Robert Kubica disappeared in a ball of spray at the head of the field. Such was their advantage, Lewis only dropped to fifth after his unplanned stop on lap six. The first of two safety-car periods then brought him right onto the tail of the leaders, and at the restart, despite running on a much heavier fuel load, he was able to keep them in sight.

Such was his pace that when Felipe Massa and Robert Kubica pitted for their first planned stop, and Kimi Räikkönen was penalised for changing tyres a fraction too late on the dummy grid, Lewis moved into the lead for the first time. He now needed to establish enough of an advantage that he could make his final stop and rejoin ahead.

This was the cue for some virtuoso brilliance from Lewis, who literally threw his McLaren-Mercedes between Monaco's unforgiving walls with sideways perfection. A gap in the region of 25 seconds was the target, but by the time Lewis actually pitted – a few laps earlier than intended, as the track was drying and dry tyres were proving quicker – he was 40 seconds up the road!

Having timed the change to dries to perfection, Lewis now only needed to steer clear of trouble to claim a tremendous victory in the most prestigious grand prix of them all. That was without factoring in another safety-car period, this time after Nico Rosberg hit the wall hard and scattered shards of carbonfibre across the track.

OPPOSITE TOP **Lewis went to Monaco determined to win after missing out in 2007.**

OPPOSITE BOTTOM **The crown jewels! Lewis's diamond-encrusted helmet.**

BELOW **A dominant display ahead of the lapped cars of Button and Alonso.**

ABOVE Lewis navigates through the wreckage from Rosberg's accident at the Swimming Pool.

BELOW Celebrating a virtuoso drive to victory with a clearly delighted Ron Dennis.

OPPOSITE Leaping ahead – victory in Monaco gave Lewis the championship lead.

While Lewis duly fended off Kubica at the restart, running over Rosberg's debris had, in fact, given him yet another flat tyre. But this is where luck intervened for the second time. Two safety cars and a slippery track had slowed the race pace considerably, so rather than running for the full 78 laps, the race was stopped at the two-hour mark on lap 76. Lewis's tyre deflated on his victory celebration lap. Had the race gone to its full distance, instead of now topping the points table, he could have left Monaco empty-handed.

"I am absolutely over the moon," said a delighted Lewis. "To win here in Monaco is the highlight of my career and an occasion I will always remember. I want to thank everybody in the team for their fantastic job. It was a very eventful race. I started well and immediately overtook Kimi, and also saw a chance to attack Felipe, but then the rain got heavier and visibility worsened.

"Fortunately, the first safety-car period helped me to close the gap to the front. We changed our strategy, and I had to make only one more stop. When I was about 40 seconds ahead, the team told me over the radio to take it easy. The second safety-car period brought more excitement, but I was able to control the race also after the second restart. What a day and what a result!"

MONACO GRAND PRIX
MONTE CARLO

RACE DATE 25th May 2008
CIRCUIT LENGTH 2.075 miles
NO. OF LAPS 78 laps
RACE DISTANCE 161.850 miles
WEATHER Raining then damp, 21°C
TRACK TEMP 23°C

Practice

Session 1 – Thursday

1	Kimi Räikkönen	Ferrari	1m15.948s
2	**Lewis Hamilton**	**McLaren-Mercedes**	**1m16.216s**
3	Heikki Kovalainen	McLaren-Mercedes	1m16.248s

Session 2 – Thursday

1	**Lewis Hamilton**	**McLaren-Mercedes**	**1m15.140s**
2	Nico Rosberg	Williams-Toyota	1m15.533s
3	Kimi Räikkönen	Ferrari	1m15.572s

Session 3 – Saturday

1	Heikki Kovalainen	McLaren-Mercedes	1m16.567s
2	**Lewis Hamilton**	**McLaren-Mercedes**	**1m17.084s**
3	Kimi Räikkönen	Ferrari	1m17.177s

Qualifying

1	Felipe Massa	Ferrari	1m15.787s
2	Kimi Räikkönen	Ferrari	1m15.815s
3	**Lewis Hamilton**	**McLaren-Mercedes**	**1m15.839s**

Race

1	**Lewis Hamilton**	**McLaren-Mercedes**	**2h00m42.742s**
2	Robert Kubica	BMW Sauber	+3.069s
3	Felipe Massa	Ferrari	+4.811s
4	Mark Webber	Red Bull-Renault	+19.264s
5	Sebastian Vettel	Toro Rosso-Ferrari	+24.657s
6	Rubens Barrichello	Honda	+28.408s
7	Kazuki Nakajima	Williams-Toyota	+30.180s
8	Heikki Kovalainen	McLaren-Mercedes	+33.191s

Fastest Lap

Kimi Räikkönen	Ferrari	1m16.689s

World Championship Positions

1	**Lewis Hamilton**	**McLaren-Mercedes**	**38 points**
2	Kimi Räikkönen	Ferrari	35 points
3	Felipe Massa	Ferrari	34 points
4	Robert Kubica	BMW Sauber	32 points
5	Nick Heidfeld	BMW Sauber	20 points
6	Heikki Kovalainen	McLaren-Mercedes	15 points
	Mark Webber	Red Bull-Renault	15 points
8	Jarno Trulli	Toyota	9 points
	Fernando Alonso	Renault	9 points

vodafone
JOHNNIE WALKER
JOHNNIE WALKER
vodafone

2008 ROUND 7

CANADIAN GRAND PRIX

MONTREAL

Rtd

POINTS TOTAL **38**
POINTS POSITION **3rd**
SEASON WINS **2**

Lap 1 Hamilton makes a clean start from pole to lead into Turn One. Kubica holds off Räikkönen to retain second and Rosberg vaults to fourth, ahead of Alonso, Massa, Kovalainen and Barrichello.

Lap 7 Hamilton is 3.3s clear of Kubica, with another 2.8s to Räikkönen. Rosberg is 3.5s further adrift in fourth, 1.6s clear of Alonso.

Lap 10 Hamilton leads by 5.0s.

Lap 14 After a string of personal bests, Räikkönen has closed to within 1.4s of Kubica.

Lap 17 After Sutil stops at Turn 3, the safety car is deployed.

Lap 19 Hamilton, Kubica, Räikkönen, Rosberg, Alonso, Massa, Kovalainen, Piquet, Bourdais and Button pit. Räikkönen and Kubica get away before Hamilton, but stop at the red pit exit light where Hamilton runs into Räikkönen and Rosberg then clips Hamilton. Hamilton and Räikkönen are out.

Lap 22 Restart. Heidfeld leads from Barrichello, Nakajima, Webber, Coulthard, Trulli, Glock, Fisichella, Vettel and Kubica.

Lap 27 Heidfeld has extended his lead to 12.3s.

Lap 29 Heidfeld and Webber pit. Barrichello leads from Nakajima and Coulthard.

Lap 31 Kubica passes Heidfeld to lie seventh – the leading driver with a pit stop under his belt.

Lap 36 Barrichello pits. Coulthard leads.

Lap 46 After numerous lead changes, and with most of the field having made a stop, Kubica leads Heidfeld by 20.7s. Coulthard, third, is catching the German.

Lap 49 Kubica pits, after lapping consistently two seconds quicker than the rest of the field and extending his lead to 25.1s – and rejoins with his lead intact.

Lap 54 Kubica leads from Heidfeld, Coulthard, Barrichello, Glock, Trulli, Massa, Vettel, Rosberg and Kovalainen.

Lap 70 One year after his serious accident at the same venue, Kubica scores his maiden F1 victory. Heidfeld is second from Coulthard, Glock, Massa, Trulli, Barrichello and Vettel.

For the opening 16 laps of the Canadian Grand Prix there looked to be one clear winner – Lewis Hamilton. From pole position he sped away, leaving the chasing pack in his dust around the wall-lined Circuit Gilles Villeneuve.

All that changed when Adrian Sutil's Force India ground to a halt on track, causing the deployment of the safety car. Lewis, like the rest of the frontrunners, was brought into the pits, and given his overwhelming advantage in the early stages of the race, McLaren opted to add a large amount of fuel, knowing this would benefit their man as the race panned out.

With Ferrari and BMW Sauber choosing the short-fuel option for Kimi Räikkönen and Robert Kubica respectively, Lewis found himself behind his rivals as he was released from his pit. At this moment the race was lost.

The red light was on at the end of the pitlane, so both Räikkönen and Kubica were stationary as Lewis approached at around 50mph. Realising too late that the pitlane exit was closed, Lewis slammed on the brakes, locking his wheels. He tried desperately to aim for a gap to Kimi's left that was just wide enough for an F1 car. But he turned just fractionally too late and smashed into the rear of the Ferrari, causing terminal damage to both cars.

"I had two guys in front of me and suddenly they stopped as I looked at the red light," explained Lewis. "Personally, I think the rule is silly. We are in the race. How can you have a red light at the end of the pitlane? But that's the rule and I accept it."

Lewis was handed a 10-place grid penalty for the following French GP, while his non-score dropped him to second in the drivers' championship behind the race winner and new championship leader Robert Kubica.

LEFT, FROM TOP Lewis's mum, Carmen, was there to support her son during the Canadian GP weekend; from pole position, Lewis leads the pack away at the start; all is under control as the pit crew attend to Lewis's car, fuelling him long, during his ill-fated pit stop after the deployment of the safety car.

RIGHT Lewis climbs from his damaged car at the end of the pitlane to face the wrath of the unfortunate Kimi Räikkönen.

CANADIAN GRAND PRIX
MONTREAL

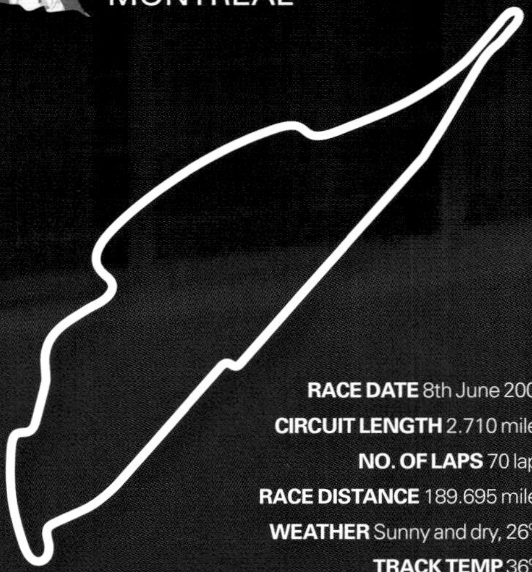

RACE DATE 8th June 2008
CIRCUIT LENGTH 2.710 miles
NO. OF LAPS 70 laps
RACE DISTANCE 189.695 miles
WEATHER Sunny and dry, 26°C
TRACK TEMP 36°C

Practice

Session 1 – Friday

1	Felipe Massa	Ferrari	1m17.553s
2	Robert Kubica	BMW Sauber	1m17.809s
3	Heikki Kovalainen	McLaren-Mercedes	1m18.133s
6	**Lewis Hamilton**	**McLaren-Mercedes**	**1m18.303s**

Session 2 – Friday

1	**Lewis Hamilton**	**McLaren-Mercedes**	**1m15.752s**
2	Robert Kubica	BMW Sauber	1m16.023s
3	Kimi Räikkönen	Ferrari	1m16.093s

Session 3 – Saturday

1	Nico Rosberg	Williams-Toyota	1m16.555s
2	Kimi Räikkönen	Ferrari	1m16.589s
3	**Lewis Hamilton**	**McLaren-Mercedes**	**1m16.725s**

Qualifying

1	**Lewis Hamilton**	**McLaren-Mercedes**	**1m17.886s**
2	Robert Kubica	BMW Sauber	1m18.498s
3	Kimi Räikkönen	Ferrari	1m18.735s

Race

1	Robert Kubica	BMW Sauber	1h36m24.447s
2	Nick Heidfeld	BMW Sauber	+16.495s
3	David Coulthard	Red Bull-Renault	+23.352s
4	Timo Glock	Toyota	+42.627s
5	Felipe Massa	Ferrari	+43.934s
6	Jarno Trulli	Toyota	+47.775s
7	Rubens Barrichello	Honda	+53.597s
8	Sebastian Vettel	Toro Rosso-Ferrari	+54.120s
Rtd	**Lewis Hamilton**	**McLaren-Mercedes**	**Lap 19 Accident**

Fastest Lap

Kimi Räikkönen	Ferrari	1m17.387s

World Championship Positions

1	Robert Kubica	BMW Sauber	42 points
2	Felipe Massa	Ferrari	38 points
3	**Lewis Hamilton**	**McLaren-Mercedes**	**38 points**
4	Kimi Räikkönen	Ferrari	35 points
5	Nick Heidfeld	BMW Sauber	28 points
6	Heikki Kovalainen	McLaren-Mercedes	15 points
	Mark Webber	Red Bull-Renault	15 points
8	Jarno Trulli	Toyota	12 points

vodafone
SAP

2008 ROUND 8

FRENCH GRAND PRIX

MAGNY-COURS

10th

POINTS TOTAL **38**
POINTS POSITION **4th**
SEASON WINS **2**

Lap 1 Räikkönen leads away from pole position. Massa settles into second, but Alonso is passed by both Trulli and Kubica. The Spaniard repasses Kubica at the hairpin exit. Glock makes a good start to take sixth from Webber, Piquet, Kovalainen and Hamilton (starting from tenth after a grid penalty for hitting Räikkönen in the pitlane in Canada), who passes Vettel at Turn Seven.

Lap 5 Hamilton passes Kovalainen.

Lap 10 Räikkönen leads by 3.2s. Trulli is a further 8.5s adrift.

Lap 13 Hamilton is given a drive-through penalty for missing the apex of Turn Seven on Lap 1 and gaining an advantage over Vettel. He comes in straight away and drops to 13th.

Lap 15 Alonso makes the race's first scheduled stop. He drops to 12th.

Lap 19 Hamilton makes a scheduled stop and drops to 19th, temporarily one lap down.

Lap 30 With all the leading drivers having made their first stops, Räikkönen leads by 6.6s from Massa. Trulli is half a minute behind the leader in third.

Lap 36 Massa closes to within 2.2s of Räikkönen, who has a broken exhaust. Trulli, Kubica, Alonso and Webber run third to sixth.

Lap 39 Massa passes Räikkönen.

Lap 54 Massa is the last of the leading drivers to make his second stop, retaining the lead. Hamilton passes Vettel for 11th.

Lap 55 Massa leads Räikkönen by 13.4s. Trulli is third, with Kovalainen closing.

Lap 57 Hamilton passes Glock for 10th.

Lap 70 Massa wins by 17.9s from Räikkönen. Trulli is third from Kovalainen, Kubica, Webber, Piquet, Alonso, Coulthard, and Hamilton.

ABOVE Serious looks from Hamiltons Jr and Sr as Lewis's championship challenge suffers a further setback.

BELOW Lewis scythes past Timo Glock to take 10th place.

OPPOSITE Preparing for battle on Saturday.

Lewis Hamilton went into the French Grand Prix weekend knowing that he faced an uphill battle – and left it facing an even bigger struggle for the World Championship.

It was a race to forget for Lewis, despite the fact that during free practice and qualifying he'd been the only driver to take the fight to the dominant Ferraris. But his 10-place grid penalty for his Canadian GP misdemeanour meant he was never in the hunt for the race win.

From 13th on the grid, Lewis knew he had it all to do in the early laps of the race, when the cars are tightly bunched and it's easier to pick up places. With his McLaren much quicker than the cars around it, it was a question of picking the right time and place to make his moves. Unfortunately, as he out-dragged the Toro Rosso of Sebastian Vettel into the Nürburgring chicane he slightly misjudged it.

Carrying too much speed to safely turn in ahead of Vettel, Lewis opted to cut inside the kerb before rejoining the track. The race stewards felt he had short-cut the track and gained an advantage, and promptly issued Lewis with a drive-through penalty. In one hit his slim chances of racing into the points disappeared.

"My drive-through penalty was an extremely close call," he admitted. "I felt I'd got past Vettel fairly and was ahead going into the corner. But I was on the outside and couldn't turn-in in case we both crashed, then I lost the back end and drove over the kerb."

For the remaining laps of the race Lewis pushed on, but he was too far back to challenge for points, and he eventually came home 10th. His second no-score in succession meant he dropped to fourth in the points standings, 10 behind Felipe Massa, who inherited victory in France when Kimi Räikkönen's exhaust broke late on.

"I've been out of the points for three races now – but there are still 10 to go," said Lewis. "Kimi came from behind to win last year's championship, so there's no reason to be disheartened. I'm 10 points behind, but I'm determined to bounce back at Silverstone in front of my home crowd."

FRENCH GRAND PRIX
MAGNY-COURS

RACE DATE 22nd June 2008
CIRCUIT LENGTH 2.741 miles
NO. OF LAPS 70 laps
RACE DISTANCE 191.870 miles
WEATHER Damp then rain, 25°C
TRACK TEMP 31°C

Practice

Session 1 – Friday

1	Felipe Massa	Ferrari	1m15.306s
2	**Lewis Hamilton**	**McLaren-Mercedes**	**1m16.002s**
3	Heikki Kovalainen	McLaren-Mercedes	1m16.055s

Session 2 – Friday

1	Fernando Alonso	Renault	1m15.778s
2	Felipe Massa	Ferrari	1m15.854s
3	Kimi Räikkönen	Ferrari	1m15.999s
4	**Lewis Hamilton**	**McLaren-Mercedes**	**1m16.232s**

Session 3 – Saturday

1	Nelson Piquet Jr	Renault	1m15.750s
2	Mark Webber	Red Bull-Renault	1m15.759s
3	Sebastian Vettel	Toro Rosso-Ferrari	1m15.827s
7	**Lewis Hamilton**	**McLaren-Mercedes**	**1m16.182s**

Qualifying

1	Kimi Räikkönen	Ferrari	1m16.449s
2	Felipe Massa	Ferrari	1m16.490s
3	Fernando Alonso	Renault	1m16.840s
13*	**Lewis Hamilton**	**McLaren-Mercedes**	**1m16.693s**

* PENALISED 10 POSITIONS FOR CAUSING ACCIDENT IN CANADIAN GP

Race

1	Felipe Massa	Ferrari	1h31m50.245s
2	Kimi Räikkönen	Ferrari	+17.984s
3	Jarno Trulli	Toyota	+28.250s
4	Heikki Kovalainen	McLaren-Mercedes	+28.929s
5	Robert Kubica	BMW Sauber	+30.512s
6	Mark Webber	Red Bull-Renault	+40.304s
7	Nelson Piquet Jr	Renault	+41.033s
8	Fernando Alonso	Renault	+43.372s
10	**Lewis Hamilton**	**McLaren-Mercedes**	**+54.538s**

Fastest Lap

Kimi Räikkönen	Ferrari	1m16.630s

World Championship Positions

1	Felipe Massa	Ferrari	48 points
2	Robert Kubica	BMW Sauber	46 points
3	Kimi Räikkönen	Ferrari	43 points
4	**Lewis Hamilton**	**McLaren-Mercedes**	**38 points**
5	Nick Heidfeld	BMW Sauber	28 points
6	Heikki Kovalainen	McLaren-Mercedes	20 points
7	Jarno Trulli	Toyota	18 points
	Mark Webber	Red Bull-Renault	18 points

1948-2008

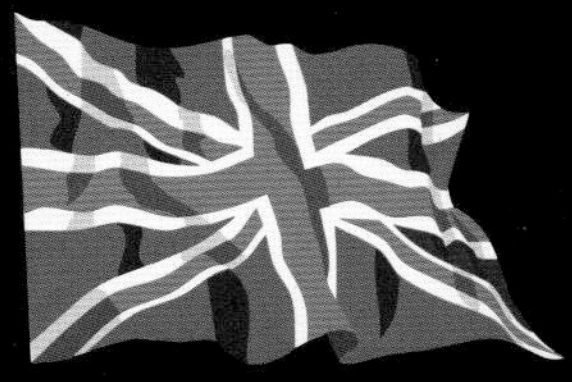

2008 ROUND 9

BRITISH GRAND PRIX

SILVERSTONE

1st

POINTS TOTAL **48**
POINTS POSITION **=1st**
SEASON WINS **3**

Lap 1 On a wet track, Kovalainen leads the intermediate-shod field away. Hamilton makes a fantastic start from fourth and almost passes his team-mate at Copse, but settles into second. Räikkönen lies third and Webber drops to the tail of the field after spinning at Chapel. Heidfeld is fourth from Piquet, Alonso, Trulli, Kubica, Glock and Barrichello. Massa spins at Abbey.

Lap 2 Kovalainen leads by 0.1s. Hamilton is barely visible in his spray. Alonso passes Piquet.

Lap 3 Alonso passes Heidfeld. Massa spins at Woodcote and drops to the tail of the field.

Lap 5 Hamilton takes the lead from Kovalainen into Stowe.

Lap 10 Hamilton leads by 6.0s. Kovalainen spins at Abbey and loses second to Räikkönen. Webber sets the fastest lap.

Lap 13 Räikkönen closes to within 4.5s of Hamilton.

Lap 21 Hamilton, Räikkönen and Massa pit.

Lap 22 Heidfeld and Piquet pit. Hamilton leads Rosberg.

Lap 23 Hamilton leads by 4.6s. It starts to rain. Kubica pits.

Lap 27 Heidfeld passes both Räikkönen and Kovalainen before the two Finns swap places.

Lap 32 Hamilton leads Heidfeld, Kovalainen, Kubica, Piquet, Barrichello, Glock and Trulli.

Lap 36 After heavy rain, Hamilton and Kubica run onto the grass. Piquet spins off at Abbey. Massa spins again.

Lap 38 Hamilton pits and opts for fresh intermediates. Heidfeld and Kubica pit. Räikkönen spins at Woodcote.

Lap 40 Kubica spins off at Abbey. Barrichello – on extreme wets – passes Alonso for fourth.

Lap 43 Having passed Trulli two laps earlier, Barrichello passes Heidfeld for second.

Lap 46 Barrichello pits for intermediates. Kovalainen passes Alonso for fifth.

Lap 48 Hamilton leads Heidfeld by 62.9s.

Lap 60 Hamilton wins by 68.5s from Heidfeld and Barrichello – the only other drivers to go the distance. Räikkönen is fourth from Kovalainen and Alonso.

After Lewis Hamilton swept to victory in the rain-soaked British Grand Prix, triple World Champion and Formula 1 legend Jackie Stewart said: "Lewis demonstrated that he's unquestionably the best wet-weather driver of the current generation."

Following his failure to score in the previous two races, Lewis knew he needed a strong result in front of a passionate home crowd. Yet during free practice and qualifying it was Lewis's team-mate Heikki Kovalainen leading the McLaren charge. But on race day the grey clouds overhead and the wet track surface meant the practice form would count for nothing.

At the start, the two McLarens shot into the lead, touching slightly as Kovalainen defended the first corner from Hamilton's attack. But while Heikki led, Hamilton was swarming all over him, clearly faster. Eventually he made his move for the lead and, with the championship at stake, Heikki put up no resistance as Lewis dived down the inside into the fast right-hander at Stowe.

Lewis now pulled away at over half a second per lap, but while his lead was building comfortably, in the cockpit it was far from easy work. "No matter what I did, the right-hand side of my visor kept fogging over," he revealed. "I was having to lift it between turns one and two and clean the inside, then put it down for Maggotts/Becketts, then open it and clean it again before Stowe. I was doing that every lap."

BELOW **Conditions were attrocious at Silverstone, but Lewis kept his cool.**

OPPOSITE, FROM TOP **The Brit pack – Lewis and Jenson Button fool around with David Coulthard; the partisan crowd shrugged off the conditions to marvel at Lewis's performance; a young Hamilton fan poses for the cameras.**

To add to his woes, the track was now drying rapidly, and preserving his intermediate wet-weather tyres became paramount. Also, as the track dried, so Kimi Räikkönen's pace increased, and the Ferrari was right on Lewis's tail as the first pit stops approached.

Lewis just kept his lead following the stops and, as the rain started to fall, he began to increase his advantage once again.

The harder the rain fell, the more Lewis pulled away. At one stage he was lapping five or six seconds a lap faster than Räikkönen. In fact, Lewis was more than two seconds a lap faster than anyone until the experienced Honda driver Rubens Barrichello made the unilateral call to change to extreme wets.

ABOVE Lewis (left) battles with Kovalainen during the opening laps.

BELOW Nick Hamilton congratulates his brother.

OPPOSITE Getting wet again on the podium.

Conditions were now treacherous, and cars were spinning off the track all around the circuit, including Lewis, who went straight on at the Abbey chicane, but rejoined with his lead intact.

Despite this brief off, Lewis kept on pushing, and by the end of the 60th and last lap, he'd lapped everyone bar Nick Heidfeld's BMW Sauber in second, and Barrichello in third. Having spun twice, Räikkönen was back in fourth, while Ferrari team-mate Felipe Massa spun five times and was the last classified finisher, two laps in arrears. The fourth title chaser, Robert Kubica, ended his race in the Abbey gravel trap.

All this meant that Lewis now headed the championship, albeit tied with Räikkönen and Massa, with Kubica just two points behind.

"Lewis did a stupendous job," said McLaren CEO Martin Whitmarsh. "He had a number of boxes he wanted to tick. Winning Monaco was one of them, winning the British Grand Prix was another, and the other is winning the championship."

With 90,000 jubilant fans cheering him across the line, it was one of the most emotional victories of Lewis's career.

"This was the toughest race, but also one of the best ones I have ever driven. I had troubles with my visor and tried to clean it a couple of times every lap. I thank my team for a great job; they did fantastic work and we always made the right decisions with the tyres in the difficult conditions. When I came round the last time, I saw the crowd standing up and I prayed: 'Just finish, just finish.'

"It was a very emotional moment to win my home grand prix and I want to dedicate this victory to my family. As everybody knows I had some troubles over the past few weeks and they have been always there for me and supported me."

BRITISH GRAND PRIX
SILVERSTONE

RACE DATE 6th July 2008
CIRCUIT LENGTH 3.194 miles
NO. OF LAPS 59 laps
RACE DISTANCE 188.446 miles
WEATHER Overcast, then rain 15°C
TRACK TEMP 16°C

Practice

Session 1 – Friday

1	Felipe Massa	Ferrari	1m19.575s
2	Heikki Kovalainen	McLaren-Mercedes	1m19.587s
3	**Lewis Hamilton**	**McLaren-Mercedes**	**1m19.623s**

Session 2 – Friday

1	Heikki Kovalainen	McLaren-Mercedes	1m19.989s
2	Mark Webber	Red Bull-Renault	1m20.520s
3	**Lewis Hamilton**	**McLaren-Mercedes**	**1m20.543s**

Session 3 – Saturday

1	Fernando Alonso	Renault	1m20.740s
2	Mark Webber	Red Bull-Renault	1m20.988s
3	Heikki Kovalainen	McLaren-Mercedes	1m21.266s
5	**Lewis Hamilton**	**McLaren-Mercedes**	**1m21.668s**

Qualifying

1	Heikki Kovalainen	McLaren-Mercedes	1m21.049s
2	Mark Webber	Red Bull-Renault	1m21.554s
3	Kimi Räikkönen	Ferrari	1m21.706s
4	**Lewis Hamilton**	**McLaren-Mercedes**	**1m21.835s**

Race

1	**Lewis Hamilton**	**McLaren-Mercedes**	**1h39m09.440s**
2	Nick Heidfeld	BMW Sauber	+1m08.577s
3	Rubens Barrichello	Honda	+1m22.273s
4	Kimi Räikkönen	Ferrari	+1 lap
5	Heikki Kovalainen	McLaren-Mercedes	+1 lap
6	Fernando Alonso	Renault	+1 lap
7	Jarno Trulli	Toyota	+1 lap
8	Kazuki Nakajima	Williams-Toyota	+1 lap

Fastest Lap

Kimi Räikkönen	Ferrari	1m32.150s

World Championship Positions

1	**Lewis Hamilton**	**McLaren-Mercedes**	**48 points**
	Felipe Massa	Ferrari	48 points
	Kimi Räikkönen	Ferrari	48 points
4	Robert Kubica	BMW Sauber	46 points
5	Nick Heidfeld	BMW Sauber	36 points
6	Heikki Kovalainen	McLaren-Mercedes	24 points
7	Jarno Trulli	Toyota	20 points
8	Mark Webber	Red Bull-Renault	18 points

Panasonic
Panasonic
Panasonic
Panasonic
Panasonic
BRIDGESTONE
BRIDGESTONE
Santander

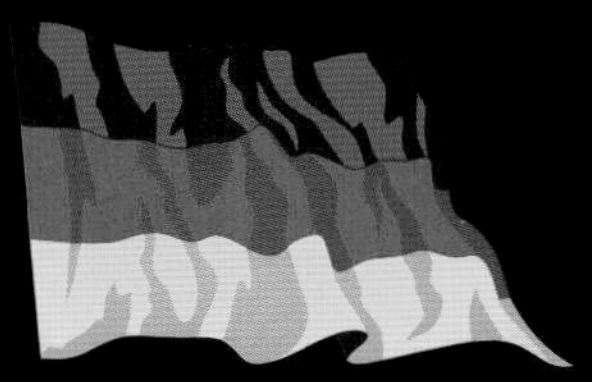

2008 ROUND 10

GERMAN GRAND PRIX
HOCKENHEIM

1st

POINTS TOTAL **58**
POINTS POSITION **1st**
SEASON WINS **4**

Lap 1 Hamilton makes a flying start from pole to lead Massa and Kovalainen. The Englishman leads by 1.8s at the lap's end. Kubica is fourth from Trulli, Alonso, Räikkönen and Vettel.

Lap 4 Hamilton leads by 3.7s. Alonso has a sideways moment at Turn One and subsequently loses a place to Räikkönen.

Lap 17 Hamilton leads by 11.0s.

Lap 18 Hamilton and Kubica pit. Massa leads. Hamilton rejoins fourth, behind Trulli.

Lap 19 Trulli and Alonso pit.

Lap 20 Massa pits. Kovalainen leads by 10.2s from Hamilton.

Lap 21 Kovalainen pits. Hamilton regains the lead.

Lap 22 Räikkönen pits. Kovalainen passes Heidfeld.

Lap 28 Hamilton leads by 10.5s from Massa.

Lap 34 Hamilton leads Massa, Kovalainen, Kubica, Räikkönen, Trulli, Vettel and Glock.

Lap 35 Glock loses control at the final corner and he spins into the pit wall. The safety car deployed.

Lap 39 Many drivers pit under the safety car. Hamilton leads Heidfeld, Piquet, Massa, Kubica, Kovalainen, Trulli and Vettel.

Lap 42 The race resumes.

Lap 45 Hamilton leads Heidfeld by 3.7s.

Lap 50 Hamilton pits and drops to fifth, 0.4s behind Kovalainen and 4.8s behind Massa.

Lap 52 Heidfeld leads. Hamilton passes Kovalainen.

Lap 53 Heidfeld pits and slips to fourth. Piquet leads by 2.0s from Massa and Hamilton.

Lap 56 Piquet is 1.8s clear of Massa, 2.2s ahead of Hamilton.

Lap 57 Hamilton passes Massa. The Brazilian attempts to respond but goes across the kerbs.

Lap 59 Piquet leads by 0.4s.

Lap 60 Hamilton passes Piquet at the hairpin to take the lead.

Lap 67 Hamilton wins by 5.5s from Piquet, Massa, Heidfeld, Kovalainen, Räikkönen, Kubica and Vettel.

ABOVE Leading the chasing pack away from pole position.

OPPOSITE TOP Lewis's fans show their colours in the Hockenheim stadium.

OPPOSITE BOTTOM Number one. Lewis shows his joy in *parc fermé* after the race.

Lewis Hamilton backed up his brilliant British GP win with another commanding performance in the German GP at Hockenheim. And just like his Silverstone triumph, the race was far from straightforward…

It didn't look like it would be much of a struggle. From pole position Lewis simply disappeared into the distance in the early stages of the race, the mid-season developments carried out to his McLaren making the car much more to his liking than it had been before.

Growing at half a second a lap, his advantage was such that McLaren called him in early for the first of his two scheduled stops, a tactic designed to nullify the impact of any safety-car period that might occur.

Having taken on a heavy fuel load, Lewis lost a little time to the chasing Felipe Massa, but he was still comfortably ahead when Timo Glock's Toyota suffered a mechanical failure coming out of the final corner and smashed heavily into the pit wall. Glock was winded and stunned, but otherwise unhurt, but debris from his wrecked car was strewn across the circuit and a safety car was inevitable.

When the pitlane opened, all the leading runners, bar Lewis, opted to make their final stop. It seemed the logical decision at the time, but McLaren boss Ron Dennis thought otherwise.

"With hindsight we probably wouldn't have done it that

way," he explained. "But the thinking was that the safety car wasn't going to be out for as long as it was. The Toyota was behind the barriers and we thought the safety car was about to come in the lap after the pitlane was opened. We felt Lewis had enough pace and enough fuel to build up enough of a lead to stay out and extend his lead sufficiently to stay in front."

As the race restarted, Lewis quickly sprinted away. But he would have to pit again, whereas his main rivals could run to the finish. Needing to build up a 23-second advantage in just seven laps, it looked as though a sure-fire win had been lost. But Lewis got his head down and lapped flat-out for those crucial seven laps.

ABOVE Joy in the McLaren garage after Lewis's momentous fightback to victory.

BELOW Outbraking Piquet into the hairpin to take the lead.

OPPOSITE Pushing hard on the way to pole.

He wasn't able to make his stop and rejoin in the lead, but the leaders were in sight and there were still 14 laps to go. The race was on.

Lewis exited the pits behind team-mate Heikki Kovalainen, who eventually let him pass after a lap with the sister McLaren in his mirrors. This moved Lewis into third, behind the Ferrari of Felipe Massa, and the leading Renault of Nelson Piquet, who'd shot into the lead from 17th on grid after his one-stop strategy worked perfectly with the safety-car interruption.

Lewis soon caught Massa, and wasted no time in scything past his title rival. He lined the Ferrari up on the run to the hairpin, where he simply out-braked the Brazilian, before running him out wide on the exit, preventing any chance of a repass.

It took a couple more laps for Piquet to fall prey to the same move. The Renault man had endured a troubled season so far, so could not afford to throw away a safe second place and offered only token resistance.

Lewis eventually crossed the line five seconds clear of Piquet to claim his eighth career win. It was a remarkable fightback and a drive that earned him a clear four-point lead in the championship.

"I nailed it this afternoon," said Lewis. "When the team told me I had to build a 23-second gap in just seven laps, I knew I had to drive over the limit – and I did. But I knew we had the best car this weekend and felt comfortable pushing hard to make up the gap. When the safety car came out, I questioned whether I should pit but I trusted the team to make the best decision on strategy. It didn't quite work out, but I knew we had the pace in the car to keep pushing. I was able to slipstream past Felipe and then thought my work was done; then I had to do it all again to get past Nelson. But I made a couple of textbook moves to get past them both. We couldn't have asked for more today."

GERMAN GRAND PRIX
HOCKENHEIM

RACE DATE 20th July 2008
CIRCUIT LENGTH 2.842 miles
NO. OF LAPS 67 laps
RACE DISTANCE 190.433 miles
WEATHER Cloudy and dry, 24°C
TRACK TEMP 29°C

Practice

Session 1 – Friday

1	Lewis Hamilton	McLaren-Mercedes	1m15.537s
2	Heikki Kovalainen	McLaren-Mercedes	1m15.666s
3	Felipe Massa	Ferrari	1m15.796s

Session 2 – Friday

1	Lewis Hamilton	McLaren-Mercedes	1m15.025s
2	Felipe Massa	Ferrari	1m15.722s
3	Kimi Räikkönen	Ferrari	1m15.760s

Session 3 – Saturday

1	Heikki Kovalainen	McLaren-Mercedes	1m15.621s
2	Felipe Massa	Ferrari	1m15.693s
3	Lewis Hamilton	McLaren-Mercedes	1m15.839s

Qualifying

1	Lewis Hamilton	McLaren-Mercedes	1m15.666s
2	Felipe Massa	Ferrari	1m15.859s
3	Heikki Kovalainen	McLaren-Mercedes	1m16.143s

Race

1	Lewis Hamilton	McLaren-Mercedes	1h31m20.874s
2	Nelson Piquet	Renault	+5.586s
3	Felipe Massa	Ferrari	+9.339s
4	Nick Heidfeld	BMW Sauber	+9.825s
5	Heikki Kovalainen	McLaren-Mercedes	+12.411s
6	Kimi Räikkönen	Ferrari	+14.403s
7	Robert Kubica	BMW Sauber	+22.682s
8	Sebastian Vettel	Toro Rosso-Ferrari	+33.299s

Fastest Lap

Nick Heidfeld	BMW Sauber	1m15.987s

World Championship Positions

1	Lewis Hamilton	McLaren-Mercedes	58 points
2	Felipe Massa	Ferrari	54 points
3	Kimi Räikkönen	Ferrari	51 points
4	Robert Kubica	BMW Sauber	48 points
5	Nick Heidfeld	BMW Sauber	41 points
6	Heikki Kovalainen	McLaren-Mercedes	28 points
7	Jarno Trulli	Toyota	20 points
8	Mark Webber	Red Bull-Renault	18 points

vodafone

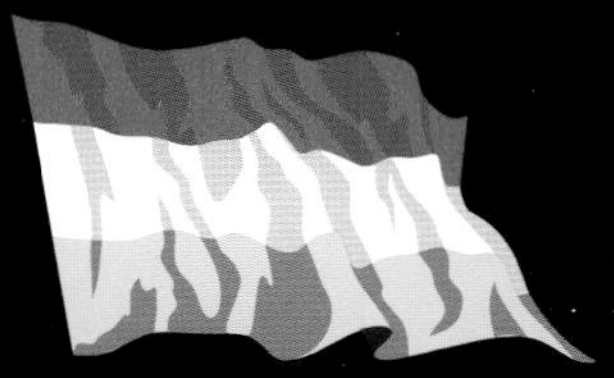

2008 ROUND 11

HUNGARIAN GRAND PRIX

BUDAPEST

5th

POINTS TOTAL **62**
POINTS POSITION **1st**
SEASON WINS **4**

Lap 1 Hamilton leads initially from pole, but Massa, starting from third on the grid, sweeps around the outside to take the lead at Turn One. Kovalainen lies third from Glock, Kubica, Alonso, Räikkönen, Webber, Trulli and Piquet.

Lap 10 Massa leads Hamilton by 2.8s and Kovalainen by 7.8s.

Lap 18 Massa pits and rejoins fourth, ahead of Alonso. Kubica and Webber refuel, too.

Lap 19 Hamilton pits and slips to sixth.

Lap 20 Kovalainen leads. Glock pits.

Lap 21 Kovalainen pits. Massa leads again.

Lap 22 Alonso and Räikkönen pit. Alonso rejoins just ahead of the Finn.

Lap 24 Massa leads by 3.1s from Hamilton. Trulli pits.

Lap 26 Piquet pits from his third place. He rejoins eighth, behind Räikkönen.

Lap 35 Massa leads Hamilton by 4.0s. Kovalainen, Glock, Alonso, Räikkönen, Piquet and Trulli run third to eighth.

Lap 41 Hamilton runs wide at Turn Five, slows down and pits. He has a punctured front-left tyre. He rejoins 10th. Heidfeld makes his first stop.

Lap 44 Massa, leading by 23.6s, pits. He rejoins second, between Kovalainen and Glock.

Lap 47 Glock and Webber pit.

Lap 48 Kovalainen pits. Massa leads again.

Lap 51 Räikkönen pits.

Lap 52 Massa leads Kovalainen by 15.4s.

Lap 54 Piquet pits and rejoins alongside Trulli. The Brazilian wins their battle through Turn One.

Lap 65 Massa leads by 7.2s. Glock is 0.8s ahead of Räikkönen.

Lap 68 Massa's engine blows just after he crosses the start/finish line. Kovalainen leads.

Lap 70 Kovalainen scores his maiden F1 win, 11.0s clear of Glock. Räikkönen is third from Alonso, Hamilton, Piquet, Trulli and Kubica.

ABOVE Checking data in the garage; Anthony Hamilton looks on as Lewis takes another pole.

BELOW Massa passes Lewis around the outside through the first corner after a stunning getaway.

OPPOSITE Lewis and Heikki Kovalainen congratulate each other on a 1–2 in qualifying.

After his stunning back-to-back wins in Britain and Germany, Lewis Hamilton went into the Hungarian Grand Prix confident of securing his first-ever Formula 1 hat-trick. And when he stuck his McLaren on pole position – a comfortable 0.3sec faster than team-mate Heikki Kovalainen – he seemed set fair.

Overtaking at the Hungaroring has verged on the impossible since the track opened in 1986, so the drivers know the start is even more crucial than normal. Lewis got away well, but from third Felipe Massa made an amazing getaway and was level with Lewis as they entered the first corner.

For a moment it looked as though Massa was heading off into the gravel, but he held it together and found a way around the outside of Lewis. After a brief attempt at trying to take the place back, Lewis slotted back into Massa's wake and the two leaders left the chasing pack in their dust.

Massa was setting a scorching pace, but Lewis was able to keep within a second or so of the Ferrari, while at the same time saving fuel. This allowed Lewis to pit a lap later than Massa when they made the first of two scheduled stops, which in turn allowed McLaren to put more fuel in Lewis's car and create the possibility of getting ahead of the Ferrari during the second stops.

Unfortunately, the theory could not be put to the test. Lewis's longer stop initially dropped him back from Massa, but once some of his extra fuel load had burned off he was reeling the Ferrari back in when, without warning, his left-front tyre deflated. Lewis had to complete almost an entire lap with a puncture, which cost him any chance of winning.

It also enforced a long final stint on the softer option tyre, which meant he'd have to be careful to preserve his tyres as he sought to fight his way back. With just three laps to go, Lewis was resigned to finishing sixth. But, amazingly, with victory in sight, Massa's engine exploded. This handed Kovalainen his first-ever F1 win, and bumped Lewis up to fifth.

"Congratulations to Heikki for his first and very well-deserved grand prix win," said Lewis. "The race could have been better for me. My start was okay, but Felipe's was better and he managed to overtake me. I managed to maintain the gap during the first stint and felt comfortable in the second stint because I was matching his times but was going to be running longer to the final stops. I feel I could have had a go at passing him, but the damaged tyre halted my progress. But at least I scored four points and maintained my lead in the championship, so this result is not too bad for me."

HUNGARIAN GRAND PRIX
BUDAPEST

RACE DATE 3rd August 2008
CIRCUIT LENGTH 2.722miles
NO. OF LAPS 70 laps
RACE DISTANCE 190.551 miles
WEATHER Sunny and dry, 29°C
TRACK TEMP 44°C

Practice

Session 1 – Friday

1	Felipe Massa	Ferrari	1m20.981s
2	Kimi Räikkönen	Ferrari	1m21.345s
3	Heikki Kovalainen	McLaren-Mercedes	1m21.410s
4	**Lewis Hamilton**	**McLaren-Mercedes**	**1m21.535s**

Session 2 – Friday

1	**Lewis Hamilton**	**McLaren-Mercedes**	**1m20.554s**
2	Nelson Piquet Jr	Renault	1m20.748s
3	Heikki Kovalainen	McLaren-Mercedes	1m20.760s

Session 3 – Saturday

1	**Lewis Hamilton**	**McLaren-Mercedes**	**1m20.228s**
2	Felipe Massa	Ferrari	1m20.567s
3	Timo Glock	Toyota	1m20.623s

Qualifying

1	**Lewis Hamilton**	**McLaren-Mercedes**	**1m20.899s**
2	Heikki Kovalainen	McLaren-Mercedes	1m21.140s
3	Felipe Massa	Ferrari	1m21.191s

Race

1	Heikki Kovalainen	McLaren-Mercedes	1h37m27.067s
2	Timo Glock	Toyota	+11.061s
3	Kimi Räikkönen	Ferrari	+16.856s
4	Fernando Alonso	Renault	+21.614s
5	**Lewis Hamilton**	**McLaren-Mercedes**	**+23.048s**
6	Nelson Piquet Jr	Renault	+32.298s
7	Jarno Trulli	Toyota	+36.449s
8	Robert Kubica	BMW Sauber	+48.321s

Fastest Lap

Kimi Räikkönen	Ferrari	1m21.195s

World Championship Positions

1	**Lewis Hamilton**	**McLaren-Mercedes**	**62 points**
2	Kimi Räikkönen	Ferrari	57 points
3	Felipe Massa	Ferrari	54 points
4	Robert Kubica	BMW Sauber	49 points
5	Nick Heidfeld	BMW Sauber	41 points
6	Heikki Kovalainen	McLaren-Mercedes	38 points
7	Jarno Trulli	Toyota	22 points
8	Fernando Alonso	Renault	18 points

Santander
vodafone
BOSS
aigo

2008 ROUND 12

EUROPEAN GRAND PRIX
VALENCIA

2nd POINTS TOTAL **70**
POINTS POSITION **1st**
SEASON WINS **4**

Lap 1 Massa leads from pole position. Hamilton gets away well from the dirtier side of the track and slots into second ahead of Kubica, Kovalainen, Räikkönen, Vettel, Trulli and Rosberg. Alonso is hit by Nakajima at Turn Four and retires.

Lap 2 Massa leads Hamilton by 1.4s.

Lap 9 Massa leads by 3.6s. Kubica lies third.

Lap 15 Massa pits and rejoins fourth, ahead of Räikkönen. Hamilton leads.

Lap 17 Hamilton pits. He rejoins just behind the Ferraris. Vettel comes in too.

Lap 18 Kubica and Räikkönen pit, Kovalainen leads.

Lap 20 Kovalainen pits. Massa leads again.

Lap 21 Massa leads Hamilton by 3.5s, with Kubica and Heidfeld (yet to stop) next up.

Lap 22 Heidfeld pits.

Lap 23 Massa extends his lead over Hamilton to 5.1s.

Lap 36 Massa's lead has grown to 10.2s. Hamilton has 19.3s in hand over Kubica.

Lap 37 Massa makes his second stop. He comes close to colliding with Sutil as he leaves his pit.

Lap 38 Hamilton leads Massa by 13.4s. Rosberg pits. The stewards launch an investigation into the manner of Massa's pitlane exit.

Lap 39 Hamilton and Vettel pit. Massa leads again.

Lap 40 Massa leads Hamilton by 5.9s. Kubica pits from third.

Lap 42 Sutil crashes at Turn Two. The stewards defer the Massa investigation until after the race.

Lap 43 Running 1.1s apart, Kovalainen and Räikkönen pit together. During the Ferrari pit stop, a mechanic is knocked down. The Finn loses a place to Trulli by the time he rejoins.

Lap 46 Räikkönen's engine blows up.

Lap 57 Massa wins by 5.6s from Hamilton, Kubica, Kovalainen, Trulli, Vettel, Glock and Rosberg.

ABOVE Massa leads away from pole with Lewis in hot pursuit.

BELOW Lewis prepares himself for qualifying on Saturday afternoon.

OPPOSITE Pressing on through the crowd-lined streets of Valencia.

When Lewis Hamilton awoke on the Saturday morning of the European Grand Prix, he didn't feel well. Muscle spasms in his neck were causing him severe discomfort, and McLaren considered asking test driver Pedro de la Rosa to take his place in the first Formula 1 race to be held at the new Valencia street circuit.

But, following some pain-killing injections, Lewis declared himself fit for action, and duly slotted himself into second place on the grid, next to the polesitting Ferrari of Felipe Massa.

At the start, Massa got away well and Lewis kept hold of second. The Ferrari was the superior machine around the harbour-front venue, and lap after lap Massa became a little smaller in Lewis's vision.

But Lewis was equally far ahead of Robert Kubica's BMW Sauber back in third. And with one eye on the championship, Lewis concentrated on driving a steady race to second.

"I can't complain with second place today," said Lewis, whose championship lead over Massa now stood at six points. "This was a strong weekend for us despite my having a few problems health-wise, but we pulled through. The track was pretty difficult to overtake on, but I maintained the gap – our lap times showed that our overall pace was good, which was encouraging. I'd describe it as a satisfactory weekend for us."

EUROPEAN GRAND PRIX
VALENCIA

RACE DATE 24th August 2008
CIRCUIT LENGTH 3.380 miles
NO. OF LAPS 57 laps
RACE DISTANCE 191.919 miles
WEATHER Dry and bright, 30°C
TRACK TEMP 44°C

Practice

Session 1 – Friday

1	Sebastian Vettel	Toro Rosso-Ferrari	1m40.496s
2	Felipe Massa	Ferrari	1m40.654s
3	**Lewis Hamilton**	**McLaren-Mercedes**	**1m40.822s**

Session 2 – Friday

1	Kimi Räikkönen	Ferrari	1m39.477s
2	Fernando Alonso	Renault	1m39.497s
3	Jenson Button	Honda	1m39.546s
5	**Lewis Hamilton**	**McLaren-Mercedes**	**1m39.712s**

Session 3 – Saturday

1	Robert Kubica	BMW Sauber	1m38.754s
2	Nico Rosberg	Williams-Toyota	1m38.877s
3	Sebastien Bourdais	Toro Rosso-Ferrari	1m39.009s
7	**Lewis Hamilton**	**McLaren-Mercedes**	**1m39.314s**

Qualifying

1	Felipe Massa	Ferrari	1m38.989s
2	**Lewis Hamilton**	**McLaren-Mercedes**	**1m39.199s**
3	Robert Kubica	BMW Sauber	1m39.392s

Race

1	Felipe Massa	Ferrari	1h35m32.339s
2	**Lewis Hamilton**	**McLaren-Mercedes**	**+5.611s**
3	Robert Kubica	BMW Sauber	+37.353s
4	Heikki Kovalainen	McLaren-Mercedes	+39.703s
5	Jarno Trulli	Toyota	+50.684s
6	Sebastian Vettel	Toro Rosso-Ferrari	+52.625s
7	Timo Glock	Toyota	+1m07.990s
8	Nico Rosberg	Williams-Toyota	+1m11.457s

Fastest Lap

Felipe Massa	Ferrari	1m38.708s

World Championship Positions

1	**Lewis Hamilton**	**McLaren-Mercedes**	**70 points**
2	Felipe Massa	Ferrari	64 points
3	Kimi Räikkönen	Ferrari	57 points
4	Robert Kubica	BMW Sauber	55 points
5	Heikki Kovalainen	McLaren-Mercedes	43 points
5	Nick Heidfeld	BMW Sauber	41 points
7	Jarno Trulli	Toyota	26 points
8	Fernando Alonso	Renault	18 points

NG
GUISSE
087 53 05 68
0495 57 88 18
Santander
Mobil 1
Mercedes-Benz
JOHNNIE WALKER
SCHÜCO
MUBADALA
Alice

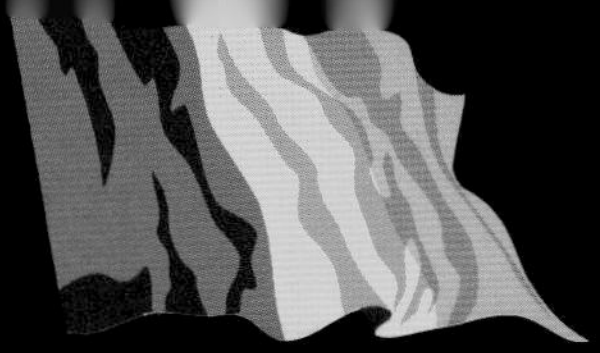

2008 ROUND 13
BELGIAN GRAND PRIX
SPA-FRANCORCHAMPS

3rd

POINTS TOTAL **76**
POINTS POSITION **1st**
SEASON WINS **4**

Lap 1 Hamilton leads from Räikkönen and Massa. Bourdais hits Trulli, who runs wide and causes a traffic jam. Kovalainen, third on the grid, is pincered and drops to 11th. Alonso is fourth from Bourdais and Piquet.

Lap 2 Hamilton spins at La Source and Räikkönen passes him on the approach to Les Combes. Webber and Kubica pass Piquet. Heidfeld passes Glock.

Lap 10 Räikkönen leads Hamilton, Massa and Alonso.

Lap 11 Hamilton makes his first pit stop.

Lap 12 Räikkönen pits, leaving Massa in the lead.

Lap 13 Massa and Alonso pit. Räikkönen leads Bourdais.

Lap 15 Bourdais and Kubica pit. Räikkönen leads, 5.6s clear of Hamilton.

Lap 25 Räikkönen and Hamilton make their second stops.

Lap 28 Massa pits for his second stop.

Lap 30 Räikkönen leads by 1.8s from Hamilton, followed by Massa, Bourdais, Kubica and Vettel.

Lap 32 Bourdais makes his second stop, as does Webber.

Lap 33 Kubica, Vettel and Kovalainen pit.

Lap 34 Räikkönen leads Hamilton, Massa, Alonso, Bourdais, Vettel, Heidfeld and Kubica.

Lap 40 Hamilton is closing on Räikkönen: he trails by 0.9s.

Lap 41 Hamilton gets very sideways at the slippery last chicane and drops away. He is 2.0s adrift.

Lap 42 Hamilton attacks Räikkönen into the chicane, but fails to pass. Heidfeld, Coulthard, Rosberg and Nakajima pit for wets.

Lap 43 It's raining heavily. Hamilton passes Räikkönen at La Source, after taking to the run-off area, emerging ahead, then letting Räikkönen through, before outbraking him to retake the lead. Both run wide later in the lap, allowing Räikkönen back ahead. The Finn then spins and rejoins, before crashing.

Lap 44 Hamilton wins by 14.4s from Massa, Heidfeld, Alonso, Vettel, Kubica, Bourdais and Glock. After the race, Hamilton is penalised for gaining an advantage when taking to the run-off area prior to passing Räikkönen, dropping him to third place.

When Lewis Hamilton crossed the finish line after 44 thrilling laps of the classic Spa-Francorchamps circuit, he thought he'd just claimed one of the greatest victories of his career.

He confounded pre-race predictions of Ferrari dominance by taking an impressive pole position, which he converted into the lead on the damp and slippery surface. Lewis had built a comfortable advantage over the chasing Kimi Räikkönen by the end of lap one, but lost most of this when he was caught out by a wet patch under braking for the La Source hairpin and spun. He got going still in the lead, but Räikkönen was now in his slipstream and the Ferrari moved into the lead under

braking for the tight right-hander at Les Combes.

The reigning World Champion built up a small but comfortable lead, and it seemed no matter how hard Lewis pushed, he just couldn't quite match Kimi's pace.

Both Ferrari and McLaren opted to run the 'prime' hard tyre for their final stint of the race, and Lewis was instantly more comfortable on these than the leader. He slashed the deficit to Kimi from five seconds to just under two in three laps. But Kimi then upped his pace.

"I was beginning to think 'I can't catch this guy'," admitted Lewis. "But I thought 'it's not over till it's over'. I was praying for rain, I could see the clouds coming and knew we'd be in better shape if the rain came."

His prayers were answered. With three laps remaining, it started to drizzle.

"I noticed Kimi backing off a bit. He was braking much earlier for Turn 8 and that was when I really knew the fight was on."

Kimi's cautiousness allowed Lewis to close right up on the Ferrari, so much so that as they approached the Bus Stop Chicane, Lewis was forced to go around the outside to avoid a collision. But this line also allowed him a chance of a pass, until Kimi aggressively shut the door, forcing Lewis to take to the escape road or crash into the Ferrari.

He chose to take to the run-off, which actually

OPPOSITE TOP Lewis closes in on Kimi Räikkönen before their controversial battle.

OPPOSITE BOTTOM Anthony Hamilton looks delighted as his son celebrates on the podium.

ABOVE Lewis punches the air to celebrate a short-lived victory.

BELOW Still wearing his winner's cap, a subdued Lewis leaves the circuit.

BELOW Powering round the La Source hairpin.

OPPOSITE Focusing on the task ahead.

brought him out ahead of Räikkönen. Lewis then backed off, allowing the Ferrari to retake the lead as they crossed the start/finish line, before pulling out of his tow and diving into the lead at the hairpin.

Lewis now scampered off into the lead as the rain started to fall more heavily. Räikkönen was being left in his spray, but then, as Lewis entered the fast Fagnes right-hander, he found the road full of Nico Rosberg's spinning Williams. Lewis was forced to take avoiding action, and Räikkönen's Ferrari flashed by before he could get back up to speed. But a corner later Lewis was ahead again, as the increasingly tricky conditions caught out Räikkönen, who had a quick spin.

Conditions were deteriorating rapidly, but with only two laps to go the leaders couldn't risk a late change to wet tyres. Lewis was tip-toeing around the track, but with Räikkönen's Ferrari now out of contention following yet another spin and contact with the barriers, all he had to do was get to the finish line for his ninth career win.

Lewis duly took the chequered flag, and then sprayed the winner's champagne on the podium, but before he'd packed up and left the track came the stunning news that he'd been given a 25-second penalty for gaining an advantage when he was forced off the track by Räikkönen. McLaren appealed the decision, and for an agonising three weeks the result of the Belgian GP was the in balance. But after hearing all of McLaren's arguments, the FIA Court of Appeal ruled that the appeal was inadmissible, and Ferrari's Felipe Massa, who had barely been a factor at Spa, was confirmed as the winner.

The penalty dropped Lewis to third place, and reduced his lead over Massa in the title fight to just two points.

BELGIAN GRAND PRIX
SPA-FRANCORCHAMPS

RACE DATE 7th September 2008
CIRCUIT LENGTH 4.352 miles
NO. OF LAPS 44 laps
RACE DISTANCE 191.491 miles
WEATHER Overcast, then rain, 15°C
TRACK TEMP 16°C

Practice

Session 1 – Friday

1	Felipe Massa	Ferrari	1m47.284s
2	Kimi Räikkönen	Ferrari	1m47.623s
3	**Lewis Hamilton**	**McLaren-Mercedes**	**1m47.878s**

Session 2 – Friday

1	Fernando Alonso	Renault	1m48.454s
2	Felipe Massa	Ferrari	1m48.504s
3	Heikki Kovalainen	McLaren-Mercedes	1m48.740s
4	**Lewis Hamilton**	**McLaren-Mercedes**	**1m48.805s**

Session 3 – Saturday

1	Nick Heidfeld	BMW Sauber	1m47.876s
2	Heikki Kovalainen	McLaren-Mercedes	1m48.165s
3	Fernando Alonso	Renault	1m48.307s
4	**Lewis Hamilton**	**McLaren-Mercedes**	**1m48.356s**

Qualifying

1	**Lewis Hamilton**	**McLaren-Mercedes**	**1m47.338s**
2	Felipe Massa	Ferrari	1m47.678s
3	Heikki Kovalainen	McLaren-Mercedes	1m47.815s

Race

1	Felipe Massa	Ferrari	1h22m59.394s
2	Nick Heidfeld	BMW Sauber	+9.383s
3*	**Lewis Hamilton**	**McLaren-Mercedes**	**+10.539s**
4	Fernando Alonso	Renault	+14.576s
5	Sebastian Vettel	Toro Rosso-Ferrari	+15.037s
6	Robert Kubica	BMW Sauber	+16.735s
7	Sebastien Bourdais	Toro Rosso-Ferrari	+42.776s
8	Mark Webber	Red Bull-Renault	+1m07.045s

* 25-SECOND PENALTY ADDED TO HAMILTON'S RACE TIME, DROPPING HIM FROM FIRST TO THIRD

Fastest Lap

Kimi Räikkönen	Ferrari	1m47.930s

World Championship Positions

1	**Lewis Hamilton**	**McLaren-Mercedes**	**76 points**
2	Felipe Massa	Ferrari	74 points
3	Robert Kubica	BMW Sauber	58 points
4	Kimi Räikkönen	Ferrari	57 points
5	Nick Heidfeld	BMW Sauber	49 points
6	Heikki Kovalainen	McLaren-Mercedes	43 points
7	Jarno Trulli	Toyota	26 points
8	Fernando Alonso	Renault	23 points

"I noticed Kimi backing off a bit. He was braking much earlier for Turn 8 and that was when I really knew the fight was on."

Santander
Santander

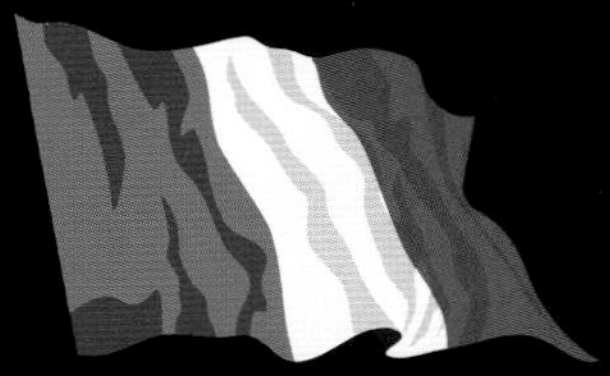

2008 ROUND 14

ITALIAN GRAND PRIX

MONZA

7th POINTS TOTAL **78**
POINTS POSITION **1st**
SEASON WINS **4**

Lap 1 Safety-car start. Pole-sitter Vettel leads Kovalainen, Webber, Rosberg, Massa and Trulli. Hamilton is 13th.

Lap 3 The safety car pulls in. Vettel pulls 2.0s clear.

Lap 4 Räikkönen and Hamilton pass Coulthard.

Lap 9 Räikkönen passes Fisichella into Turn One.

Lap 10 Vettel leads by 6.6s. Hamilton passes Fisichella.

Lap 11 Hamilton passes Räikkönen for 11th.

Lap 16 After swapping places several times, Massa repasses Rosberg once more. Hamilton passes Glock.

Lap 17 Hamilton passes Kubica. He now lies eighth.

Lap 18 Vettel pits and drops to fourth. Kovalainen leads.

Lap 19 Hamilton passes Alonso. Glock passes Kubica.

Lap 22 The top three all pit. Vettel leads. Hamilton passes Trulli into Turn One, but misses the apex of Turn Two and gives the place back as they exit the corner.

Lap 23 Hamilton repasses Trulli.

Lap 24 Hamilton passes Rosberg for second.

Lap 27 Hamilton pits and drops to 10th.

Lap 33 Vettel leads Kovalainen. Massa, Glock and Rosberg pit.

Lap 35 Webber spins at Ascari. Räikkönen and Trulli pit.

Lap 36 Vettel pits and rejoins with his lead intact. Hamilton and Piquet also pit.

Lap 37 Vettel leads Kovalainen by 9.5s. Kubica, Alonso, Heidfeld, Massa, Hamilton and Webber are next up.

Lap 49 Webber and Hamilton brush wheels as the Australian tries an outside pass at Turn One. He slithers down the escape road, then allows Hamilton back ahead.

Lap 53 Vettel wins, 12.5s clear of Kovalainen. Kubica is third from Alonso, Heidfeld, Massa, Hamilton and Webber.

ABOVE Lewis passes Robert Kubica early in the race, one of many passing manoeuvres during his charge through the field.

OPPOSITE Keeping an eye on championship rival Massa.

As Lewis Hamilton left the pits for his first lap in Q2 – the qualifying session that determines who will make the top-10 shoot-out, he knew he was gambling. The track had been wet throughout Q1, but there had been no more rain, so rather than stick with the full-wet tyre the others were using, he decided to opt for the intermediate in the hope that a drier line had emerged. It was a costly mistake.

With the hoped-for extra grip not there, Lewis recorded the slowest time among the 15 cars on track. It was the worst qualifying position of his career, and would make getting a result in the race extremely difficult. The only comfort he could take was that both Ferraris had struggled too – Massa starting sixth, Räikkönen in 14th.

The race started in terrible conditions – the track was saturated. In the early stages, Lewis found himself tucked up behind Räikkönen, unable to find a way out of 15th. His race seemed ruined. But finally, after 10 laps staring at the Ferrari's gearbox, Lewis pulled off a stunning move into the fast Lesmo sweepers.

Once ahead of Kimi, his race came alive. He was now the man to watch as he passed car after car in thrilling fashion. Having started so far down the order, McLaren had opted to fuel Lewis for a single stop, and his daring passes, combined with the first stops of those drivers who planned to pit twice, meant he was up to second and in contention for the win by half-distance.

This was the defining point of the race. The track was now drying significantly, but was still very wet in places, and with further rain still predicted, McLaren fitted full wets when Lewis made his one planned stop.

Had the rain fallen as predicted, he almost certainly would have won. But it didn't, and the track continued to dry. This worked out perfectly for some of the two-stoppers, in particular Sebastian Vettel, whose Toro Rosso team was able to fit intermediates at his second planned stop.

It was clear that inters were the way forward, and McLaren was forced to call in Lewis again. This dropped him from second to seventh. Initially, he caught Massa ahead of him at an incredible rate, but this took its toll on his tyres, and in the closing stages Lewis was forced to fight hard with Red Bull's Mark Webber for his two precious points.

Lewis now led the championship by a single point, but he was rightly proud of his swashbuckling performance.

"I felt I drove a really good race and was moving through the field very quickly when the circuit was at its wettest," he said. "If it had kept on raining, I feel pretty confident I probably could have even won from 15th grid position; but, as the circuit dried out, my tyres overcooked and I had to defend my position from Mark Webber. Still, today was all about damage control: I came away with some points and kept my lead in the Drivers' World Championship."

ITALIAN GRAND PRIX
MONZA

RACE DATE 14th September 2008
CIRCUIT LENGTH 3.600 miles
NO. OF LAPS 53 laps
RACE DISTANCE 190.800 miles
WEATHER Raining, then overcast, 16°C
TRACK TEMP 17°C

Practice

Session 1 – Friday

1	Adrian Sutil	Force India-Ferrari	1m32.842s
2	Rubens Barrichello	Honda	1m33.428s
3	Giancarlo Fisichella	Force India-Ferrari	1m33.695s
20	**Lewis Hamilton**	**McLaren-Mercedes**	**No time**

Session 2 – Friday

1	Kimi Räikkönen	Ferrari	1m23.861s
2	Robert Kubica	BMW Sauber	1m23.931s
3	Nick Heidfeld	BMW Sauber	1m23.947s
4	**Lewis Hamilton**	**McLaren-Mercedes**	**1m23.983s**

Session 3 – Saturday

1	Timo Glock	Toyota	1m35.464s
2	Sebastian Vettel	Toro Rosso-Ferrari	1m36.129s
3	Nico Rosberg	Williams-Toyota	1m36.347s
20	**Lewis Hamilton**	**McLaren-Mercedes**	**1m46.325s**

Qualifying

1	Sebastian Vettel	Toro Rosso-Ferrari	1m37.555s
2	Heikki Kovalainen	McLaren-Mercedes	1m37.631s
3	Mark Webber	Red Bull-Renault	1m38.117s
15	**Lewis Hamilton**	**McLaren-Mercedes**	**1m39.265s**

Race

1	Sebastian Vettel	Toro Rosso-Ferrari	1h26m47.494s
2	Heikki Kovalainen	McLaren-Mercedes	+12.512s
3	Robert Kubica	BMW Sauber	+20.471s
4	Fernando Alonso	Renault	+23.903s
5	Nick Heidfeld	BMW Sauber	+27.748s
6	Felipe Massa	Ferrari	+28.816s
7	**Lewis Hamilton**	**McLaren-Mercedes**	**+29.912s**
8	Mark Webber	Red Bull-Renault	+32.048s

Fastest Lap

Kimi Räikkönen	Ferrari	1m28.047s

World Championship Positions

1	**Lewis Hamilton**	**McLaren-Mercedes**	**78 points**
2	Felipe Massa	Ferrari	77 points
3	Robert Kubica	BMW Sauber	64 points
4	Kimi Räikkönen	Ferrari	57 points
5	Nick Heidfeld	BMW Sauber	53 points
6	Heikki Kovalainen	McLaren-Mercedes	51 points
7	Fernando Alonso	Renault	28 points
8	Jarno Trulli	Toyota	26 points

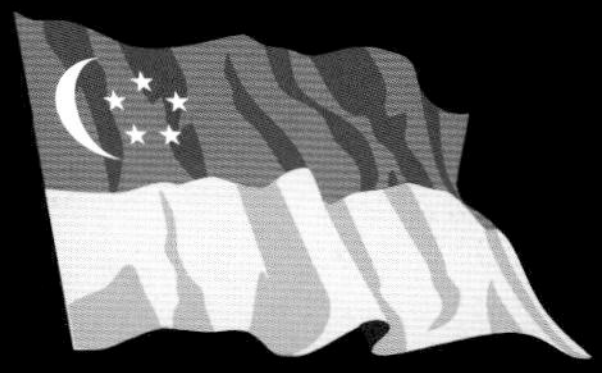

2008 ROUND 15
SINGAPORE GRAND PRIX
MARINA BAY

3rd

POINTS TOTAL **84**
POINTS POSITION **1st**
SEASON WINS **4**

Lap 1 From pole, Massa leads Hamilton and Räikkönen. After much jostling for position, Kubica lies fourth from Vettel, Glock, Kovalainen and Heidfeld.

Lap 12 Alonso makes the race's first scheduled stop.

Lap 14 Piquet crashes heavily at Turn 17. Webber, Coulthard and Barrichello pit.

Lap 15 Safety car deployed – the pitlane is now closed. Rosberg pits. Barrichello stops on the circuit.

Lap 17 Pitlane opens. Massa, Hamilton, Vettel, Glock, Räikkönen, Kovalainen, Heidfeld, Nakajima, Button and Sutil pit. Massa leaves his pit with his fuel rig still attached. He eventually leaves the pitlane after the crew free the fuel hose.

Lap 18 Behind the safety car, Rosberg leads from Trulli, Fisichella, Kubica, Alonso, Webber, Bourdais (who pits), Coulthard and Hamilton.

Lap 20 Restart. Rosberg pulls clear of Trulli to lead by 2.8s.

Lap 22 Rosberg leads by 6.9s. Rosberg and Kubica are under investigation for refuelling when the pitlane was closed.

Lap 24 Massa serves a drive-through penalty for unsafe release from the pits.

Lap 26 Rosberg leads but, along with Kubica, must serve a stop-go penalty for refuelling before the pitlane opened.

Lap 27 Kubica comes in for his penalty.

Lap 41 After a number of lead changes during the pit stops, Alonso pits. He rejoins without losing the lead.

Lap 42 Hamilton passes Coulthard. Both pit at the lap's end.

Lap 43 Alonso leads Glock by 4.8s. Hamilton lies seventh.

Lap 46 Glock pits and drops to fifth.

Lap 50 Räikkönen pits and slips to fifth. Trulli retires at the end of the lap. Massa spins at Turn 18 and rejoins just before Sutil crashes at the same spot. Safety car deployed.

Lap 54 Restart. Alonso leads Rosberg by 3.7s.

Lap 58 Räikkönen crashes at Turn 10.

Lap 44 Alonso wins by 2.9s from Rosberg, Hamilton, Glock, Vettel, Heidfeld, Coulthard and Nakajima.

ABOVE The drivers used clear visors for improved vision under the lights.

BELOW A word for former team-mate Alonso on the podium.

OPPOSITE A unique and spectacular backdrop during Friday practice.

The first-ever Singapore Grand Prix also introduced the concept of night racing to Formula 1.

With no pre-race testing, all the teams and drivers started the weekend on an equal footing, but Lewis Hamilton wasted no time in making his mark, and was the first driver ever to head an official F1 practice session held under lights. But, as usual, the Ferraris of Felipe Massa and Kimi Räikkönen were hot on his tail, and it required a great qualifying effort from Lewis to split the two red cars for a place on the front row of the grid.

In the early stages, the Singapore GP was a pretty dull affair. Massa shot away from pole, and Lewis was driving his heart out just to keep the Ferrari in sight. Behind him, Kimi Räikkönen initially dropped back, but once his tyres came into their prime he started to catch Lewis.

It was just as the leaders were approaching the first of their two pit stops that the race was thrown into chaos. Nelson Piquet spun his Renault into the wall and the safety car was scrambled as the wreckage was cleared.

As soon as the pitlane was declared open, McLaren and Ferrari brought their men in. It was a disastrous stop for Massa and Ferrari, as the Brazilian was sent out before the fuel hose was disconnected. As the Ferrari surged away it tore the hose from the refuelling tank, sending an unfortunate mechanic tumbling. Once Massa realised something was wrong, he pulled over at the end of the pitlane and could only watch as Lewis cruised by.

With his main rival now out of the running, the race was there for the taking for Lewis. However, Jarno Trulli and Giancarlo Fisichella hadn't pitted, and were now running at the head of the field, behind only Nico Rosberg's Williams and Fernando Alonso's Renault, who had shot into the lead by pitting just before Piquet crashed.

Trulli and Fisichella were heavy and slow. Lewis had rejoined behind David Coulthard's Red Bull, and the Scot was stuck in a queue behind Fisi. Lewis had to be careful on the restart not to push too hard and damage his tyres, and with Massa now out of the picture there was no sense in making a risky move.

Finally, he forced his way by Coulthard, and with Trulli and Fisichella having dropped back after making their stops, he was up to third. But the time he lost had allowed Alonso to build a big lead, while Rosberg had been far enough ahead that he was able to take a penalty, imposed for pitting while the pits were closed, and still rejoin ahead of the McLaren.

A second safety car late on – after Adrian Sutil crashed avoiding Massa, who had spun – gave Lewis a sniff of victory. But Rosberg defended second stoutly and, with third place handing Lewis a comfortable seven-point title lead, he opted for the safe option of a podium finish in one of the craziest races in recent F1 history.

"I honestly can't complain," said Lewis. "It was just a bit unfortunate to be stuck in traffic. Nevertheless, to have a podium finish in the first Singapore night race is a great result. Seven points I am quite happy with. Obviously I was trying to get as close to Nico as possible and see if there was an opportunity there. I did not need to take any risks with both Ferraris out of the points."

SINGAPORE GRAND PRIX
MARINA BAY

RACE DATE 28th September 2008
CIRCUIT LENGTH 3.148 miles
NO. OF LAPS 61 laps
RACE DISTANCE 192.028 miles
WEATHER Hot and humid, 30°C
TRACK TEMP 33°C

Practice

Session 1 – Friday

1	**Lewis Hamilton**	**McLaren-Mercedes**	**1m45.518s**
2	Felipe Massa	Ferrari	1m45.598s
3	Kimi Räikkönen	Ferrari	1m45.961s

Session 2 – Friday

1	Fernando Alonso	Renault	1m45.654s
2	**Lewis Hamilton**	**McLaren-Mercedes**	**1m45.752s**
3	Felipe Massa	Ferrari	1m45.793s

Session 3 – Saturday

1	Fernando Alonso	Renault	1m44.506s
2	**Lewis Hamilton**	**McLaren-Mercedes**	**1m45.119s**
3	Felipe Massa	Ferrari	1m45.246s

Qualifying

1	Felipe Massa	Ferrari	1m44.801s
2	**Lewis Hamilton**	**McLaren-Mercedes**	**1m45.465s**
3	Kimi Räikkönen	Ferrari	1m45.617s

Race

1	Fernando Alonso	Renault	1h57m16.304s
2	Nico Rosberg	Williams-Toyota	+2.957s
3	**Lewis Hamilton**	**McLaren-Mercedes**	**+5.917s**
4	Timo Glock	Toyota	+8.155s
5	Sebastian Vettel	Toro Rosso-Ferrari	+10.268s
6	Nick Heidfeld	BMW Sauber	+11.101s
7	David Coulthard	Red Bull-Ferrari	+16.387s
8	Kazuki Nakajima	Williams-Toyota	+18.489s

Fastest Lap

Kimi Räikkönen	Ferrari	1m45.599s

World Championship Positions

1	**Lewis Hamilton**	**McLaren-Mercedes**	**84 points**
2	Felipe Massa	Ferrari	77 points
3	Robert Kubica	BMW Sauber	64 points
4	Kimi Räikkönen	Ferrari	57 points
5	Nick Heidfeld	BMW Sauber	56 points
6	Heikki Kovalainen	McLaren-Mercedes	51 points
7	Fernando Alonso	Renault	38 points
8	Sebastian Vettel	Toro Rosso-Ferrari	27 points

Santander
Mobil 1
Mercedes-Benz
BOSS
vodafone
vodafone
vodafone

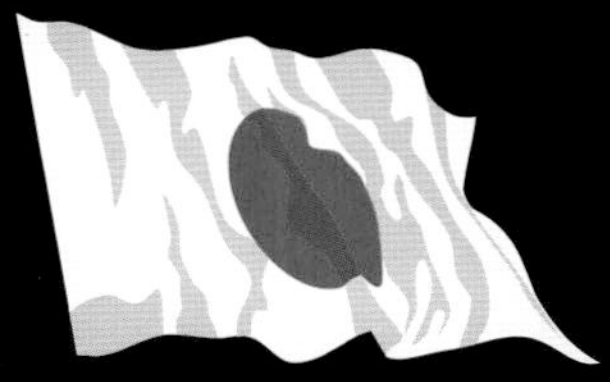

2008 ROUND 16

JAPANESE GRAND PRIX

FUJI SPEEDWAY

12th POINTS TOTAL **84**
POINTS POSITION **1st**
SEASON WINS **4**

Lap 1 Hamilton, on pole, is passed by Räikkönen. Hamilton fights back, but locks up. Both Ferraris and Kovalainen run wide. Kubica grabs the lead. Alonso is second, from Kovalainen, Trulli, Massa, Hamilton, Räikkönen and Piquet.

Lap 2 Hamilton battles with Massa at Turn 11 and the cars touch. Hamilton spins, falls to the back of the field and pits.

Lap 8 Räikkönen passes Trulli.

Lap 12 Kubica leads by 1.5s from Kovalainen and Räikkönen.

Lap 17 Kubica and Räikkönen pit. Hamilton and Massa are awarded drive-through penalties, Hamilton for forcing Räikkönen off the track, Massa for causing a collision. Hamilton pits straight away. Kovalainen retires with a smoking engine.

Lap 18 New leader Alonso pits and rejoins ahead of Kubica. Massa pits for fuel.

Lap 19 Trulli leads from Bourdais and Piquet. Massa serves his drive-through.

Lap 21 Trulli pits. Bourdais leads.

Lap 23 Bourdais pits. Piquet leads.

Lap 29 After Piquet's stop, Alonso leads Kubica by 7.2s. Räikkönen is third.

Lap 34 Webber pits from fourth. Hamilton passes Button for 13th.

Lap 40 Alonso leads Kubica by 12.6s. Räikkönen is still third. Heidfeld pits, as does Hamilton. Massa passes Webber.

Lap 50 Trulli and Bourdais pit. Bourdais rejoins just behind Massa, the cars touch and Massa spins.

Lap 56 All the leading cars have made their second stops. Alonso leads by 13.2s, from Kubica, Räikkönen, Piquet, Trulli, Bourdais, Vettel and Webber. Massa is 10th, Hamilton 12th.

Lap 60 Massa passes Heidfeld before Turn One.

Lap 65 Massa overtakes Webber for eighth place.

Lap 67 Alonso wins, 5.2s ahead of Kubica. Räikkönen is third from Piquet, Trulli, Bourdais, Vettel and Massa. Hamilton finishes 12th. After the race, Bourdais is awarded a 25s penalty for tangling with Massa, elevating Massa to seventh place.

After his considered drive to third in Singapore, McLaren spoke of a new approach for Lewis – one designed to win championships rather than races.

In qualifying Lewis was in imperious form, blasting around the Fuji circuit to claim his 12th career pole. And, with Felipe Massa struggling and only fifth on the grid, he could scarcely have hoped for a better pre-race scenario.

Yet all that was undone as the red lights went out. Lewis made a tardy start and was soon swamped by Kimi Räikkönen, while team-mate Heikki Kovalainen was forced to back off as Lewis aggressively defended his position. Heading into the first corner, Lewis tried to retake the lead, but left his braking too late, running wide into the corner as his front wheels locked under braking.

Räikkönen, Massa and a large chunk of the chasing pack took avoiding action in the run-off.

Lewis rejoined, but his front tyres were badly flat-spotted and he would have to pit for a new set. But as he fought on, he pressured Massa into running too deep on the way into the chicane. Lewis dived to the inside for the first part, and then assumed the racing line for the second part, but Massa gave no ground. Even though he had all four wheels off the track, he attempted to barge his way back past Lewis, spearing the McLaren into a spin.

Lewis had an agonising wait as the whole field passed before he could rejoin. Worse was to come, as he was slapped with a drive-through penalty for his role in the first-corner shenanigans. This dropped him to the tail of the field and, with the car slightly damaged after Massa's assault, his hopes of a good result were shot.

There was some consolation in the fact that Massa too was given a penalty for spinning Lewis out, and even though he had the fastest car in the race he could finish only seventh, reducing Lewis's title lead to five points.

"Obviously, I'm not happy after a result like today's – but I'm already getting over it, and tomorrow will be another day," Lewis stated. "Disappointingly, I didn't make a great start, but I slipstreamed Kimi and went up the inside. I braked a bit late – but so did everybody. A lot of cars went wide at Turn One – and I just went a bit wider than everyone else. But you can't undo the penalty or change today's result. On lap two, Felipe went wide and I went up the inside, giving him room, but he tapped me quite hard into a spin.

"There are positives to take from today; I've only lost two points to Felipe in the drivers' championship, so it's definitely not over. Now I'll forget today ever happened and move forward; we've got two more races to go and my target is still to win both of them."

BELOW **Lewis discusses the MP4-23's handling with his race engineer, Phil Prew.**

OPPOSITE **The calm before the storm as Lewis waits on the grid, concentrating on the task ahead.**

JAPANESE GRAND PRIX
FUJI SPEEDWAY

RACE DATE 12th October 2008
CIRCUIT LENGTH 2.852 miles
NO. OF LAPS 67 laps
RACE DISTANCE 191.084 miles
WEATHER Overcast and dry, 15°C
TRACK TEMP 17°C

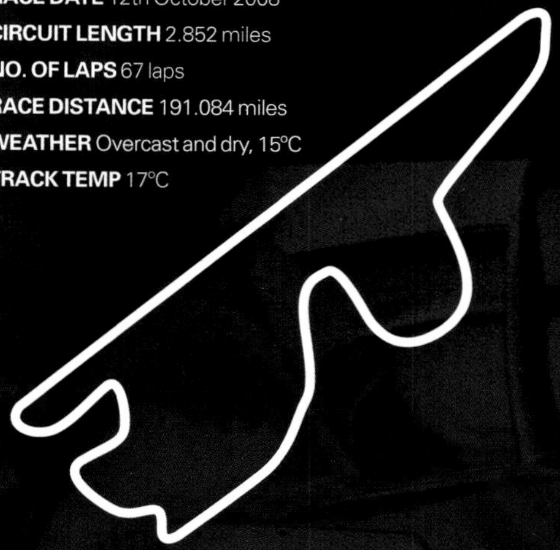

Practice

Session 1 – Friday

1	**Lewis Hamilton**	**McLaren-Mercedes**	**1m18.910s**
2	Felipe Massa	Ferrari	1m19.063s
3	Heikki Kovalainen	McLaren-Mercedes	1m19.279s

Session 2 – Friday

1	Timo Glock	Toyota	1m18.363s
2	Fernando Alonso	Renault	1m18.426s
3	**Lewis Hamilton**	**McLaren-Mercedes**	**1m18.463s**

Session 3 – Saturday

1	Robert Kubica	BMW Sauber	1m25.087s
2	Timo Glock	Toyota	1m25.171s
3	Nelson Piquet Jr	Renault	1m25.415s
11	**Lewis Hamilton**	**McLaren-Mercedes**	**1m25.901s**

Qualifying

1	**Lewis Hamilton**	**McLaren-Mercedes**	**1m18.404s**
3	Kimi Räikkönen	Ferrari	1m18.644s
3	Heikki Kovalainen	McLaren-Mercedes	1m18.821s

Race

1	Fernando Alonso	Renault	1h30m21.892s
2	Robert Kubica	BMW Sauber	+5.283s
3	Kimi Räikkönen	Ferrari	+6.400s
4	Nelson Piquet Jr	Renault	+20.570s
5	Jarno Trulli	Toyota	+23.767s
6	Sebastian Vettel	Toro Rosso-Ferrari	+39.207s
7	Felipe Massa	Ferrari	+46.158s
8	Mark Webber	Red Bull-Renault	+50.811s
12	**Lewis Hamilton**	**McLaren-Mercedes**	**+1m18.900s**

Fastest Lap

Felipe Massa	Ferrari	1m18.426s

World Championship Positions

1	**Lewis Hamilton**	**McLaren-Mercedes**	**84 points**
2	Felipe Massa	Ferrari	79 points
3	Robert Kubica	BMW Sauber	72 points
4	Kimi Räikkönen	Ferrari	63 points
5	Nick Heidfeld	BMW Sauber	56 points
6	Heikki Kovalainen	McLaren-Mercedes	51 points
7	Fernando Alonso	Renault	48 points
8	Sebastian Vettel	Toro Rosso-Ferrari	30 points
	Jarno Trulli	Toyota	30 points

vodafone
SAP

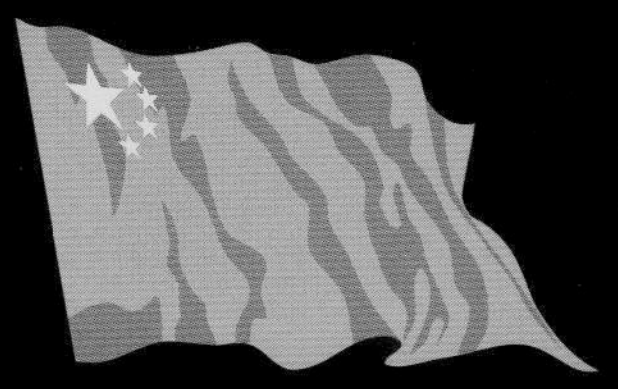

2008 ROUND 17
CHINESE GRAND PRIX
SHANGHAI

1st

POINTS TOTAL **94**
POINTS POSITION **1st**
SEASON WINS **5**

Lap 1 Hamilton makes a clean start from pole to lead Räikkönen and Massa into Turn One. Kovalainen takes fourth from Alonso, but the Spaniard claims the place back before the lap's end. Heidfeld moves up from ninth to sixth, helped by a Turn One clash between Bourdais and Trulli.

Lap 3 Hamilton leads by 2.5s.

Lap 6 Hamilton leads Räikkönen by 3.5s, with Massa another 2.6s behind.

Lap 13 Hamilton has stretched his lead to 4.1s.

Lap 14 Massa and Alonso pit.

Lap 15 Hamilton and Räikkönen pit.

Lap 16 Kovalainen leads from Heidfeld, Hamilton, Vettel and Räikkönen. Massa is seventh, behind Kubica.

Lap 17 Heidfeld pits. Kovalainen leads Hamilton by 7.2s. The latter is 0.6s faster than both Ferraris.

Lap 18 Kovalainen and Vettel pit. Hamilton leads.

Lap 19 Hamilton leads Räikkönen by 6.8s. Kubica remains third, ahead of Massa.

Lap 25 Kubica pits.

Lap 27 Räikkönen reduces the gap to 6.4s.

Lap 28 Hamilton leads Räikkönen by 6.6s and Massa by 15.5s. Alonso, Kovalainen, Heidfeld and Glock are next.

Lap 35 Kovalainen has a punctured right-front. He slowly gets back to the pits and drops towards the tail of the field.

Lap 39 After the leaders have all stopped, Hamilton leads Räikkönen by 13.0s, followed by Massa and Alonso.

Lap 40 Räikkönen reduces his arrears by 0.7s. The Ferraris are 2.6s apart.

Lap 46 With 10 laps remaining, Hamilton leads Räikkönen by 13.9s and Massa by 16.0s.

Lap 48 Massa is 1.1s behind Räikkönen.

Lap 49 Massa passes Räikkönen. Kovalainen retires.

Lap 56 Hamilton wins by 14.9s from Massa, Räikkönen, Alonso, Heidfeld, Kubica, Glock and Piquet.

Following the disappointment of Fuji, Lewis Hamilton needed a strong result at the Chinese Grand Prix, which took place just a week later in Shanghai. And that's exactly what he got.

McLaren shielded Lewis from the negative headlines that filled the British press, allowing him to keep his concentration solely on his preparations for the race weekend. It worked a treat, and Lewis was fastest in both of Friday's free-practice sessions. He maintained this form in qualifying, setting a stunning pole-position lap, despite carrying more fuel than the two Ferraris which would line up behind him.

A slow getaway had been Lewis's undoing in Fuji, but this time his start was fantastic and he shot off into a lead he would never lose. Lewis was quite simply in a different class from his rivals, and at no stage was he ever under threat from either of the Ferrari drivers.

Kimi Räikkönen led the charge for the red team, but with his hopes of defending the title already over, he backed off late in the race and handed second place to Felipe Massa. Massa's eight points prevented Lewis from wrapping up the World Championship with a round to go, but his seven-point advantage sent him into the final race of the season needing only to finish fifth to become the youngest World Champion in the 58-year history of Formula 1.

"Everything just went right this weekend," he said. "Our car has been simply phenomenal. I made one of my best-ever starts and had perfect balance during the race. I owe so much of that to the guys in the team – both at the track and back home; they did an amazing job so a big thanks to them.

"I've got a seven-point lead in the World Championship, but that doesn't allow me to take anything for granted. It might be another step towards my dream but we've still got to stay calm and keep our heads. I just hope we can pull through."

LEFT, FROM TOP Lewis leads away from pole at the start of a dominant display that would take him one step closer to the title; the expressions say it all – Massa knows he faces an uphill battle in Brazil; Lewis sprays the bubbly to celebrate equalling Massa's tally of five wins during 2008.

RIGHT Pondering the future, with just one race left to run in the battle for the World Championship, on Massa's home turf.

CHINESE GRAND PRIX
SHANGHAI

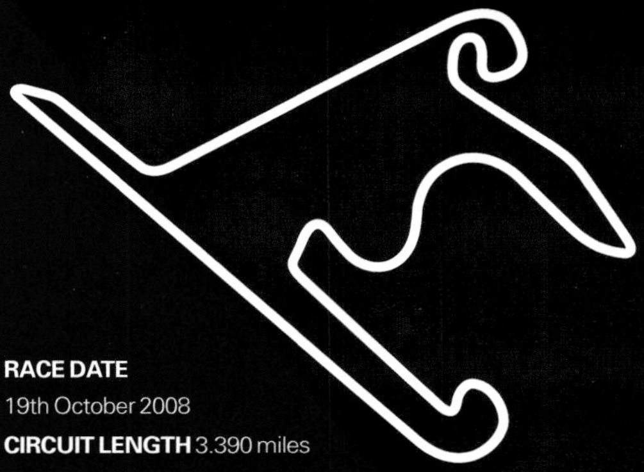

RACE DATE
19th October 2008
CIRCUIT LENGTH 3.390 miles
NO. OF LAPS 56 laps
RACE DISTANCE 189.680 miles
WEATHER Overcast and dry, 27°C
TRACK TEMP 30°C

Practice

Session 1 – Friday

1	Lewis Hamilton	McLaren-Mercedes	1m35.630s
2	Felipe Massa	Ferrari	1m36.020s
3	Kimi Räikkönen	Ferrari	1m36.052s

Session 2 – Friday

1	Lewis Hamilton	McLaren-Mercedes	1m35.750s
2	Fernando Alonso	Renault	1m36.024s
3	Nelson Piquet Jr	Renault	1m36.094s

Session 3 – Saturday

1	Nick Heidfeld	BMW Sauber	1m36.061s
2	Lewis Hamilton	McLaren-Mercedes	1m36.135s
3	Robert Kubica	BMW Sauber	1m36.150s

Qualifying

1	Lewis Hamilton	McLaren-Mercedes	1m36.303s
2	Kimi Räikkönen	Ferrari	1m36.645s
3	Felipe Massa	Ferrari	1m36.889s

Race

1	Lewis Hamilton	McLaren-Mercedes	1h31m.57.403s
2	Felipe Massa	Ferrari	+14.925s
3	Kimi Räikkönen	Ferrari	+16.445s
4	Fernando Alonso	Renault	+18.370s
5	Nick Heidfeld	BMW Sauber	+28.923s
6	Robert Kubica	BMW Sauber	+33.219s
7	Timo Glock	Toyota	+41.722s
8	Nelson Piquet Jr	Renault	+56.645s

Fastest Lap

Lewis Hamilton	McLaren-Mercedes	1m36.3256s

World Championship Positions

1	Lewis Hamilton	McLaren-Mercedes	94 points
2	Felipe Massa	Ferrari	87 points
3	Robert Kubica	BMW Sauber	75 points
4	Kimi Räikkönen	Ferrari	69 points
5	Nick Heidfeld	BMW Sauber	60 points
6	Fernando Alonso	Renault	53 points
7	Heikki Kovalainen	McLaren-Mercedes	51 points
8	Sebastian Vettel	Toro Rosso-Ferrari	30 points
	Jarno Trulli	Toyota	30 points

vodafone
LEW
1

2008 ROUND 18

BRAZILIAN GRAND PRIX
SÃO PAULO

5th POINTS TOTAL **98** POINTS POSITION **1st** SEASON WINS **5**

Lap 1 After a delayed start due to torrential rain, Massa, from pole, leads Trulli, Räikkönen, Hamilton, Vettel, Alonso and Kovalainen. Rosberg and Coulthard clash at Turn Two. Piquet crashes at Turn Three. Safety car deployed.

Lap 5 Restart. Massa leads Trulli by 0.9s. Hamilton is fourth.

Lap 11 Trulli, Räikkönen and Hamilton are among the last drivers to pit for dries.

Lap 12 Massa leads Vettel, Alonso, Räikkönen, Fisichella, Trulli, Hamilton and Glock.

Lap 13 Hamilton passes Trulli for sixth at Turn One.

Lap 18 Hamilton passes Fisichella. He's now fifth.

Lap 27 Vettel pits and drops to sixth. Kovalainen passes Trulli and Fisichella for seventh.

Lap 28 Massa leads Alonso by 4.2s.

Lap 38 Massa, Fisichella and Bourdais pit. Alonso leads.

Lap 40 Alonso and Hamilton pit, as does Barrichello.

Lap 41 Räikkönen leads by 12.5s from Massa, Vettel, Alonso, Kovalainen and Hamilton.

Lap 42 Kovalainen and Heidfeld pit.

Lap 43 Räikkönen pits, Massa leads. Trulli pits, too.

Lap 45 Massa leads Vettel, Alonso, Räikkönen and Hamilton.

Lap 51 Vettel pits.

Lap 63 It starts to rain. Fisichella pits for intermediates.

Lap 64 Heidfeld, Barrichello, Rosberg, Bourdais, Kubica and Sutil pit.

Lap 65 Kovalainen and Button pit.

Lap 66 Alonso, Räikkönen, Hamilton and Vettel pit for intermediates.

Lap 67 Massa pits. He rejoins in the lead from Alonso, Räikkönen, Glock (still on dries), Hamilton and Vettel.

Lap 69 Vettel passes Hamilton to take fifth place.

Lap 71 Massa wins by 13.2s from Alonso and Räikkönen. Glock slows in the increasing rain. Vettel and Hamilton pass the German and Hamilton recovers the point he needs to become the sport's youngest-ever World Champion.

ABOVE **The crew remain calm and collected during the critical late pit stop for intermediates. With five laps to go, the final twist in the dramatic story of the 2008 World Championship is about to unfold.**

It came down to the last corner of the last lap of the final race of the season, but in the most thrilling title decider in Formula 1 history, Lewis Hamilton clinched the World Championship.

It was a nail-biting race for Lewis's McLaren team. The track was bone dry as the cars lined up on the grid, but literally seconds before the start of the race it started to rain, soaking the tricky first couple of corners and throwing in the sort of random element that could upset Lewis's seemingly straightforward mission of taking a top-five finish.

The race start was delayed so that all teams could fit wet-weather tyres, and when the action finally got underway Lewis made a satisfactory start and slotted into fourth place, keeping well out of trouble on the slippery Interlagos track surface.

Title rival Felipe Massa was doing exactly what he had to do, and was out front in his Ferrari, but fourth was more than enough for Lewis. After the brief shower, the rain stopped and it soon became time for the switch to dry tyres. McLaren acted with caution, and monitored its rivals' performance before calling Lewis in.

This gave those who had gambled with an earlier switch to dries the advantage, and when Lewis rejoined he was down to sixth – and no longer World Champion in waiting.

Force India had gambled on a very early stop for Giancarlo Fisichella, and the veteran Italian was now running ahead of Lewis. The track was still wet off-line through the Senna Esses that form the first two corners, but Lewis had a great tow out of the final corner, and he pulled off a ballsy move to dive down the inside on the wet track to take the fifth place he needed.

Lewis gained a further place as Sebastian Vettel made the second of his three pit stops. The Toro Rosso man caught Lewis in the final stages, but Lewis defended fourth resolutely, until, with just seven laps to go it started to rain again. The rain was light, and was only falling on the final part of the track. It was an agonising call for McLaren – did it bring Lewis in and lose 30 seconds for a change to wet tyres, or did it keep him on dries and hope the rain didn't get any stronger?

Having been cautious all weekend, McLaren opted for the safer option of bringing Lewis in. Vettel followed Lewis into the pits, but great McLaren pitwork meant Lewis exited with an increased lead. But he was now back in fifth once again…

Though the three cars ahead of Timo Glock had also pitted, Toyota gambled on keeping their man on dries. The German was 20 seconds up the road from Lewis, but only a couple of seconds a lap slower. Unless the rain got heavier, Lewis wouldn't catch him.

TOP Everyone wants a sound-bite after Lewis qualifies in fourth place, leaving him vulnerable to first-corner attack from Räikkönen and Alonso.

ABOVE Lewis passes Giancarlo Fisichella's Force India early in the race to take the vital fifth place, but his work was far from done...

To make matters even trickier, Vettel was now right on Lewis's tail and looking for a way through. Added into the mix was BMW Sauber's Robert Kubica. The Pole was a lap down, but was flying in the slippery conditions. He forced his way by Vettel and then Lewis. This distracted Lewis and he locked a rear wheel and drifted wide. Vettel was through and Lewis was down to sixth with just a lap to go!

Massa came through to win the race comfortably, and his family celebrated as though he had won the title. But the rain was now teeming, and Glock's dries had had their day. He got massively sideways at the bottom of the hill, and was struggling for traction as Vettel and Lewis blasted by. In the space of just a couple of hundred metres, despair turned to triumph for Lewis, who at the age of 23 became the youngest World Champion in F1 history.

"Before it started to rain I was quite comfortable," he said. "My tyres were a little bit shot so I was struggling to keep the pace up, but I was able to stay ahead of Vettel. Then it started to drizzle and I didn't want to take any risks. Then he got past me and I was told that I had to get in front of him, and I couldn't believe it! Then at the last corner I managed to get past Glock and I'm telling you it was just amazing. I can only thank God.

"I don't think it has hit home yet. I just had the most intense race of my life, my heart is still racing. I'm just so thankful for the opportunity the team gave me. Huge respect to McLaren and Mercedes-Benz for giving me a wonderful opportunity, and my family who came here and supported me, and all the people back home as well. Without them I wouldn't be doing this."

LEFT, FROM TOP With Lewis still lying in sixth place approaching the end of the last lap, tension runs high in the McLaren garage as all seems lost; moments later, 2008 World Champion Lewis waves to Massa's stunned home crowd on the slowing-down lap; the realisation of a life-long dream – Lewis celebrates with father Anthony, brother Nick and the McLaren team.

RIGHT Job done! Ten years after signing a long-term agreement with McLaren-Mercedes, Lewis repays the team's faith in him by climbing triumphantly from his MP4-23 to enter the history books as the youngest-ever Formula 1 World Champion.

BRAZILIAN GRAND PRIX
INTERLAGOS

RACE DATE 2nd November 2008
CIRCUIT LENGTH 2.677 miles
NO. OF LAPS 71 laps
RACE DISTANCE 190.067 miles
WEATHER Rain, dry, rain, 30°C
TRACK TEMP 33°C

Practice

Session 1 – Friday

1	Felipe Massa	Ferrari	1m12.305s
2	**Lewis Hamilton**	**McLaren-Mercedes**	**1m12.495s**
2	Kimi Räikkönen	Ferrari	1m12.507s

Session 2 – Friday

1	Fernando Alonso	Renault	1m12.296s
2	Felipe Massa	Ferrari	1m12.353s
3	Jarno Trulli	Toyota	1m12.435s
9	**Lewis Hamilton**	**McLaren-Mercedes**	**1m12.787s**

Session 3 – Saturday

1	Fernando Alonso	Renault	1m12.141s
2	**Lewis Hamilton**	**McLaren-Mercedes**	**1m12.212s**
3	Heikki Kovalainen	McLaren-Mercedes	1m12.225s

Qualifying

1	Felipe Massa	Ferrari	1m12.368s
2	Jarno Trulli	Toyota	1m12.737s
3	Kimi Räikkönen	Ferrari	1m12.825s
4	**Lewis Hamilton**	**McLaren-Mercedes**	**1m12.830s**

Race

1	Felipe Massa	Ferrari	1h34m11.435s
2	Fernando Alonso	McLaren-Mercedes	+13.298s
3	Kimi Räikkönen	Ferrari	+16.235s
4	Sebastian Vettel	Toro Rosso-Ferrari	+38.011s
5	**Lewis Hamilton**	**McLaren-Mercedes**	**+38.907s**
6	Timo Glock	Toyota	+44.368s
7	Heikki Kovalainen	McLaren-Mercedes	+55.074s
8	Jarno Trulli	Toyota	+1m08.433s

Fastest Lap

Felipe Massa	Ferrari	1m13.376s

World Championship Positions

1	**Lewis Hamilton**	**McLaren-Mercedes**	**98 points**
2	Felipe Massa	Ferrari	97 points
3	Kimi Räikkönen	Ferrari	75 points
4	Robert Kubica	BMW Sauber	75 points
5	Fernando Alonso	Renault	61 points
6	Nick Heidfeld	BMW Sauber	60 points
7	Heikki Kovalainen	McLaren-Mercedes	53 points
8	Sebastian Vettel	Toro Rosso-Ferrari	35 points